GENERAL EDITOR: CHRISTOPHER RICKS

CATULLUS IN ENGLISH

GAIUS VALERIUS CATULLUS was Rome's first major lyric poet. He lived from about 82 BC to about 52 BC. The ancient sources say that he was born in Verona and died in Rome, but little more is known about his life. Through the ages, however, readers have always felt that they knew Catullus himself, for few ancient poets have written of emotions and personal experience with such intensity. His most moving subjects are the death of his brother and his unhappy love for a woman he calls Lesbia, but his work also includes scurrilous lampoons of politicians like Caesar and Pompey, attacks on bad poets and praise of good ones, obscene invective and long learned poems in the Alexandrian mode. Catullus' poetry exercised great influence on Virgil and Horace in the Augustan Age and on Martial's epigrams at the end of the first century AD, but after the second century it disappeared from the historical record for over a thousand years. It survived the Middle Ages in a single manuscript which was discovered around 1300.

JULIA HAIG GAISSER was educated at Brown University, Harvard University, and the University of Edinburgh, where she was a Marshall Scholar. She is Professor of Latin and Eugenia Chase Guild Professor in the Humanities at Bryn Mawr College (Bryn Mawr, Pennsylvania). Her previous books include *Catullus and his Renaissance Readers* and *Pierio Valeriano on the Ill Fortune of Learned Men: A Renaissance Humanist and His World*.

CATULLUS IN ENGLISH

Edited by JULIA HAIG GAISSER

PENGUIN BOOKS

PENGUIN BOOKS

Published by the Penguin Group
Penguin Books Ltd, 27 Wrights Lane, London W8 5TZ, England
Penguin Putnam Inc., 375 Hudson Street, New York, New York 10014, USA
Penguin Books Australia Ltd, Ringwood, Victoria, Australia
Penguin Books Canada Ltd, 10 Alcorn Avenue, Toronto, Ontario, Canada M4V 3B2
Penguin Books India (P) Ltd, 11, Community Centre, Panchsheel Park, New Delhi – 110 017, India
Penguin Books (NZ) Ltd, Private Bag 102902, NSMC, Auckland, New Zealand
Penguin Books (South Africa) (Pty) Ltd, 5 Watkins Street, Denver Ext 4, Johannesburg 2094, South Africa

Penguin Books Ltd, Registered Offices: Harmondsworth, Middlesex, England

Published in Penguin Classics 2001
1
Editorial matter copyright © Julia Haig Gaisser, 2001

All rights reserved

The acknowledgements on pp. x–xii constitute an extension of this copyright page

The moral right of the editor has been asserted

Set in 10/12.5 pt PostScript Monotype Bembo
Typeset by Rowland Phototypesetting Ltd, Bury St Edmunds, Suffolk
Printed in England by Clays Ltd, St Ives plc

Except in the United States of America, this book is sold subject
to the condition that it shall not, by way of trade or otherwise, be lent,
re-sold, hired out, or otherwise circulated without the publisher's
prior consent in any form of binding or cover other than that in
which it is published and without a similar condition including this
condition being imposed on the subsequent purchaser

CONTENTS

Acknowledgements x
Preface xiii
Introduction xv
A Note on Catullus' Metres xlii
Further Reading xlix

TRANSLATIONS AND IMITATIONS

SIR WALTER RALEGH 3
SIR PHILIP SIDNEY 4
MATTHEW GWINNE 5
GEORGE CHAPMAN 9
THOMAS CAMPION 10
BEN JONSON 13
HENRY PEACHAM 17
SAMUEL SHEPPARD 21
ROBERT HERRICK 23
ANONYMOUS (1612) 24
RICHARD CRASHAW 25
RICHARD LOVELACE 26
ABRAHAM COWLEY 32
NAHUM TATE 35
JOHN OLDHAM 38
WILLIAM WALSH 40
TOM BROWN 41
JOHN GLANVILL 43
JONATHAN SWIFT 44

SAMUEL SAY 45
JOHN GAY 47
ANONYMOUS IN *THE GENTLEMAN'S JOURNAL* (1692, 1693) 48
ANONYMOUS (1693) 51
NICHOLAS AMHURST 54
ANONYMOUS (1702) 55
THOMAS COOKE 59
THE ADVENTURES OF CATULLUS 62
ANONYMOUS (1717) 68
CHRISTOPHER SMART 72
ROBERT LLOYD 73
JOHN NOTT 74
JOHN HOOKHAM FRERE 81
SAMUEL TAYLOR COLERIDGE 86
WALTER SAVAGE LANDOR 87
CHARLES ABRAHAM ELTON 93
THOMAS MOORE 106
LEIGH HUNT 109
GEORGE LAMB 116
GEORGE GORDON, LORD BYRON 123
THE RIGHT HON. W. E. GLADSTONE 126
WILLIAM JAMES LINTON 127
CHARLES BADHAM 129
SIR THEODORE MARTIN 131
SIR RICHARD BURTON 136
JAMES CRANSTOUN 139
THOMAS HARDY 145
G. S. DAVIES 146
EUGENE FIELD 147
HUGH MACNAGHTEN 148
ARTHUR SYMONS 151
AUBREY BEARDSLEY 155
MAURICE BARING 156
MARY STEWART 158
FRANKLIN P. ADAMS 162

JAMES ELROY FLECKER 163
EZRA POUND 165
F. L. LUCAS 167
HORACE GREGORY 169
BASIL BUNTING 172
JACK LINDSAY 175
STEVIE SMITH 178
LOUIS ZUKOFSKY 179
QUINTIN HOGG (LORD HAILSHAM) 185
FRANK O. COPLEY 186
JAMES LAUGHLIN 192
GUY LEE 193
DAVID FERRY 194
PETER WHIGHAM 195
JAMES K. BAXTER 215
JAMES MICHIE 216
RODNEY GOVE DENNIS 223
FREDERIC RAPHAEL AND KENNETH McLEISH 226
ROBERT CLAYTON CASTO 234
DOROTHEA WENDER 239
ROBERT MEZEY 242
HUMPHREY CLUCAS 243
BENITA KANE JARO 246
CHARLES MARTIN 247
JANE WILSON JOYCE 250
MARCIA KARP 251
ANNE CARSON 252
HUGH TOLHURST 255

Appendix: Some poems that would not have been written without Catullus

SIR WALTER RALEGH 261
ROBERT HERRICK 262
THOMAS RANDOLPH 263
ABRAHAM COWLEY 264

ANDREW MARVELL 268
ALEXANDER POPE 270
THOMAS TWINING 270
GEORGE ELLIS 273
SAMUEL TAYLOR COLERIDGE 274
WALTER SAVAGE LANDOR 275
LEIGH HUNT 277
PERCY BYSSHE SHELLEY 279
ALFRED, LORD TENNYSON 280
ALGERNON CHARLES SWINBURNE 283
ARTHUR SYMONS 286
W. B. YEATS 287
EDNA ST VINCENT MILLAY 288
DOROTHY PARKER 289
WILLIAM D. HULL, II 289
ALLEN TATE 290
R. P. BLACKMUR 291
REX WARNER 292
JOHN COTTON 292
JAMES K. BAXTER 294
THOMAS McAFEE 295
JULIA BUDENZ 296
DAVID VESSEY 299

English Editions 301
Index of Poems Translated 309
Index of Translators and Imitators 317
Index of Poets in the Appendix 321

For T.K.G.

ACKNOWLEDGEMENTS

For permission to reproduce copyright material in this book, the editor and publisher gratefully acknowledge the following:

MAURICE BARING Reproduced by permission of A. P. Watt on behalf of the Trustees of Maurice Baring Will Trust.

JAMES K. BAXTER Reproduced by permission of Oxford University Press Australia and New Zealand and Mrs J. Baxter from *Collected Poems James K. Baxter* (Oxford University Press 1980) © The Estate of James K. Baxter.

JULIA BUDENZ 'Roman Sonnet 2: A Response to Catullus' poem 5', originally published in *Rhino* 98 (1998), p. 59.
'Roman Sonnet 3', originally published in *American Voice* 45 (1998), p. 53.

BASIL BUNTING From Basil Bunting, *The Complete Poems* (Bloodaxe Books, 2000).

ANNE CARSON 'Translations of Catullus: Carmen 43, 46, 50, 86' © Anne Carson, first appeared in the January/February issue of the *American Poetry Review*. Reprinted by permission of the author.

HUMPHREY CLUCAS From *Versions of Catullus* (Hippopotamus Press, 1985).

FRANK O. COPLEY From *Gaius Valerius Catullus: The Complete Poetry* (Ann Arbor: The University of Michigan Press, 1957). Reproduced by permission of The University of Michigan Press.

JOHN COTTON Catullus at Sirmio: 'First published in *Ambit* magazine 89, in 1982'.

RODNEY GOVE DENNIS Reproduced with permission of the author.

ACKNOWLEDGEMENTS

DAVID FERRY Reproduced with permission of the author.

HORACE GREGORY Copyright © 1956, 1972 by the Estate of Horace Gregory, from his *Poems of Catullus* (W. W. Norton, 1972). Used with permission.

QUINTIN HOGG Poem reproduced with permission of the author.

WILLIAM D. HULL 'In Memoriam' first published in the *Sewanee Review* 48: 1 (Winter 1940). © 1940 by the University of the South. Reprinted with the permission of the editor.

BENITA KANE JARO Carmen 37, 52 and 80, from *The Key* (1988). Reprinted with the permission of the author.

JANE WILSON JOYCE Reproduced with permission of the author.

MARCIA KARP Reproduced with permission of the author.

JAMES LAUGHLIN 'The Country Road', from *Poems New and Selected*, © 1996 by James Laughlin. Reprinted by permission of New Directions Publishing Corp.

JACK LINDSAY Reproduced by permission of Jack Lindsay, from *The Complete Poems of Gaius Catullus* (1929) and *Catullus: The Complete Poems* (1948).

WILLIAM JAMES LINTON 'In Dispraise of a Woman', reproduced by permission of Brown University Library, Providence, Rhode Island.

F. L. LUCAS Reproduced by kind permission of Mrs E. Lucas.

THOMAS McAFEE From *My Confidant, Catullus* (1983), reproduced by permission of the English Department, University of Missouri–Columbia.

CHARLES MARTIN From *The Poems of Catullus*, pp. 14, 27, 47, 116, © 1989. Johns Hopkins University Press.

JAMES MICHIE Grateful thanks are due to James Michie to reprint from *The Poems of Catullus*, translated by James Michie (ed. Rupert Hart-Davis, 1969).

DOROTHY PARKER 'From a Letter to Lesbia', from *The Portable Dorothy Parker* by Dorothy Parker, copyright 1928, renewed © 1956 by Dorothy Parker. Used by permission of Viking Penguin, a division of Penguin Putnam Inc.

EZRA POUND Cat. 26, 43, 85 from *Translations* by Ezra Pound (Faber & Faber, 1970). Reproduced by permission.

STEVIE SMITH 'Not Waving But Drowning', from *Collected Poems of Stevie Smith*, © 1972 by Stevie Smith. Reprinted by permission of New Directions Publishing Corp.

ARTHUR SYMONS Grateful thanks to Diana P. Read for *Knave of Hearts*, 1894–1908 by Arthur Symons (William Heinemann, 1913).

ALLEN TATE 'Adaptation of a Theme by Catullus', from *Collected Poems, 1919–1976* by Allen Tate. Copyright © 1977 by Allen Tate. Reprinted by permission of Farrar, Straus and Giroux, LLC.

HUGH TOLHURST Catullus 2, 3 and 7 from *Filth and Other Poems* (Black Pepper Press, 1997). Reproduced by permission of the author and publisher.

DAVID VESSEY Reproduced by permission of the author.

REX WARNER Poem XVIII, from *Poems and Contradictions* (John Lane, 1945).

PETER WHIGHAM To Penguin Books for *The Poems of Catullus* translated by Peter Whigham (Penguin Classics, 1966).

W. B. YEATS 'The Scholars', reproduced by permission of A. P. Watt on behalf of Michael B. Yeats.

LOUIS ZUKOFSKY From *Complete Short Poetry* © 1991, The Johns Hopkins University Press.

Every effort has been made to trace or contact all copyright holders. The publishers will be glad to make good any omissions brought to our attention in future editions.

PREFACE

In 1931 Ezra Pound proclaimed: 'There is no useful English version of Catullus.' There are *useful* versions today (though Pound might not agree), but there is still no *satisfactory* version, by which I mean a translation that does justice to the poet in all his parts. Catullus is a poet of great delicacy and charm, of violent, obscene (and sometimes extremely funny) abuse, of passionate feeling, of austere and moving emotional restraint, and of complicated and recherché learning in the manner of the Greek Alexandrians. Very often he is playing in several of these registers at once. It is not surprising, therefore, that poets – even good ones – have found him so difficult. No single poet has been able to present Catullus in English in all his voices and genres, but I hope this collection of poets may come close.

Catullus, unlike Horace and Virgil, did not exercise a decisive influence on English poetry, but he has been important to individual poets great and small in every generation including our own, with each age responding differently to him and finding different poems to enjoy and imitate. Because Catullus' surviving *oeuvre* is so small (smaller than that of any major Latin poet except Tibullus), and because most of his 116 poems are so short, it has been possible to include in the anthology at least one translation or imitation of every poem, and several translations of many, so that readers can follow the reception both of the poet and of individual poems from the sixteenth century to the present.

The anthology of translations and imitations is preceded by a note on Catullus' metres and followed by an Appendix of 'Some poems that would not have been written without Catullus'. Both the anthology and the Appendix are arranged chronologically by the birth dates of the poets (the earliest poet represented is Sir Walter Ralegh, born *c*. 1552;

the latest is Hugh Tolhurst, born in 1966). An Index of Poems Translated follows the text.

Poems have been quoted as far as possible from the earliest available printed text, or the one bearing the author's final imprint, or from authoritative modern editions based on such texts.

A list of English editions appears at the end of the volume. Spelling and punctuation have not been modernized, except that long *s* (= f without the cross-stroke) has been replaced with modern *s*, vocalic *v* is printed as *u*, and *then* (meaning *than)* is spelled *than*. When translations are part of essays or other prose passages, their context has been included and printed in italics. A date is printed after a poem if its author has included it with his translation.

It has been a great pleasure to assemble this collection of poetic responses to Catullus. Indeed, a classicist with a taste for poetry and intellectual history could hardly find a more congenial project. I am extremely grateful to Christopher Ricks for inviting me to undertake it. I also wish to thank the many friends and colleagues who have given me their generous assistance at every stage of the endeavour. I owe a special debt of thanks to Thomas Gaisser, Betty Kirkpatrick Hart, D. F. S. Thomson, Michael Putnam, Deborah Roberts, David Ferry, Helen North, Margaret Holley and Robert Mezey. I have received indispensable assistance from the staff of the Bryn Mawr College Library, but especially from Mary Leahy, Anne Slater, Charles Burke, Maggie Nerz and Andrew Patterson.

Bryn Mawr, Pennsylvania
November, 1998

INTRODUCTION

Catullus and his Poetry

Gaius Valerius Catullus was Rome's first major lyric poet. The biographical facts about him are few and easily told. He lived from about 82 BC to about 52 BC. The ancient sources say that he was born in Verona and died in Rome at the age of thirty. His father was important enough to be on terms of hospitality with Julius Caesar, as we learn from an anecdote related by Caesar's first-century biographer Suetonius. Catullus, it seems, had damaged the great man's prestige irreparably with scurrilous poems on his protégé Mamurra.[1] He apologized, and Caesar magnanimously responded both by remaining on good terms with the father and by inviting the poet himself to dinner.

This information is scanty enough (and little more is known about the lives of most ancient authors), but Catullus himself seems to make up for the deficiency. No ancient poet except Sappho writes of emotions and personal experience with such intensity. The poems present a complicated emotional landscape with two figures at the centre: Catullus' brother, whose death has banished all his interest in both love and poetry (a loss recounted in poems about the separation and grief of lovers); and his mistress Lesbia, whom he loves and wants to respect – and who betrays him in every alley in Rome. Catullus' brother is otherwise unknown, but Lesbia is generally identified with the notorious Clodia whose high pedigree and low morals Cicero satirized in his oration *Pro Caelio*. There are also lesser loves – Ipsitilla, invited obscenely to a midday rendezvous, and the boy Juventius, coy and unfaithful. Catullus' poetry abounds with the names of friends and enemies, many

---

[1] Probably *Carmina* 29 and 57.

of whom are historical personages – politicians like Caesar and Cicero, fellow poets like Cinna and Calvus, and the historian Cornelius Nepos, to whom the work is dedicated. We can even glean a few dates. Catullus mentions serving in Bithynia as a member of the staff of Gaius Memmius, who governed the province in 57–56 BC, and he refers to Pompey's consulship of 55 BC and to Caesar's invasion of Britain, probably the campaign of 54 BC.[2]

Catullus' vividness and detail invite the manufacture of biographies. From at least the end of the seventeenth century to the present many poets and critics have believed both that Catullus revealed his own character and emotions in the poems and that his biography could be reconstructed in the form of a narrative that we may call 'The story of Catullus'.[3] 'The story of Catullus' appears sometimes in novels, but more often in translators' and scholars' introductions, or in rearrangements of the poems to correspond to a narrative line. But the effort is misguided, for poems have always been unreliable witnesses. 'We know how to tell many lies like the truth, and we know how to tell the truth when we please,' say Hesiod's Muses in the *Theogony*. Catullus puts it differently:

> I'll show you boys who's a man,
> You catamite Aurelius and pervert Furius,
> Who think I'm not upstanding enough
> Since my verses are a little soft.
> The dedicated poet ought to be chaste –
> His verses are a different matter.   (*Carmen* 16.1–6)[4]

But it hardly matters if the poet hides behind his *persona* and mocks biographers. It is less useful to the historian to arrange the Lesbia poems, for example, in a romantic chronology than to see Catullus' poetry as

---

[2] Catullus' brother: *Carmina* 65, 68, 101. Lesbia's betrayals: especially *Carmina* 37 and 58. Ipsitilla: *Carmen* 32. Juventius: *Carmina* 24, 48, 61, 99. Serving with Memmius: *Carmina* 10, 28, 31, 46. Pompey's consulship: *Carmen* 113. Caesar in Britain: *Carmina* 11, 29.
[3] See T. P. Wiseman, *Catullus and his World: A Reappraisal* (Cambridge, 1985) 218–41.
[4] Here and elsewhere in the Introduction, unattributed translations are by the editor, J.H.G.

a work of the imagination that evokes, but does not chronicle, a portion of the world and society of late republican Rome. Catullus' world has been well characterized in modern scholarship.[5] It is urban and urbane, violently partisan, morally lax, but with powerful undercurrents of old Roman values – family, the obligations of friendship and the acceptance of duty.

It is also a world of poets and poetry – a certain kind of poetry. For Catullus and his friends (Cinna, Calvus and the rest) were part of a poetic revolution that ostentatiously rejected Roman models in favour of the Hellenistic Greek poet Callimachus and his fellow Alexandrians, and they were as partisan in their poetics as in their politics. The 'New Poets', or neoterics, turned whole-heartedly and self-consciously to the principles of learning, craftsmanship and attention to detail sponsored by Callimachus. Like Callimachus, they eschewed epic in favour of smaller genres – particularly lyric, elegy, epigram and a species of miniature erotic 'epic' termed *epyllion* by modern scholars; they wrote love poems, satirized politicians (the more important the better), attacked bad poets and praised the Alexandrians and one another. Their metres were various and for the most part familiar (hexameters, elegiac couplets, iambics), but their hallmark was the Phalaecean hendecasyllable, an eleven-syllable verse little used before in either Greek or Latin poetry.

The hendecasyllable is the Catullan metre *par excellence*, and the one for which later generations would remember him best. About two-thirds of his lyrics, the so-called polymetrics (short poems in various metres), are in hendecasyllables. Their content is various (from the erotic to the scatological), but the metre is always light, graceful, intimate – perfectly suited to the cultivated ease and informality of the Catullan *persona*. (Indeed, the great German scholar Wilamowitz, apparently thinking that such a graceful and elegant metre had something French about it, attributed Catullus' facility in it to his Gallic ancestry.[6]) But the hendecasyllabics are as studied and carefully wrought – as Alexandrian – as anything in Catullus. Like the rest of the corpus

---

[5] See especially Wiseman, *Catullus and his World* 1–14; D. O. Ross, jun., *Style and Tradition in Catullus* (Cambridge, Mass., 1969) 80–95.
[6] Ulrich von Wilamowitz-Moellendorf, *Griechische Verskunst* (Berlin, 1921) 139.

they are both a product and an assertion of neoteric poetics. The programme is announced in the opening lines of the first poem, a dedication to Cornelius Nepos:

> To whom shall I give my charming new little book,
> Just now well polished with dry pumice?   (*Carmen* 1.1–2)

'Charming' and 'new' are catchwords in the neoteric vocabulary; 'well polished' puns on the polish given the papyrus roll and that applied to its contents by the artful poet; the diminutive 'little book' (*libellus*) announces that Catullus plans a work on a small (i.e., Alexandrian) scale.

We cannot tell what the book announced in the programme poem would have looked like, for the merest scraps of Latin poetic papyri have survived from antiquity. Catullus' word *libellus* suggests that the book was small – that is, that the papyrus roll it occupied would have been rather short. The facts of ancient book production make it almost certain that the *libellus* included only a portion of Catullus' poetry. Single books of poetry were written on separate rolls (e.g., a book of the *Aeneid*, a book of Horace's *Odes*, etc.), with a typical length of about 750 lines and an upper limit of around 1100. There are some exceptions: the books of Lucretius' *De Rerum Natura* range between 1092 and 1455 verses; Book 4 of Apollonius Rhodius contains 1779. Simply by adding more lengths of papyrus it would have been possible to manufacture a roll to contain a work much longer than even Apollonius 4, but the result would have been almost impossibly cumbersome for a book of poetry. The nearly 2300 verses of Catullus that we have today would constitute a book longer by a third than the longest extant book of ancient poetry, and they would require a roll substantially longer than the 10.5 metres usually taken to be the upper limit for classical papyri.[7] Such a book, if it ever existed, could scarcely be described as a *libellus*.

It is quite likely, therefore, that Catullus' poems appeared originally in several (probably at least three) books or rolls, which were joined

---

[7] F. G. Kenyon, *Books and Readers in Ancient Greece and Rome* (Oxford, 1951) 54–5. For further discussion see Julia Haig Gaisser, *Catullus and his Renaissance Readers* (Oxford, 1993) 5 and 277.

together when the work was transferred from roll to codex long after
his death, and that the dedication originally intended for a single *libellus*
was used for the whole. The exact contents and arrangement of each
book are unknown, but there are some probabilities. Catullus' poetry
easily falls into three sections that might well have appeared in separate
libelli. Poems 1–60 (about 850 lines) contain the polymetrics, 61–64
(795 lines) ambitious Alexandrian set-pieces (epithalamia, the Attis
poem, the miniature epic, or *epyllion*), and 65–116 (around 650 lines)
elegies and epigrams. Whether these groups were arranged and published as books by Catullus or another is open to question. Catullus
died young, and it is possible that the *libellus* announced in *Carmen* 1
(evidently the polymetrics) was the only one published in his lifetime.
The book shows signs of careful arrangement, but it may also include
poems added after his death by an editor. There are no dedications for
the other groups of poems, which perhaps were posthumously arranged.
It is likely, for example, that the *epyllion* (*Carmen* 64) originally occupied
a roll by itself. There is an additional complication. The principles of
arrangement discerned in the collection have been derived (naturally
enough) from the extant poems, but there is a possibility, at least, that
some of Catullus' poems did not survive. He has frequently been
credited with *priapea* (poems to the ithyphallic garden god, Priapus),
and it is probable that a quatrain preserved by Terentianus Maurus and
two one-line fragments found in Nonius and Porphyrion are genuine.[8]
The place of such poems in the collection is problematic; perhaps they
failed to survive simply because they were circulated separately.

From Antiquity to the Renaissance

Catullus had a profound influence on the Augustan poets in the next
generation – Virgil, Horace and the elegists. But it was Martial, a
hundred years later, in the Silver Age, who had the greatest influence
on Catullus. For it was Martial who created the portrait of Catullus that

---

8 Modern editors print them as fragments 1–3. Many earlier editors followed Marc-
Antoine de Muret (1554) in printing fragment 1, together with two non-Catullan *priapea*,
after *Carmen* 17.

would survive the Middle Ages and form the basis of the Renaissance Catullus in Italy and France. To paint this portrait, Martial did as every imitator and interpreter does: he looked in the mirror. In its reflection he saw not the elegant features of a learned and self-conscious Alexandrian, but the broader lineaments of a popular and racy epigrammatist.

Martial claims Catullus as his principal model throughout his *Epigrams* – by invoking his name, by imitating his themes and turns of phrase, and by his frequent use of the hendecasyllable to lend a Catullan flavour to his verse. But Martial's poetry is very different from Catullus', and its very Catullan *color* emphasizes the sense of distance and disjunction. Part of the difference lies in the *personae* of the two poets. This is what the sixteenth-century commentator and poet Muret felt when he remarked: 'there is as much difference between the writings of Martial and Catullus as between the words of some wag on the street-corner and the well-bred jests of a gentleman, seasoned with sophisticated wit'.[9]

But their two worlds differ as well. Catullus was a young man whose property and social position allowed him to move in the highest (if most morally lax) levels of Roman society. He could afford to be in the literary avant-garde, to live for his poetry and to insult anyone he liked – from Caesar and Pompey to the demagogue Publius Clodius, the brother and lover of his Lesbia. Martial, writing several generations later, lived by his wits on the fringes of society, without independent means, social prestige or a steady patron. He had to be a careful man, for he published ten of his twelve books of epigrams during the reign of the vicious emperor Domitian. His epigrams, however offensive, are designed to offend no one in particular: the butts of his satire and obscene jests are types; real people receive pleasantries and compliments.

Catullus, or rather, Martial's Catullus, was popular in the Silver Age. Poets liked to use him as a model for light and sometimes naughty verse, although some critics found his style harsh or rough. Writers of the period considered Catullus' learned Alexandrianism passé, and

---

9 Muret, *Catullus et in eum Commentarius* (Venice, 1554) iii. See Gaisser, *Catullus and his Renaissance Readers* 155 and 201.

seldom mentioned the long poems, but they unceasingly imitated and discussed the polymetrics and epigrams. They had their favourites: Catullus' dedication poem (*Carmen* 1), an obscene attack on Caesar and Mamurra (*Carmen* 29), his claim that the poet's life is separate from his poetry (*Carmen* 16), and, above all, his kiss poems to Lesbia (*Carmina* 5 and 7) and the two poems on Lesbia's sparrow (*Carmina* 2 and 3).

Thus diminished, Catullus entered the second century, where Aulus Gellius and Apuleius were among his readers. From this point on, however, Catullus goes underground for a thousand years. A few later writers mention his name or quote a verse or phrase at second hand, and there are various scraps of evidence for the transmission of the text; but after the second century we know of only two people for the next millennium who undoubtedly read Catullus: the scribe of a ninth-century anthology containing poem 62, and the scribe of the single manuscript we know of that survived the Middle Ages. No one else displays clear and direct knowledge of so much as a single poem.

The explanation for Catullus' eclipse seems to be – not censorship, as is sometimes suggested – but merely literary taste and a change in fashion. The qualities that the modern age, at least, values in him – his elegant urbanity, his learned Alexandrianism, his passionate emotion – had not appealed to Martial and his contemporaries in the Silver Age. Instead they admired and promoted him exclusively as a poet of light verse. Before long, he was supplanted by his chief imitator. Why read an old-fashioned and sometimes difficult poet like Catullus, when one could so easily enjoy Martial's smooth and racy epigrams? In any era a poet with few readers soon becomes unavailable. No doubt texts were already becoming scarce in the time of Apuleius and Aulus Gellius, and we can be sure that fewer still were preserved when scribes transferred the works of ancient authors from roll to codex around the fourth century AD.

We know that Catullus made the journey from antiquity to the Renaissance – he arrived, after all – but we do not know how or by what route. It is as if we were tracing a submarine or an underground stream – our evidence a faint blip of sonar or a telltale puddle – a mention here, a possible sighting there, a dubious one somewhere else. But at last, around 1300, Catullus washed up on the shores of the

Renaissance, with only the poor manuscript he stood up in and a few laudatory testimonia from Antiquity. We do not know what his manuscript looked like, for it was copied soon after its discovery and then lost or destroyed; and we do not know who found it, or where.

A contemporary epigram preserved in two of our earliest manuscripts commemorates the discovery and identifies the discoverer – but in the form of a riddle, which no one yet has managed to solve.

> *The Verses of Master Benvenuto Campesani of Vicenza on the Resurrection of the poet Catullus of Verona*
>
> An exile, I come to my country from distant lands.
> A fellow-countryman was the cause of my return,
> A man whom France assigned a name from the reeds,
> And one who marks the journey of the passing crowd.
> With all your might celebrate your Catullus,
> Whose light had been hidden under a bushel.

Only one point in the riddle is clear: someone from Catullus' home city of Verona discovered the manuscript 'in distant lands' and brought it back to Verona. Confusion surrounds the rest.

Catullus in Italy and France

The discovery of Catullus was greeted with enthusiasm, for he was one of the most celebrated poets of antiquity and he had been lost for a thousand years. The difficulty was that no one knew what to do with him. Scholars copied his manuscripts, but at a very slow rate. (We have only four manuscripts from the first hundred years after his discovery, and only half a dozen more from the next fifty.) They tried to correct the text, collected quotable verses for their anthologies, and included Catullus in lists of obscene poets when they sought either to excuse or to condemn scandalous verse. For the most part, however, they did not imitate or try to interpret his poetry – largely because they could not read it. Catullus' text was notoriously corrupt. Poems were run together; there were metrical problems without number; the point –

and often even the subject – of many poems was lost. Furthermore, although the humanists admired the learning of Catullus' poetry – or rather, admired the *idea* that it was learned – they were vague about the details. They knew that the poet was called *doctus Catullus* ('learned Catullus') by other ancient writers, but they had little notion of what his learning entailed. Greek studies were in their merest infancy, and much that we take for granted about Alexandrian literature was unknown. (In fact, two of the texts most important for understanding Catullus' learned Alexandrianism were discovered only in the twentieth century. Both are from the *Aitia* of Callimachus: the prologue, which sets out Callimachus' poetic programme, and the *Lock of Berenice*, which Catullus translated in *Carmen* 66.)

At the same time, however, Catullus' imitator Martial was meeting with a very different reception. Many manuscripts of Martial were available in the fourteenth and fifteenth centuries; he had been studied by Boccaccio in the 1370s, and by nearly every humanist afterwards; and his epigrams were widely imitated. If no one was reading Catullus, everyone was reading Martial.

The humanists gradually began to improve Catullus' text, and the process accelerated after the appearance of the first edition in 1472, which made the poet more widely available than he had been at any time in his history. But the real breakthrough came in the middle of the fifteenth century when the Neapolitan scholar and poet Giovanni Gioviano Pontano (1429–1503) took the obvious and fateful step of using Martial as a guide to Catullus. He accepted the portrait of Catullus he saw in Martial, read Catullus' poetry through Martial's imitations, and wrote his own Latin imitations of Martial's Catullus. Pontano's treatment would ultimately become the dominant way of reading Catullus well into the sixteenth century. But the Catullus perceived by Pontano and his successors was not identical with Martial's Catullus. The civilization of Catullus and Martial was gone, and with it the basic cultural assumptions that they had shared both with their ancient readers and with each other. Pontano and the other humanists were Italians, not Romans, and they saw both Martial and Martial's Catullus with Renaissance eyes. We might think of them as reading Catullus through both Martial's lens and their own – seeing neither a versatile Alexandrian nor a poet of light and racy verse, but rather a new figure, the Renaissance Catullus.

The Renaissance Catullus was above all a sensualist, largely divested of both powerful emotion and confusing Alexandrianism. The Italian poets (soon followed by the French) created him from Martial's Catullus, using as the basis of their creation a mere handful of poems which they read through Martial's imitations – *Carmen* 16, the sparrow poems (*Carmina* 2 and 3), and the kiss poems to Lesbia (*Carmina* 5 and 7).

Carmen 16 provided Italian and French poets with two essential justifications for risqué and obscene verse: first, the idea that poetry should be an aphrodisiac ('verses have charm and wit if they are soft and not too chaste and can titillate not just boys, but even sluggish old men', lines 7–9); and second, the principle that poetry does not reveal the morals of the poet ('the dedicated poet ought to be chaste; his verses are a different matter', lines 5–6).[10] The second idea had a long afterlife in Renaissance Catullan poetry, both in Latin and in the vernaculars. Sometimes it appeared in Martial's formulation ('my page is naughty; my life is pure', 1.4.8), but the poets more often quoted Catullus himself. In France, for example, Pierre Ronsard used *Carmen* 16, verses 5–6 as the motto of his *Folastries* ('Little Follies', 1553), which were conceived as French counterparts of the Catullan hendecasyllable.

Catullus' sparrow and kiss poems had been popular in antiquity. In the Renaissance they inspired almost as many imitations as the stars and sands invoked as images of innumerability by the poets. There were scores of poems on sparrows and doves and literally hundreds on kisses, including nearly a dozen kiss poems by Pontano as well as the influential Latin kiss cycle (*Basia*) by the Dutch poet Johannes Secundus (1511–36), which inspired still more imitations in both Latin and the vernaculars. Often, the sparrow (or dove) was combined with the kissing theme to speak more or less openly of both homosexual and heterosexual intercourse. Here too, Martial was the source – although it would be more accurate to say that the Italian humanist Angelo Poliziano (1454–94) bore equal responsibility, since it was he who created the

---

10 Cf. Martial 1.35 and 1.4.

Renaissance vogue for obscene evocations of the sparrow. He did so in the following chapter of his philological work, the *Miscellanea* (1489):

> *In what sense the sparrow of Catullus is to be understood, and a passage pointed out in Martial*

That sparrow of Catullus in my opinion allegorically conceals a certain more obscene meaning which I cannot explain with my modesty intact. Martial persuades me to believe this in that epigram of which these are the last verses:

> Give me kisses, but Catullan style.
> And if they be as many as he said,
> I will give you the sparrow of Catullus. [Martial 11.6.14–16]

For he would be too inept as a poet (which it is wrong to believe) if he said he would give the sparrow of Catullus, and not the other thing I suspect, to the boy after the kisses. What this is, for the modesty of my pen, I leave to each reader to conjecture from the native salaciousness of the sparrow. (*Miscellanea* 1.6)

But the sensual Catullus was not to everyone's taste. Poliziano's obscene interpretation of the sparrow appalled almost as many as it convinced, and many found the excuse for salacious verse from *Carmen* 16 unacceptable – either for contemporary poetry or for Catullus himself. Reactions to obscenity in the Renaissance varied from decade to decade and city to city, and even from one person to another. Some of Catullus' readers embraced it enthusiastically (the obscene passages in Catullus were explained more frankly and explicitly in the period from 1450 to 1520 than they would be for the next 450 years); but others wanted their poetry chaste and could excuse Catullus' obscenity only as a lamentable defect of his times.

Discomfort with Catullus and what he represented intensified throughout the sixteenth century, and humanists began to feel it increasingly necessary to find excuses for studying him. In his lectures at the University of Rome in 1521 the Italian humanist, Pierio Valeriano, tried to replace the image of Catullus the sensualist with that of Catullus the teacher. Like Catullus' other interpreters, Valeriano created a

Catullus in his own image. Valeriano saw himself as a teacher with a fatherly concern for his charges, in whom he wanted to instil both literary ambition and moral excellence. His Catullus had a similar beneficial purpose:

The poet is certainly useful when he celebrates virtues and does not allow the achievements of illustrious men to perish, by whose example others might be kindled to a desire for glory. He is useful when he chastises vice, criticizes evil ways, and attempts to deter mankind from imitating the wicked men he chastises in his poetry.[11]

In Counter-Reformation Rome a generation or so later it was somewhat more difficult to find excuses for the poet. In the preface to his commentary on Catullus (1566), the Portuguese humanist and papal secretary Achilles Statius claimed to have studied classical poetry in order to master lyric metres in preparation for his own Latin verse translation of the *Psalms*. After his friends urged him to use his notes to write commentaries on the poets, he began with Catullus on the grounds that 'it was the verdict of every earlier age that he surpassed all poets in elegance'. And he continued:

as to the fact that he wrote somewhat racily and voluptuously, this was the habit of those times, or rather the licence and defect, although he says of himself as if in embarrassment: 'The dedicated poet ought to be chaste – / His verses are a different matter.' (Statius, *Catullus* A3)

Statius' language exactly (and no doubt deliberately) reflects the terms in which the Council of Trent (1545–63) had excluded ancient authors from its general ban on obscene literature: elegance of style and the acknowledged licentiousness of paganism.[12]

But if Catullus could be embarrassing to a papal secretary in Rome, he required still more care from a northern Protestant. Joseph Scaliger, Catullus' most famous Renaissance editor, claimed in his commentary (1577) to have begun work on Catullus, Tibullus and Propertius ('the triumvirate of Love', as he called them) as a diversion after an illness

---

11 See Gaisser, *Catullus and his Renaissance Readers* 117.
12 *Ibid.* 170–71.

– drawn by their elegance of style, while hating the lasciviousness characteristic of their age. 'I compare the reading of poets to the sea,' he says:

There are reefs in it, but the experienced sailor never runs his ship aground on them. In poetry there are some indecent words on which the virtuous mind does not stumble, but briskly sails past unconcerned.

(Scaliger, *Castigationes* a5)

Catullus' frequent obscenity and his reputation as a sensualist were the most obvious bar to Catullan studies in the later sixteenth century, but even when his poetry was not obscene it was uncongenial to the general spirit of the age, which was increasingly concerned with serious moral, philosophical and theological issues. Catullus' subjects are poetry and personal emotions. The poet places himself in the centre of a world of friends, enemies, lovers and other poets, where the highest values are personal and aesthetic – the bonds of trust and obligation between individuals, and a poetic credo founded on learning, craftsmanship, and, above all, charm and wit. There is no room in his poetic landscape for large moral or national themes, no reference to ideals or claims beyond those of the individual. Such poetry serves, and can be made to serve, no utilitarian purpose except that of teaching elegant Latin style.

Catullus in England

Catullus came late to England. No doubt at least some of his poems were known in the fifteenth century, but we find the first direct allusion by an English scholar only in the sixteenth, when Nicholas Udall quoted and explained four verses from *Carmen* 84 in his *Floures for Latine Spekynge* (1533).[13] Texts were not always easy to get, even on the continent; and Lluellen's rhyme from *Marrow of the Muses* testifies to a general scarcity in England as late as 1660:

[13] Nicolas Udall, *Floures for Latine Spekynge Selected and Gathered oute of Terence* (London, 1533) 62. See James A. S. McPeek, *Catullus in Strange and Distant Britain* (Cambridge, Mass., 1939) 129 and 325.

> *Catullus*, and *Tibullus*, and that other
> Whose Name for want of Rime to't I must smother,
> Put them together, pray, *if you can get 'em*,
> And if you thinke they meane to fight eene let 'em.[14]

The scarcity continued until 1684, when a text of Catullus was finally printed in England. This edition, by the Dutch scholar Isaac Voss, made Catullus generally available for the first time and opened a new era for English readers, poets and translators.

Puritan strictures against erotic and frivolous poetry no doubt helped to delay the publication of Catullus, but lack of demand must have been the deciding factor, as we can see by comparing Catullus' publication history with Martial's. By 1700 Catullus had only the Voss edition of 1684, but there had been at least eight printings of Martial in England (three for use in Westminster School), and at least nine printings of translations of the *Epigrams*. It was Catullus' lack of moral utility – even more than his obscenity – that limited his popularity. Martial, after all, is often much more obscene than Catullus, but his epigrams (with some judicious surgery) were regarded as suitable school texts. The difference is that Martial is a satirist and that he is interested not in his own emotions but in the foibles of society. Suitably censored and selected, his epigrams have interesting and amusing moral – or at least, social – lessons to teach. His popularity in England during the sixteenth and seventeenth centuries was further assured by the contemporary taste for wit and a general enthusiasm for both Latin and English epigrams.[15] Catullus, with none of these factors to recommend him, was destined to move in much narrower circles.

From the beginning, Catullus' reception in England was very different from his reception in Italy. The difference in historical circumstances is obvious. Catullus appeared in Italy in a period that was receptive to erotic and personal poetry; by the time he arrived in England, such poetry was becoming suspect even on the continent. This change in

---

14 Quoted by McPeek, *Catullus in Strange and Distant Britain* 275.
15 See *Martial in English*, J. P. Sullivan and A. J. Boyle, eds. (Harmondsworth, 1996) xx–xxx; J. P. Sullivan, *Martial, The Unexpected Classic: A Literary and Historical Study* (Cambridge, 1991) 282–95.

attitudes ensured that English Catullan poetry would be less overtly sensual than its continental counterpart. *Carmen* 16, for example, is no longer used as a blanket excuse for obscenity or explicit sexual references. Instead, the principles culled from it by the continental poets are generally reversed or rejected. Thus, Abraham Cowley (1618–67) refuses to separate the character of the poet from that of his verse: "tis just / The Author blush, there where the Reader must' (*On Wit*). He presents poetry as an aphrodisiac for his readers ('My Lines of amorous desire / I wrote to kindle and blow others fire') – but in a poem lamenting that he has succumbed to the very emotions he counterfeited (*The Dissembler*). Sparrows and other birds abound, beginning with John Skelton (1460?–1529) and his *Boke of Phyllyp Sparowe* (c. 1505), but their lives and deaths have no obscene overtones. The many kiss poems deriving from *Carmina* 5 and 7 now tend less to assume consummation than to argue for it, and take as their subject seduction, not the intensification of an existing sexual affair.[16]

A second difference is still more important. Catullus appeared in Italy virtually out of nowhere, with no baggage of recent imitation, interpretation or scholarship; and the Italian humanists first interpreted him through Martial's imitations. He arrived in England surrounded by generations of European (predominantly Italian) literary and scholarly interpretation and there was no possibility for English readers and poets to have an unmediated encounter with him. They came to him with their minds full not only of Martial, but of 150 years of European poetry – from Pontano, Sannazaro and Marullo, to Tasso, Ronsard and Johannes Secundus, and many more besides. The large number of modern imitations both in Latin and in the vernaculars both lessened the importance of Martial for Catullus and complicated the English tradition of Catullan poetry. Modern Catullan poets imitated each other as well as Catullus; by now many of Catullus' themes had been treated so often that they had become part of a general poetic currency. As a consequence, when we find them in English poems, it is not always possible to identify Catullus as the primary model, or even as a model

---

16 See Gordon Braden, '*Vivamus, mea Lesbia* in the English Renaissance', *English Literary Renaissance* 9 (1979) 199–204.

at all. The English poems in turn became part of the stock for other imitations and translations.

One of the most striking examples of this process is the case of John Skelton's *Boke of Phyllyp Sparowe*. Skelton identified himself as 'the British Catullus'[17] and wrote on the death of a young woman's sparrow, but it is not clear that he had actually read Catullus himself or that anything in his 1380-verse lament owes a direct debt to Catullus' poems on Lesbia's sparrow (*Carmina* 2 and 3). He comes closest in these verses, which critics have compared with *Carmen* 2.1–2 ('Sparrow, the darling of my girl, with which she plays, which she holds in her lap'):

> It had a velvet cap,
> And wold syt upon my lap,
> And seke after small wormes,
> And somtyme white bred crommes;
> And many tymes and ofte
> Betwene my brestes softe
> It wolde lye and rest –
> It was propre and prest.[18] (verses 120–27)

But the parallel is not striking. Perhaps Skelton was thinking of Catullus. More likely, however, he was recalling something in one of Catullus' many European imitators. The important point, however, as McPeek observed long ago, is that Skelton's Phyllyp Sparowe soon became elided with Catullus' sparrow, so that for several decades the mention of the one evoked the other.[19] A pleasant offshoot of this tradition is Thomas Campion's Latin epitaph for Sir Philip Sidney, whom he mourns in an imitation of Catullus' lament for Lesbia's sparrow (*Carmen* 3); the name Philip provides the link.[20]

---

17 He awards himself the title in the Latin address to his book *Garlande or Chapelet of Laurell*: 'Ite, Britannorum lux O radiosa, Britannum / Carmina nostra pium vestrum celebrate Catullum!' (verses 1521–2). 'Go, shining light of the Britons, and celebrate, our songs, your worthy British Catullus!' See *John Skelton: The Complete English Poems*, John Scattergood, ed. (Harmondsworth, 1983). But in the next verses he calls himself Adonis and Homer.
18 *propre and prest*: 'pretty and neat'.
19 McPeek, *Catullus in Strange and Distant Britain* 56–67.
20 *De obitu Phil: Sidnaei equitis aurati generosissimi* (*Epig*. II.xi). *Campion's Works*, ed. Percival Vivian (Oxford, 1909) 273. Quoted by McPeek, 296.

Before the middle of the seventeenth century we find a relatively small number of actual translations, and these of a rather small number of poems: *Carmina* 5 and 7 (on kisses), *Carmen* 8 (Catullus' renunciation of Lesbia), *Carmen* 51 (the translation of Sappho), portions of *Carmina* 61 and 62 (the epithalamia), and snippets of other poems probably taken from commonplace books. This last category deserves some explanation. Renaissance readers enjoyed classical authors for their own sake, but also as ornaments for their own speech and writings. As they read, they copied into their commonplace books useful phrases, memorable lines, and, above all, pithy sentiments and aphorisms. Although Catullus lent himself to this treatment less well than poets like Martial or Horace or Virgil, even his earliest Renaissance readers found and collected quotable verses. The process began in Italy within a few years of the discovery of Catullus, when the Paduan judge, Geremia da Montagnone, excerpted seven Catullan passages for the commonplace book that he compiled around 1300.[21] Readers might make collections for themselves or supplement their own reading by borrowing from anthologies already in circulation. Ralegh's translation from *Carmen* 5 and Randolph's parody of the same verses (see Appendix), Sidney's translation of *Carmen* 70, and Herrick's translation from *Carmen* 22 were probably all made from originals in commonplace books.[22] The Catullan quotations from Montaigne translated by Matthew Gwinne perhaps have a similar origin.

Soon after 1650, however, both Lovelace and Cowley added to the stock of translated poems. Lovelace wrote literal translations of thirteen poems, only one of which (*Carmen* 70) had been translated before. Cowley freely translated *Carmen* 45 (on Septimius and Acme) and included an imitation of *Carmen* 4 (on Catullus' yacht) in his ode, *Sitting and Drinking in the Chair, made out of the Reliques of Sir Francis Drake's Ship* (see Appendix). The publication of Voss's edition in 1684 inspired still more translations and imitations; and, according to one count, by

---

21 See Gaisser, *Catullus and his Renaissance Readers* 19.
22 For Ralegh's verses from *Carmen* 5 see Braden, '*Vivamus, mea Lesbia* in the English Renaissance' 208–9. The verses translated by Herrick (*Carmen* 22.20–21) were excerpted by Geremia da Montagnone and probably by many others.

1750 around half of Catullus' 116 poems had been translated.[23] Apart from Lovelace, however, no single poet before the end of the eighteenth century translated more than one or two poems. The first collection of translations was published in 1707, in the anonymous *Adventures of Catullus*, which was translated from a French novel entitled *Les Amours de Catulle* (1680) and contained forty-six poems in renderings by an unknown number of different translators. The first complete translation appeared only in 1795. It was printed anonymously, but is generally acknowledged to be the work of a physician and scholar named John Nott.

The very late appearance of a complete translation can be partially but not entirely explained by Catullus' obscenity. The diversity of Catullus' poetry must bear equal responsibility. Not only does his work fall into three large and distinct categories (lyrics, Alexandrian set-pieces and epigrams), but the poems within each category vary widely in subject, tone and diction. The work of Martial, by contrast, belongs to the single genre of epigram; and that of Horace is fairly consistent within each of its several genres (epodes, satires, odes, epistles). To translate all of Catullus, a poet must command a wide range of genres and diction; to wish to translate him, he must have an even greater range of tastes, interests and sympathies.

Some of Catullus' poems command attention at every period – for example, *Carmina* 2, 3, 5 and 7 (the sparrow poems and the kiss poems to Lesbia), but others seem to have much more appeal in some periods and places than others. The explanation for such shifts in taste is not always obvious. A reader coming from Catullan poetry on the continent to that of the early English tradition, for example, finds some surprising omissions. Catullus' dedication (*Carmen* 1) was a favourite model for imitation both in antiquity and for Renaissance poets on the continent; yet English poets before the eighteenth century generally ignored it. *Carmen* 4 inspired the only parody of a whole poem that has survived from antiquity, *Catalepton* 10, generally attributed to Virgil in the Renaissance. On the continent original and parody alike received

---

[23] McPeek (*Catullus in Strange and Distant Britain* 288) says that forty-seven poems were imitated or alluded to, and sixty-two were 'translated'.

dozens of Latin imitations and parodies, and whole books were devoted to them from the end of the sixteenth to the middle of the seventeenth century.[24] The English poets, with the exception of Cowley, were apparently not interested. Later poets produced several imitations of *Carmen* 4, but neither it nor *Carmen* 1 ever became a favourite in the English tradition.

A few of Catullus' epigrams were translated early, and more than once, but most did not receive any attention before the eighteenth century. Epigrams were undoubtedly in vogue, but their model was Martial rather than Catullus. Martial's epigrams were witty, pointed and satirical. Catullus', by contrast, were emotional and personal. For the most part they lacked both general applicability and epigrammatic 'point' – the witty surprise or 'sting in the tail' that so endeared Martial to his many imitators. Continental poets hotly debated the merits of the two styles of epigram, ranging Martial on one side and Catullus and the poets of the *Greek Anthology* on the other, but in England Martial's supremacy in the genre was uncontested.[25]

The long poems, *Carmina* 61–8, experienced various fates. *Carmen* 67 (a conversation with the door of an adulterous household) has generally been ignored, but has been well translated by Michie in the twentieth century. The wedding poems, *Carmina* 61 and 62, were imitated by Chapman and Jonson and other writers of epithalamia in the sixteenth and seventeenth centuries, but their importance declined with that of the English epithalamium. Catullus' Alexandrian masterpiece, *Carmen* 64, was simply too long, too convoluted and too learned to attract sympathetic attention from early translators. This miniature epic tells two stories, one within the other: the wedding of Peleus and Thetis and the tragic tale of Ariadne and Theseus, which is embroidered on the coverlet of Thetis' marriage bed. It ends with the wedding-song of the Fates who prophesy the birth and career of Peleus and Thetis' son Achilles, and a surprising conclusion on the decline of human morality since the age of heroes. The poem as a whole has yet to receive a satisfactory English interpretation, although parts of it have been well

---

24 See Gaisser, *Catullus and his Renaissance Readers* 255–71.
25 For the debate see Sullivan, *Martial: The Unexpected Classic* 269–73; Gaisser, *Catullus and his Renaissance Readers* 155.

translated (see Elton, Bunting and Whigham). The earliest attempt to render a substantial portion of it is probably *The Complaint of Ariadna* by William Bowles (d. 1705). Bowles's effort was not a success. As McPeek aptly remarks after quoting part of it: 'Such lines witness the fascination of evil.'[26]

Carmina 65, 66 and 68 fared little better than 64, and for the same reasons. *Carmen* 65 introduces 66, Catullus' translation of Callimachus' elegy on the *Lock of Berenice*, a curl first dedicated to the gods and then transported to the skies as a constellation. The subject inspired Pope's *Rape of the Lock* (see Appendix), but did not find a satisfactory translation until the twentieth century (see Whigham). *Carmen* 68 (on Catullus' passion, his brother's death and the tragic love of Laodamia and Protesilaos) was extravagantly praised by Marc-Antoine de Muret and admired in France,[27] but its complex Alexandrianism attracted little attention in England; like 65 and 66, it has been translated best in the twentieth century (see Raphael and McLeish).

Carmen 63, however, has had a more appreciative reception. This poem, the only complete ancient example of the strange and hypnotic galliambic metre (see A Note on Catullus' Metres), relates the tragedy of the Greek youth Attis – from his ecstatic self-castration and religious frenzy in devotion to the mother goddess Cybele to his subsequent regret and ultimate enslavement to the goddess. Although Latin poets on the continent from Marullo to Muret imitated its galliambic metre to celebrate Bacchus and other ecstatic divinities,[28] *Carmen* 63 began to attract serious attention in England only at the end of the eighteenth century. It is tempting to attribute the origin of this interest to Gibbon, since both Nott and Hunt claim the authority of his praise.[29] Gibbon mentions Catullus in a footnote to his discussion of Neoplatonic interpretations of myths, including the story of Attis:

---

26 McPeek, *Catullus in Strange and Distant Britain* 245.
27 Gaisser, *Catullus and his Renaissance Readers* 159–61.
28 D. A. Campbell, 'Galliambic Poems of the 15th and 16th Centuries: Sources of the Bacchic Odes of the Pléiade School', *Bibliothèque d'humanisme et renaissance* 22 (1960) 490–510.
29 [John Nott], *The Poems of Caius Valerius Catullus in English Verse* (2 vols.; London, 1795) 1.206–7. Leigh Hunt, *Velluti to his Revilers* (*The Examiner*, 7 August 1825).

But all the allegories which ever issued from the Platonic school are not worth the short poem of Catullus on the same extraordinary subject. The transition of Atys from the wildest enthusiasm to sober pathetic complaint for his irretrievable loss, must inspire a man with pity, an eunuch with despair. (*Decline and Fall of the Roman Empire*, chapter 23, note 18)

Hunt published his important translation of the poem in 1810, and produced a remarkable imitation on a modern Attis in 1825 (*Velluti to his Revilers*; see Appendix). Twenty years after Hunt's *Velluti*, Walter Savage Landor closed his essay on Catullus with an ecstatic vision inspired by *Carmen* 63:

They who have listened patiently and supinely, to the catarrhal songsters of goose-grazed commons will be loth and ill-fitted to mount up with Catullus to the highest steeps in the forests of Ida, and will shudder at the music of the Corybantes in the temple of the Great Mother of the Gods.[30]

As Wiseman observes: 'The *Attis* has become the crucial text.'[31] Landor's enthusiasm was shared by his disciple Swinburne, who evoked Catullus' hypnotic fervour in *Dolores* (see Appendix). Both Tennyson and Meredith imitated the galliambic metre – Tennyson in *Boädicea* (see Appendix) and Meredith in *Phaéthôn* (see Note on Metres).

Carmen 63, however, was not the only poem to come into its own in the nineteenth century. *Carmina* 31 (Catullus' return to Sirmio), 46 (his departure from Bithynia) and 101 (his lament for his brother), all little noticed before 1800, have received great attention in the nineteenth and twentieth centuries. But *Carmen* 101 has achieved the greatest popularity. In 1842 Landor admired its 'sorrowful but . . . quiet solemnity', but it was the next generation of poets who took it to heart.[32] Swinburne both imitated it and used it to celebrate his 'brother poet', Baudelaire (see Appendix). Tennyson combined it with *Carmen*

---

30 Walter Savage Landor, 'The Poems of Catullus', *Foreign Quarterly Review* (1842), quoted from *The Complete Works of Walter Savage Landor*, ed. T. Earle Welby and Stephen Wheeler (16 vols.; London, 1927–36) 11.225.
31 Wiseman, *Catullus and his World* 214.
32 Landor, 'The Poems of Catullus' 220.

31 to lament the death of his own brother (see Appendix). Symons and Beardsley translated it at the turn of the century, and it has received scores of translations since.

The reception of some poems was retarded or complicated by their obscenity, as we can see in the representative cases of *Carmen* 32 and *Carmen* 16. In the early tradition English poets neglected *Carmen* 32, no doubt appalled by Catullus' invitation of Ipsitilla to 'nine fuckings one after the other'. They avoided *Carmen* 16, which had been so popular on the continent, not only because it claimed that poetry's purpose was the sexual titillation of its readers and separated the poet's character from his verses, but for its explicit threats of fellatio and sodomy against the catamites Furius and Aurelius. Both poems were translated, albeit with some euphemism, in the eighteenth century. In *The Adventures of Catullus* (1707), Ipsitilla is instructed, unambiguously, but without obscenity, to 'prepare to meet repeated Joy, continued bliss without Alloy'.[33] Nott (1795) translates *Carmen* 16, but softens Catullus' threat:

> I'll treat you as 'tis meet, I swear,
> Lascivious monsters as ye are!

But attitudes had hardened again already by the early nineteenth century. George Lamb omitted from his translation (1821) over twenty poems that he considered indecent, but contented himself with rewriting *Carmina* 16 and 32, expunging the threat of the one and the sexual invitation of the other. His excuse in each case is that a literal translation could not be tolerated.[34]

The change between Nott and Lamb reflects not only an increasing moral conservatism around the turn of the eighteenth century but also a difference in their approaches to translation.[35] Lamb wished to make the poet elegant and charming to his own readers and was willing to rewrite his poetry to secure the desired effect. Nott, by

---

[33] *The Adventures of Catullus* (London, 1701) 71.
[34] George Lamb, *The Poems of Caius Valerius Catullus* (2 vols.; London, 1821) 1.141 and 154.
[35] See Lawrence Venuti, *The Translator's Invisibility: A History of Translation* (London and New York, 1995) 81–98.

contrast, argued for the necessity of presenting Catullus as he was in his own time:

When an ancient classic is translated, and explained, the work may be considered as forming a link in the chain of history: history should not be falsified, we ought therefore to translate him somewhat fairly; and when he gives us the manners of his own day, however disgusting to our sensations, and repugnant to our natures they may oftentimes prove, we must not in translation suppress, or even too much gloss them over, through a fastidious regard to delicacy.[36]

Lamb's method had more adherents in the nineteenth century than Nott's, but with two interesting exceptions – James Cranstoun (1867) and Sir Richard Burton (1894). Cranstoun, a Scottish schoolmaster, allowed himself some departures from strict verbal accuracy for what he termed 'obvious reasons', but argued against rewritings and omissions:

His expressions, it is true, are often intensely sensuous, sometimes even grossly licentious, but to obliterate these and to clothe him in the garb of purity would be to misrepresent him entirely. He would be Atys, not Catullus.[37]

Burton, whose purpose was to produce a literal and completely unexpurgated translation, made an even stronger case for historical honesty than Nott:

A Scholar lively, remembered to me, that *Catullus* translated word for word, is an anachronism, and that a literal English rendering in the nineteenth century could be true to the poet's letter, but false to his spirit. I was compelled to admit that something of this is true; but it is not the whole truth. 'Consulting modern taste' means really a mere imitation, a re-cast of the ancient past in modern material. It is presenting the toga'd citizen, rough, haughty, and careless of any approbation not his own, in the costume of to-day, – boiled shirt, dove-tailed coat, black-cloth clothes, white pocket-handkerchief, and diamond ring. Moreover, of these transmogrifications we have already enough and to spare. But we have not, as far as I

---

36 [Nott], *The Poems of Caius Valerius Catullus in English Verse* 1.xi.
37 James Cranstoun, *The Poems of Valerius Catullus* (Edinburgh, 1867) vi.

know, any version of Catullus which can transport the English reader from the teachings of our century to that preceding the Christian Era.[38]

But neither Cranstoun nor Burton lived up to his promise. In Cranstoun the threat of *Carmen* 16 is reduced to 'Base Furius and Aurelius! hence, away!'; and Catullus' obscene request to Ipsitilla becomes: 'Caresses rare for me prepare, / Be three times three the number.' Burton, on the other hand, was thwarted by his wife. He died before his manuscript was sent to press, and his wife deleted the obscenities from his text, leaving dots of omission in their place. Ipsitilla apparently survived unscathed ('for us prepare / Nine-fold continuous love-delights'), but only dots were left for Furius and Aurelius:

> I'll . . . you twain and . . .
> Pathic Aurélius! Fúrius, libertines!

Not surprisingly, the last hundred years have tended towards greater tolerance and openness in the treatment of Catullus' obscenity. There have been some egregious exceptions, especially among scholars. Every American who read Catullus in college in the 1950s and '60s remembers Merrill's famous note on *Carmen* 32: 'Contents, execrable. Date, indeterminable. Metre, Phalaecean'.[39] Fordyce is notorious on both sides of the Atlantic for omitting thirty-two poems from his otherwise distinguished commentary (1961).[40] Twentieth-century poets and translators, on the other hand, generally approached Catullus' obscenity frankly, even when they were not being strictly literal (as in Whigham's instructions to Ipsitilla: 'prepare yourself to come nine times straight off together'). Sometimes their frankness verged on enthusiasm, exaggerating or outdoing Catullus himself. Several translations (not included in this anthology) by Carl Sesar and Raphael and McLeish are in this category. In more than one case a translator's enthusiasm for Catullus'

---

[38] Sir Richard Burton and Leonard Smithers, *The Carmina of Caius Valerius Catullus* (London, 1894) ix.

[39] *Catullus*, ed. Elmer Truesdell Merrill (Cambridge, Mass., 1893; reprinted 1951).

[40] C. J. Fordyce, *Catullus: A Commentary* (Oxford, 1961). He omitted the poems in deference to headmasters and headmistresses who thought them unsuitable for the classroom; see D. F. S. Thomson, *Catullus: Edited with a Textual and Interpretative Commentary* (Toronto, 1997) 59.

obscenity exceeded his understanding of it. In *Carmen* 16, for example, Catullus uses his threats of fellatio and sodomy to demonstrate dominance and masculine superiority over unwilling passive partners ('I'll show you boys who's a man!') and to prove that his effeminate verses are no indication of his own character. Translations suggesting that Catullus will be the passive partner mistake the point of the poem.[41]

Obscene language was not the only stumbling block for translators. Homosexual or pederastic themes, even without obscenity, were equally problematic. In general, eighteenth- and nineteenth-century translators reacted to them as they did to obscenity – but with one exception, Catullus' boy Juventius, who proved to be an embarrassment to the open and squeamish alike. *The Adventures of Catullus*, generally so frank, argues that 'Juventius' was really the nickname given to a woman named Crastinia, who just happened to resemble a young man named Juventius. Nott entitles each of the four Juventius poems (*Carmina* 24, 48, 81, 99) 'To his Favourite' and avoids any reference to gender. Lamb depicts Juventius as merely a friend in 24 and 81, but suppresses his name and changes his sex in 48 and 99, both on the subject of kisses (in 99 Juventius becomes 'dearest maid of my soul'). Cranstoun, for all his avowed honesty, follows Lamb, although he is at least consistent: he depicts Catullus' darling as always anonymous and always female (in 99 she is 'fair honey'd maid'). Burton alone is honest about the gender and the situation; his collaborator Leonard Smithers clarifies matters still further with his note on *Carmen* 99: 'This poem shews beyond contradiction that Catullus himself was not free from the vice of paederasty, so universal amongst the Roman youth.'[42]

Thus, apart from Burton, even translators who could treat obscenity and homosexuality frankly according to the standards of their time could not stomach Juventius. They could render the homosexual invective Catullus hurled against his enemies, but they could not allow a homosexual romance to the poet himself. The reason is to be sought in the vividness and immediacy of the *persona* of Catullus created in the poems and the way in which readers identified with it. From at least the end

---

41 Thus Sisson and Raphael and McLeish.
42 Burton and Smithers, *The Carmina of Caius Valerius Catullus* 313.

of the seventeenth century, poets and critics both believed in the reality of the *persona* and saw in Catullus someone with their own emotions and moral values – or perhaps it is better to say, with the emotions and moral values *they professed* in accordance with the standards of their time. Like both Martial and the readers of the Italian Renaissance before them, they created a Catullus in their own image. Before the end of the nineteenth century, this Catullus, whatever else he did, could not possibly indulge in homosexual love, and he most certainly could not plead with a young boy for kisses, as the poet does in *Carmina* 48 and 99.

The picture of Catullus created by his readers has changed with the times. In *The Adventures of Catullus* he was a seventeenth-century French courtier in English translation. In Lamb he appeared to be a man of aristocratic manners and temperament living in an uncongenial age, as if he were a high-minded English gentleman transplanted into a somewhat unsavoury period:

we may fairly describe him as irascible but forgiving; careless and imprudent; affectionate to his kindred, warm in friendship, but contemptuous and offensive to those whom he disliked; grateful, but not cringing, to his patrons; and inclined to constancy in love, had his constancy met with return. He seems to have been as little sullied by the grossness of the age, as was possible for one invited to the pleasures of the times by the patronage of his superiors: as far as we know, he gave in to no vice which was then stigmatized as disgraceful; and pure indeed must that mind naturally have been, which, amidst such coarseness of manners, could preserve so much expressive delicacy and elevated refinement.[43]

Other nineteenth-century poets and translators pictured their Catullus in similar terms, although he became somewhat more sentimental as the century progressed – more Victorian, one might say. In 1861 Theodore Martin criticized Lamb for presenting 'not Catullus, but the graceful sarcasms of a well-bred gentleman of the days of the Regency', and depicted an equally anachronistic Catullus of his own.[44] Martin's

---

43 Lamb, *The Poems of Caius Valerius Catullus* 1.xliii.
44 Theodore Martin, *The Poems of Catullus Translated into English Verse* (London, 1861) xxx.

Catullus was an embodiment of 'manliness', a strange conglomerate of English public-school virtues that attained almost the status of a cult in England from about 1860 to 1900:

Impulsive, irascible, intense, wayward, and hasty, but at all times hearty, frankly spoken, generous, and manly, it is impossible not to be drawn towards him, and to forget his faults in our sympathy with his warm heart and thoroughly genial temperament.[45]

Only Burton saw that Catullus was not a nineteenth-century English gentleman complete with 'boiled shirt, dove-tailed coat, black-cloth clothes, white pocket-handkerchief, and diamond ring'.

By the early twentieth century Catullus had become a full-blown Romantic. In both Symons and Yeats (see Appendix) we find him a passionate lover scornful of the limits of bourgeois society. (The American Catullus at the same period is generally a lighter and more cheerful character, to judge from the translations of Field, Stewart and Adams.) After about 1930 Catullus began to speak in many voices, American and Australian as well as English, and to take on a variety of characters from the austere (Lucas) to the jokey (Copley). Since around 1960 he has become increasingly and sometimes defiantly explicit in his language and hostile in his invective, more devoted to his brother, and correspondingly more cynical about Lesbia – in both his variety and his emotions, a Catullus of our time.

---

45 Martin, *The Poems of Catullus Translated into English Verse* xxvi. For more on manliness see D. Newsome, *Godliness and Good Learning* (London, 1961) 195–239; Gaisser, 'The Roman Odes at School: The Rise of the Imperial Horace', *Classical* 87 (1994) 443–56.

A NOTE ON CATULLUS' METRES

Latin metre is quantitative. It uses patterns not of stressed and unstressed syllables as English metre does, but of syllables regarded as long or short. (The conventional notation is – for long, u for short and x for a syllable that may be either long or short.) Strictly speaking, long syllables are held or pronounced for a longer period of time than short syllables, not more strongly stressed or accented. The distinction, however, is not always easy to maintain, both since the ears of English speakers are more attuned to accentual than to quantitative rhythms and because the Latin language itself is strongly accentual. Often in Latin poetry the quantitative metre of longs and shorts clashes with or contradicts the natural accent of the words to produce a complex rhythmical counterpoint.

In reading Latin poetry one runs together or 'elides' a vowel or *m* at the end of a word with a vowel at the beginning of the next word, making one syllable out of two for metrical purposes. The Romans probably lightly pronounced or slid over the elided vowel.

Catullus uses several different metres. Some of the most important are described and illustrated with English examples below. (The English poets substitute stressed and unstressed syllables for Catullus' longs and shorts.)

Hendecasyllables

About two-thirds of Catullus' lyrics or polymetrics (*Carmina* 1–60) are in hendecasyllables, a light and graceful eleven-syllable line. The metrical beat and word accent usually coincide, producing a naturalistic, conversational effect. (The pattern is described thus: x x – u u – u – u – –.)

> Quaeris, quot mihi basiationes
> tuae, Lesbia, sint satis superque. (*Carmen* 7.1–2)

Several nineteenth-century poets imitated the metre, including Tennyson (see Appendix), George Meredith:

> The sweet smell of the woodland haunts me ever. (*Fragment* 68)

and Swinburne:

> In the month of the long decline of roses
> I, beholding the summer dead before me,
> Set my face to the sea and journied silent. (*Hendecasyllabics*, 1–3)

Sapphic Stanza

Only *Carmina* 11 and 51 are in sapphics. The stanza consists of three eleven-syllable lines (– u – x – u u – u – –) and a short fourth line (– u u – –), which gives the metre its characteristic shape.

> Ille mi par esse deo videtur,
> ille, si fas est, superare divos,
> qui sedens adversus identidem te
> spectat et audit (*Carmen* 51.1–4)

Zukofsky, Charles Martin, Bunting, Dennis and Mezey have all reproduced the effect of the stanza in their translations. Here is a sapphic stanza from Swinburne:

> All the night sleep came not upon my eyelids,
> Shed not dew, nor shook nor unclosed a feather,
> Yet with lips shut close and with eyes of iron
> Stood and beheld me. (*Sapphics*, 1–4)

Glyconics and Pherecrateans

Catullus uses combinations of these metres in *Carmina* 17, 30, 34 and 61. The basic element is a measure called a choriamb (– u u –), which is also found in both hendecasyllables and sapphics. A glyconic is x x – u u – u – ; a pherecratean is one syllable shorter: x x – u u – –. Each line of *Carmen* 17 consists of a glyconic followed by a pherecratean; an obligatory diaeresis (break between words, represented ||) separates the two units:

> O Colonia, quae cupis || ponte ludere longo.   (*Carmen* 17.1)

Badham uses a very similar metre in his translation, but breaks up the line into shorter units. *Carmen* 30 is in glyconics with the insertion of two additional choriambs:

> Alfene immemor atque unanimis false sodalibus.   (*Carmen* 30.1)

Carmina 34 and 61 are in stanzas. *Carmen* 34 has three glyconic lines followed by a pherecratean. In *Carmen* 61 there are four glyconics and a pherecratean:

> Collis o Heliconii
> cultor, Uraniae genus,
> qui rapis teneram ad virum
> virginem, o Hymenaee Hymen,
> o Hymen Hymenaee.   (*Carmen* 61.1–5)

Tennyson used glyconics alone in alternate stanzas in the 'Jubilee Ode'.

> You then joyfully, all of you,
> Set the mountain aflame tonight,
> Shoot your stars to the firmament,
> Deck your houses, illuminate
> All your towns for a festival.
>   ('On the Jubilee of Queen Victoria', 15–19)

Iambics

Catullus has several poems in iambics (the pattern is u –), a metre also natural to English. *Carmina* 4 and 29 are in pure iambic trimeter – six iambic feet with no substitutions:

> Quis hoc potest videre, quis potest pati,
> nisi impudicus et vorax et aleo,
> Mamurram habere quod comata Gallia
> habebat uncti et ultima Britannia?   (*Carmen* 29.1–4)

Burton translated the verses into iambic pentameter:

> Who e'er could witness this (who could endure
> Except the lewdling, dicer greedy-gut
> That should Mamurra get what hairy Gaul
> And all that farthest Britons held whilòme?)
>   ('To Caesar of Mamurra, called Mentula', 1–4)

Eight poems, including *Carmina* 8, 37 and 39, are in 'limping iambics' (*scazons*). This iambic trimeter verse allows some substitutions and resolutions, but its characteristic feature is the substitution of a long for a short in the last foot (not u – but – –), which gives the line its dragging, limping effect.

> Egnatius, quod candidos habet dentes,
> renidet usque quaque. si ad rei ventum est   (*Carmen* 39.1–2)

Goold's translation preserves the metre:

> Ignatius is the owner of superb white teeth,
> With which he gives to all he meets a big broad smile.

Galliambics

Only one complete poem in galliambics survives from antiquity, *Carmen* 63. The metre is supposed to have been used for hymns sung to Cybele by her castrated priests, the *Galloi*. It consists of two groups of eight syllables divided by an obligatory diaeresis (||). It follows the pattern u u – u – u – – || u u – u u u u x, but u u and – are often interchanged. The diaeresis preceded by two long syllables in the centre of the verse helps to create a compelling hypnotic rhythm; the large number of short syllables throughout the verse, but especially at the end of the line, produces a rushing, frenzied effect. The example below is from Attis' ecstatic speech to his comrades.

> mora tarda mente cedat: || simul ite sequimini
> Phrygiam ad domum Cybebes, || Phrygia ad nemora deae,
> ubi cymbalum sonat vox, || ubi tympana reboant,
> tibicen ubi canit Phryx || curvo grave calamo,
> ubi capita Maenades vi || iaciunt hederigerae,
> ubi sacra sancta acutis || ululatibus agitant,
> ubi suevit illa divae || volitare vaga cohors,
> quo nos decet citatis || celerare tripudiis. (*Carmen* 63.19–26)

Tennyson approximated the effect of the metre in 'Boädicea' (see Appendix). Meredith also imitated it in 'Phaéthôn':

> Lo, lo, increasing lustre, torrid breath to the nostrils; lo,
> Torrid brilliancies thro' the vapours lighten swifter, penetrate
>   them,
> Fasten merciless, ruminant, hueless, on earth's frame crackling
>   busily.
> He aloft, the frenzied driver, in the glow of the universe,
> Like the paling of the dawn-star withers visibly, he aloft:
> Bitter fury in his aspect, bitter death in the heart of him.
>   ('Phaéthôn', 103–8)

Dactylic Hexameter

Carmina 62 and 64 are in hexameters. The line consists of six feet. Each of the first four may be either a dactyl (– u u) or a spondee (– –). The fifth foot is usually a dactyl and the sixth is always a spondee. Since the hexameter is traditionally the metre of epic poetry, it was the natural choice for Catullus' miniature epic, *Carmen* 64. Catullus' hexameter tends to have a high proportion of spondees, since Latin has a large number of long syllables. In the example below the last five feet of the third verse are all spondees. (*Aeeteos* has four long syllables.)

> Peliaco quondam prognatae vertice pinus
> dicuntur liquidas Neptuni nasse per undas
> Phasidos ad fluctus et fines Aeeteos. (*Carmen* 64.1–3)

English hexameters are much lighter, as Coleridge complained:

> All my hexameters fly, like stags pursued by the stag-hounds,
> Breathless and panting, and ready to drop, yet flying still onwards,
> I would full fain pull in my hard-mouthed runaway hunter;
> But our English Spondeans are clumsy yet impotent curb-reins;
> And so to make him go slowly, no way have I left but to lame him.
> (*Hexameters*, 10–14)

Elegiac couplets

Catullus uses elegiacs for the long poems, *Carmina* 65–8, and for the epigrams, *Carmina* 69–116. The couplet consists of a dactylic hexameter and a so-called 'pentameter': – u u – u u – ‖ – u u – u u –. The pentameter is divided by an obligatory diaeresis, with two and one-half dactylic feet on either side. In the first half, dactyls and spondees are interchangeable; dactyls are obligatory in the second. The hexameter line of the couplet seems to have a forward, even rapid, movement. The pentameter echoes it, but with a retarding effect produced by the diaeresis and the single long syllable at line end.

> Nulli se dicit mulier mea nubere malle
>   quam mihi, non si se Iuppiter ipse petat. (*Carmen* 70.1–2)

Sidney tried to translate this epigram (included in this volume) into English quantitative metre, but the characteristic rising and falling quality of the couplet appears to better effect in the verses Coleridge translated from Schiller's imitation:

> In the hexameter rises the fountain's silvery column;
>   In the pentameter aye falling in melody back.
>
> ('The Ovidian Elegiac Metre')

Now Schiller:

> Im Hexameter steigt des Springquells flüssige Säule;
>   Im Pentameter drauf fällt sie melodisch herab. ('Das Distichon')

The starting and stopping effect of the pentameter is captured in a wicked Victorian parody:

> All men alike hate slops, particularly gruel.

FURTHER READING

Eleanor Shipley Duckett. *Catullus in English Poetry*. Smith College Classical Studies 6. Northampton, Massachusetts, 1925.

John Bernard Emperor. *The Catullian Influence in English Lyric Poetry, Circa 1600–1650*. The University of Missouri Studies 3. Columbia, Missouri, 1928.

J. Ferguson. 'Catullus and Tennyson'. *English Studies in Africa* 12 (1961) 41–58.

William Fitzgerald. *Catullan Provocations: Lyric Poetry and the Drama of Position*. Berkeley, California, 1995.

Julia Haig Gaisser. *Catullus and his Renaissance Readers*. Oxford, 1993.

G. P. Goold, ed. *Catullus*. London, 1983.

James W. Halporn, Martin Ostwald and Thomas G. Rosenmeyer. *The Meters of Greek and Latin Poetry*. New York, 1963.

James A. S. McPeek. *Catullus in Strange and Distant Britain*. Harvard Studies in Comparative Literature 15. Cambridge, Massachusetts, 1939.

Kenneth Quinn. *The Catullan Revolution*. Cambridge, 1969.

George M. Ridenour. 'Swinburne's Imitations of Catullus'. *The Victorian Newsletter*, Fall 1988, 51–7.

J. P. Sullivan. *Martial, The Unexpected Classic: A Literary and Historical Study*. Cambridge, 1991.

Lawrence Venuti, *The Translator's Invisibility: A History of Translation*. London and New York, 1995.

T. P. Wiseman, *Catullus and his World: A Reappraisal*. Cambridge, 1985.

TRANSLATIONS AND IMITATIONS

SIR WALTER RALEGH
(c. 1552–1618)

Ralegh, courtier and adventurer, historian and poet, fell in and out of favour with Queen Elizabeth, but was always out of favour with King James I, who kept him in the Tower of London for thirteen years, then sent him on an impossible mission to Guiana, and finally had him beheaded. His translation of three lines from *Carmen 5* was probably made from a commonplace book (see Introduction). He used it in *The History of the World*, which he wrote and published anonymously while he was imprisoned.

From *The History of the World* (1614), 1.2.5.

Carmen 5.4–6

That Man is (as it were) a little world: with a digression touching our mortalitie . . . For this tide of mans life, after it once turneth and declineth, ever runneth with a perpetuall ebbe and falling streame, but never floweth againe: our leafe once fallen, springeth no more, neither doth the Sunne or the Summer adorne us againe, with the garments of new leaves and flowers . . . of which Catullus, Epigram 53:

The Sunne may set and rise:
But we contrariwise
Sleepe after our short light
One everlasting night.

SIR PHILIP SIDNEY (1554–86)

Sidney was an energetic courtier and adviser of Queen Elizabeth I and an ardent supporter of the Protestant cause, for which he died a chivalrous and premature death fighting for the Dutch against the Spaniards. He wrote most of his poetry, including the selection below, in the period 1578–82, when he was often absent from the court.

Sidney translates *Carmen* 70 literally. The selection here identified as an imitation of *Carmen* 51 has sometimes been called a translation of Sappho's *Fragment* 31 (of which *Carmen* 51 is a translation). Both Sappho's poem (first published in 1554) and Catullus' translation were frequently translated and imitated in France in the second half of the sixteenth century, and Sidney probably has both poems in mind. His translations show the influence of his membership in the Areopagus (a group promoting the use of classical metres in English), for both are in quantitative verse. The first is in a metre Sidney called 'Anacreon's kind of verses'; the pattern (u – u – u – –) is achieved by relying almost exclusively on monosyllables. The second, probably the earliest English translation of Catullus, is in elegiac couplets.

Carmen 51 is from *The Second Eclogues* of *The Countess of Pembroke's Arcadia* (1593). *Carmen* 70 is from *Certain Sonnets*, first printed with *The Countess of Pembroke's Arcadia* (1598).

Carmen 51.5–12

My muse what ails this ardour?
My eys be dym, my lyms shake,
My voice is hoarse, my throte scorcht,
My tong to this my roofe cleaves,
My fancy amazde, my thought dull'd,
My harte doth ake, my life faints,
My sowle beginnes to take leave.
So great a passion all feele,
To think a soare so deadly
10 I should so rashly ripp up.   (*Second Eclogues* 32.9–18)

Carmen 70

Out of Catullus

Unto no body my woman saith she had rather a wife be,
    Than to my selfe, not though *Jove* grew a suter of hers.
These be her words, but a woman's words to a love that is
    eager,
    In wind or water streame do require to be writ.

MATTHEW GWINNE (1558?–1627)

Gwinne was the first professor of physic at Gresham College in London, enjoyed a large medical practice and served as a commissioner in charge of inspecting tobacco. He is best known, however, for his friendship with John Florio and for his contribution to Florio's translation of Montaigne. Florio credited Gwinne with tracing the sources of Montaigne's many quotations from Greek, Latin, Italian and French literature; and it is generally thought that he provided the translations for them as well.

The selections below from Florio's *Montaigne* have a double pedigree since they are French in their selection and Elizabethan in their language and sensibility. Catullus was better known in France than in England, and had long been imitated in both French and neo-Latin poetry, but Montaigne seems to have made a deliberate effort to avoid quoting from the short Catullan lyrics popular with contemporary continental poets. He quotes from thirteen different poems, but never from the kiss poems (*Carmina* 5, 7 and 48) or from the popular epigrams (70, 72, 85). Instead, he favours the long elegies, especially 68, which he quotes twelve times. His preference for *Carmen* 68 was probably influenced by the enthusiasm of his fellow countryman, Marc-Antoine de Muret, who described it in his commentary (1554) as 'perhaps the most beautiful elegy to be found in the whole Latin language'.

From Michel de Montaigne, *The Essays: or Morall, Politike and Millitarie Discourses*, John Florio, trans. (1603).

Carmen 51.5–12 from Montaigne 1.2: 'Of Sadnesse or Sorrowe'

>   miserably from me
> This bereaves all sence: for I can no sooner
> Eie thee my sweete heart, but I wot not one word
>   to speake amazed.
> Tongue-tide as in a trance, while a sprightly thin flame
> Flowes in all my joynts, with a selfe-resounding
> Both my eares tingle, with a night redoubled
>   Both mine eies are veild.

Nor is it in the liveliest and most ardent heate of the fit, that wee are able to display our plaints and perswasions, the soule being then aggravated with heavie thoughts, and the body suppressed and languishing for love. And thence is sometimes engendered that casuall faintnes, which so unseasonably surpriseth passionate Lovers, and that chilnesse, which by the power of an extreme heate doth seize on them in the verie midst of their joy and enjoying. All passions that may be tasted and digested, are but meane and slight.

Carmen 64.405–6 from Montaigne 3.5: 'Upon Some Verses of Virgil'

Our maistery and absolute possession, is infinitly to be feared of them [women]: After they have wholy yeelded themselves to the mercy of our faith and constancie, they have hazarded something: They are rare and difficult vertues: so soone as they are ours, we are no longer theirs.

51.4 *to speake amazed* translates a fifteenth-century supplement (*quod loquar amens*) for a verse lacking in Catullus

The lust of greedy minde once satisfied,
They feare no words; nor reke othes falsified.

Carmen 65.19–24 from Montaigne 3.5: 'Upon Some Verses of Virgil'

To conclude this notable commentarie, escaped from me by a flux of babling: a flux sometimes as violent as hurtfull,

As when some fruite by stealth sent from hir friend,
From chaste lap of a virgin doth descend,
Which by hir, under her soft aprone plast,
Starting at mothers comming thence is cast
And trilling down in hast doth head-long goe,
A guiltie blush in hir sad face doth floe.

Carmen 66.15–18 from Montaigne 1.37: 'How we weepe and laugh at one selfe-same thing'

And what gentle flame soever doth warme the heart of young virgines, yet are they hardly drawne to leave and forgoe their mothers, to betake them to their husbands: whatsoever this good fellow say;

Doe yong Brides hate indeede fresh *Venus* toyes,
   Or with false teares delude their parents joyes,
Which in their chambers they powre out amaine?
   So helpe me God, they doe not true complaine.

64.2 *They* i.e., men

A mosaic of verses from *Carmina* 68 and 65 on the death of Catullus' brother (68.20, 23–4, 21–2, 25–6, 65.[9]–11) from Montaigne 1.27: 'Of Friendship', in which he laments the death of his friend Étienne de La Boétie

O brother reft from miserable me,
All our delight's are perished with thee,
Which thy sweete love did nourish in thy breath.
Thou all my good hast spoiled in thy death:
With thee my soule is all and whole enshrinde,
At whose death I have cast out of minde
All my mindes sweete meates, studies of this kinde;
Never shall I heare thee speake, speake with thee?
Thee brother than life dearer never see?
10   Yet shalt thou ever be belov'd of mee.

Carmen 68.125–8 from Montaigne 3.5: 'Upon Some Verses of Virgil'

. . . there is nor quaint phrase, nor choise word, nor ambiguous figure, nor patheticall example, nor love-expressing gesture, nor alluring posture, but they [women] knowe them all better than our bookes: It is a cunning bred in their vaines and will never out of the flesh . . . which these skill-infusing Schoole-mistresses nature, youth, health and opportunitie, are ever buzzing in their eares, ever whispering in their mindes: They neede not learne, nor take paines about it; they beget it, with them it is borne.

No Pigeons hen, or paire, or what worse name
You list, makes with hir Snow-white cock such game,
With biting bill to catch when she is kist,
As many-minded women when they list.

68.1 *paire* mate

> *Had not this naturall violence of their desires bin somwhat held in awe, by feare and honor, wherewith they have beene provided, we had all beene defamed.*

GEORGE CHAPMAN (c. 1560–1634)

Chapman, like his friend Jonson, was a prolific poet, dramatist and translator. He completed Christopher Marlowe's *Hero and Leander*, and his works include *The Shadow of Night* and important translations of Petrarch, Juvenal, Hesiod and, above all, Homer.

Catullus' *Carmen* 62 is a wedding-song for alternating choruses of youths and maidens. Chapman freely adapts the youths' lines at the beginning and end in the following selection from *Epithalamion Teratos* in *Hero and Leander*. He imitates most closely at lines 16–20, where he plays with Catullus' conceit that the maiden holds only a third share in her virginity. Catullus, however, awards the other two thirds to her parents, while Chapman, perhaps more romantically, gives equal parts to the parents, the girl and her husband.

From the end of the Fifth Sestiad of *Hero and Leander* (1598).

Carmen 62.1–3 and 62–5, adapted

The Evening starre I see:
Rise youths, the Evening starre,
Helps Love to summon warre,
Both now imbracing bee.
Rise youths, loves right claimes more than banquets, rise.
Now the bright Marygolds that deck the skies,
Phoebus celestiall flowrs, that (contrarie
To his flowers here) ope when he shuts his eie,
And shut when he doth open, crowne your sports:
10   Now love in night, and night in love exhorts
Courtship and Dances: All your parts employ,
And suite nights rich expansure with your joy,

>   Love paints his longings in sweet virgins eyes:
>   Rise youths, loves right claims more than banquets, rise.
>   Rise virgins, let fayre Nuptiall loves enfold
>   Your fruitles breasts: the maidenheads ye holde
>   Are not your owne alone, but parted are;
>   Part in disposing them your Parents share,
>   And that a third part is: so must ye save
> 20 Your loves a third, and you your thirds must have.
>   Love paints his longings in sweet virgins eyes:
>   Rise youths, loves right claims more than banquets, rise.

THOMAS CAMPION (1567–1620)

Campion claimed pre-eminence in the three arts of Apollo, describing himself as 'Campion the musician, the poet and the doctor' (*Epigram* 1.167). He studied at Cambridge and at Gray's Inn (as much an academy of music, poetry and manners as a school of law), and took his medical degree at the University of Caen in France (better known for its music and pageantry than as a medical school). He achieved a reputation as a Latin poet through his *Poemata* (1595), which included an epitaph for Sir Philip Sidney recalling Catullus' *Carmen* 3 on the death of Lesbia's sparrow (see Introduction). His greatest accomplishment, however, was as a writer of words and music for the lute song. His works include several *Bookes of Ayres*, as well as masques for the court and nobility.

Campion's three imitations are lute songs. *Carmen* 5, the most imitated and translated of Catullus' poems, had already inspired scores of imitations in Europe. Between 1601 and 1612 versions by Campion, Ben Jonson and Anonymous (1612) would appear in three separate collections of airs. Catullus' poem treats three themes: kisses (the most important to his European imitators), censorious old men and the shortness of human life. Campion translates Catullus only in his first stanza, omitting the kissing theme and the second half of Catullus' poem. (For a full translation see Crashaw.) His second and third stanzas develop themes from Propertius and Tibullus. The subject in *Carmen* 7 is kisses, which are to be as many as the sands of Libya or the stars that see stolen loves. Campion follows Catullus only in lines 11–16 and 21–4; lines 16–20 recall *Carmen* 48.

Carmen 5 is from *A Booke of Ayres* (1601). *Carmina* 7 and 8 are from *Two Bookes of Ayres* [1612/13].

Carmen 5

My sweetest Lesbia, let us live and love,
And, though the sager sort our deedes reprove,
Let us not way them; heav'ns great lampes doe dive
Into their west, and strait againe revive,
But, soone as once set is our little light,
Then must we sleepe one ever-during night.

If all would lead their lives in love like mee,
Then bloudie swords and armour should not be,
No drum nor trumpet peaceful sleepes should move,
10   Unles alar'me came from the campe of love:
But fooles do live, and wast their little light,
And seeke with paine their ever-during night.

When timely death my life and fortune ends,
Let not my hearse be vext with mourning friends,
But let all lovers, rich in triumph, come,
And with sweet pastimes grace my happie tombe;
And, Lesbia, close up thou my little light,
And crowne with love my ever-during night.

Carmen 7

Come, you pretty false-ey'd wanton,
    Leave your crafty smiling:
Think you to escape me now
    With slipp'ry words beguiling?

No; you mock't me th' other day,
    When you got loose, you fled away;
But, since I have caught you now,
    Ile clip your wings for flying:
Smothring kisses fast Ile heape,
    And keepe you so from crying.

Sooner may you count the starres,
    And number hayle downe pouring,
Tell the Osiers of the *Temmes*,
    Or *Goodwins* Sands devouring,
Than the thicke-showr'd kisses here
    Which now thy tyred lips must beare.
Such a harvest never was,
    So rich and full of pleasure,
But 'tis spent as soone as reapt,
    So trustlesse is loves treasure.

Would it were dumb midnight now,
    When all the world lyes sleeping:
Would this place some Desert were,
    Which no man hath in keeping.
My desires should then be safe,
    And when you cry'd then would I laugh;
But if ought might breed offence,
    Love onely should be blamed:
I would live your servant still,
    And you my Saint unnamed.

7.13 *Temmes* the Thames
7.14 *Goodwins Sands* a sandbank in the Dover Strait
7.20 *trustlesse* not to be trusted, undependable

Carmen 8

Harden now thy tyred hart with more than flinty rage;
Ne'er let her false teares henceforth thy constant griefe asswage.
Once true happy dayes thou saw'st, when shee stood firme and kinde,
Both as one then liv'd, and held one eare, one tongue, one minde.
But now those bright houres be fled, and never may returne:
What then remaines, but her untruths to mourne?
Silly Tray-tresse, who shall now thy carelesse tresses place?
Who thy pretty talke supply? whose eare thy musicke grace?
Who shall thy bright eyes admire? what lips triumph with thine?
10   Day by day who'll visit thee and say, th'art onely mine?
Such a time there was, God wot, but such shall never be:
Too oft, I feare, thou wilt remember me.

BEN JONSON (1572?–1637)

Jonson was protean in both his life and art. Bricklayer, actor, homicide and womanizer, he was also a scholar and man of letters, tutor to Sir Walter Ralegh's son and pensioner of Ralegh's nemesis, James I. His works reveal similar variety and exuberance and include genres ranging from tragedy and comedy to masque, satire, epigram and lyric.

Jonson's imitation of *Carmen* 5 is sung in his comedy, *Volpone* (*The Fox*), by Volpone, in an attempt to seduce the married Celia. Like Campion, Jonson omits Catullus' theme of kisses, while keeping those of *carpe diem* and censorious voyeurs; his voyeurs are not Catullus' moralistic old men, but 'household spies', who might give away the adulterous lovers. The song was reprinted with a musical setting in Alphonso Ferrabosco's *Ayres* (1609), and again (with some changes) in *The Forrest* (1616), where it is entitled 'Song to Celia' and is immediately followed by the imitation of *Carmina* 5 and 7. In his imitation of *Carmina* 5 and 7 Jonson continues the idea of deceiving potential tattle-tales. Lines 12–18 imitate lines 1–14 in Campion's version of *Carmen* 7. Lines 19–22 first appeared in *Volpone*, where they follow 'Song to Celia' after an interruption of some fifty lines.

Jonson's translation from *Carmen* 62 was written for a masque performed for the ill-fated marriage of the Earl of Essex and Lady Frances Howard in January 1606. He substitutes the abstractions Truth and Opinion for Catullus' competing choruses of youths and maidens. (Catullus' youths easily win the contest, but Jonson's Truth is victorious only after a trial by combat and angelic intervention.)

Carmen 5 is from *Volpone* III.vii (acted 1606, printed 1607). The imitation of *Carmina* 5 and 7 is from *The Forrest* (1616). The selection from *Carmen* 62 is from *Hymenaei: or the Solemnities of Masque and Barriers* (1606).

Carmen 5

Song to Celia

Come, my Celia, let us prove,
While we can, the sports of love;
Time will not be ours, for ever,
He, at length, our good will sever;
Spend not then his gifts, in vaine.
Sunnes, that set, may rise againe:
But if, once, we lose this light,
'Tis with us perpetuall night.
Why should wee deferre our joyes?
10   Fame, and rumor are but toies.
Cannot we delude the eyes
Of a few poore houshold-spies?

Or his easier eares beguile,
Thus remooved, by our wile?
'Tis no sinne, loves fruits to steale;
But the sweet thefts to reveale:
To be taken, to be seene,
These have crimes accounted beene.

Carmina 5 and 7

To the Same

Kisse me, sweet: The warie lover
Can your favours keepe, and cover,
When the common courting jay
All your bounties will betray.
Kisse againe: no creature comes.
Kisse, and score up wealthy summes
On my lips, thus hardly sundred,
While you breath. First give a hundred,
Then a thousand, then another
10 Hundred, then unto the tother
Adde a thousand, and so more:
Till you equall with the store,
All the grasse that *Rumney* yeelds,
Or the sands in *Chelsey* fields,
Or the drops in silver *Thames*,
Or the starres, that guild his streames,

5.13 *his* the husband's
5 and 7.13 *Rumney* a town in Kent surrounded by marshy grazing land
5 and 7.14 *sands in Chelsey fields* perhaps a pun. According to the *Speculum Britanniae* (1593) of Jonson's contemporary John Norden, Chelsea (Chelsey) was so named because its 'strand is like the chesel [gravel, pebbles] which the sea casteth up of sand and pebble stones'.

In the silent sommer-nights,
When youths ply their stolne delights.
That the curious may not know
How to tell 'hem, as they flow,
And the envious, when they find
What their number is, be pin'd.

Carmen 62.39–58

OPINION

Looke, how a flower, that close in closes growes,
Hid from rude cattell, bruised with no ploughes,
Which th' *ayre* doth stroke, *sun* strengthen, *showres* shoot higher,
It many *youths*, and many *maydes* desire;
The same, when cropt by cruell hand, is wither'd,
No *youths* at all, no *maydens* have desir'd:
So a *virgin*, while untouch'd she doth remaine,
Is deare to hers; but when with bodies staine
Her chaster flower is lost, she leaves to appeare
Or sweet to young men, or to *maydens* deare.
That conquest then may crowne me in this warre,
Virgins, O *virgins*, flie from HYMEN farre.

TRUTH

Virgins, O *virgins*, to sweet HYMEN yeeld,
For as a lone vine, in a naked field,
Never extolls her branches, never beares
Ripe grapes, but with a headlong heavinesse weares

---

5 and 7.22 *pin'd* pained, vexed   **62.9** *leaves* ceases
62.15 *extolls* raises up

Her tender body, and her highest sproote
Is quickly levell'd with her fading roote;
By whom no *husbandmen*, no *youths* will dwell;
But if, by fortune, she be married well
To th'elme her *husband*, many *husbandmen*,
And many *youths* inhabit by her, then;
So whilst a *virgin* doth, untouch't abide
All unmanur'd, she growes old, with her pride;
But when to equall *wedlocke*, in fit time,
Her fortune, and endevor lets her clime,
Deare to her *love*, and *parents* she is held.
Virgins, O *virgins*, to sweet HYMEN yeeld.

HENRY PEACHAM (1576?–1643?)

Peacham was a man of many talents: schoolmaster, composer, mathematician, artist, traveller, author and poet. He was best known for the *Compleat Gentleman* (1622), a work on gentlemanly accomplishments and behaviour.

His translation of *Carmen* 61 is the third 'nuptiall hymne' in *Period of Mourning*, in which poems mourning the death of James I are combined with wedding-songs for the marriage of his daughter, Elizabeth, to Frederick, Count Palatine of the Rhine, on Valentine's Day, 1613. Peacham has abridged his model (his poem has 90 lines to Catullus' 235), but keeps its five-verse stanzas.

From *Period of Mourning* (1613).

62.24 *unmanur'd* untilled. The image is both sexual and agricultural.

Carmen 61

Nuptiall Hymne

3
URANIAS Sonne, who dwell'st upon
The fertile top of *Helicon*,
Chaste Marriage Soveraigne, and dost leade
The Virgin to her Bridall Bed.
   Io Hymen Hymenaeus.

With Marjoram begirt thy brow,
And take the Veile of yealow: now
Yee Pinie Torches with your light,
To golden day convert the night.
   Io Hymen Hymenaeus.

See how like the *Cyprian* Queene,
ELIZA comes, as when (I weene)
On *Ida* hill the prize she had
Allotted by the *Phrygian* Lad.
   Io Hymen Hymenaeus.

As *Asian* Myrtle fresh and faire,
Which *Hamadryads* with their care,
And duely tending by the flouds,
Have taught to over-looke the Woods.
   Io Hymen Hymenaeus.

61.11 *Cyprian Queene* Venus
61.14 *Phrygian Lad* Paris

Behold how *Vesper* from the skie
Consenteth by his twinckling eye:
And *Cynthia* stayes her Swans to see
The state of this Solemnitie.
   Io Hymen Hymenaeus.

Wedlocke, were it not for thee,
Wee could nor Childe nor Parent see;
Armies Countries to defend,
Or Shepheards hilly Heards to tend.
   Io Hymen Hymenaeus.

But *Hymen* call the Nymph away,
With Torches light the Children stay,
Whose sparkes (see how) ascend on hye,
As if there wanted Starres in Skye.
   Io Hymen Hymenaeus.

As virgin Vine her Elme doth wed,
His Oake the Ivie over-spread:
So chaste desires thou joynst in one,
That disunited were undone.
   Io Hymen Hymenaeus.

But see her golden foote hath past
The doubted Threshold, and at last
Shee doth approach her Bridall-bed,
Of none save *Tyber* envyed.
   Io Hymen Hymenaeus.

61.23 *Cynthia* Diana, goddess of the moon
61.44 *Of none save Tyber envyed* Rome's river, the Tiber, might envy the Protestant marriage of Elizabeth and Frederick.

Chast Mariage-bed, he sooner tels
The Starres, the *Ocean* Sand, or shels,
That thinkes to number those delights
Wherewith thou shortnest longest nights.
    Io Hymen Hymenaeus.

With richest *Tyrian* Purple spred,
Where her deare Spouse is laid on bed,
Like yong *Ascanius*, or the Lad
Her Love the Queene of *Cyprus* had:
    Io Hymen Hymenaeus.

Young *Frederick* of Royall Ligne,
Of *Cassimires*, who on the *Rhine*
To none are second said to be,
For Valour, Bounty, Pietie.
    Io Hymen Hymenaeus.

Come Bride-maide *Venus* and undoe
Th' Herculean knot with fingers two,
And take the girdle from her wast,
That Virgins must for goe at last,
    Io Hymen Hymenaeus.

Scatter Nuts without the Dore,
The Married is a Childe no more
For whosoere a wife hath wed,
Hath other businesse in his head.
    Io Hymen Hymenaeus.

61.53 *Lad* Adonis, the youth loved by Venus

    Where passe ye many an happy night,
    Untill Lucina brings to light,
    An hopefull Prince who may restore,
    In part, the losse we had before,
       Io Hymen Hymenaeus.

    That one day we may live to see,
    A *Frederick Henry* on her knee,
    Who mought to *Europe* give her law,
    And keepe encroaching Hell in awe.
       Io Hymen Hymenaeus.

    Upon whose Brow may Envie read,
    The reconcile of Love and Dread,
    And in whose Rosie cheeke we see,
    His Mothers gracefull Modestie,
       Io Hymen Hymenaeus.

    But Muse of mine we but molest
    I doubt, with ruder song their rest,
    The Dores are shut, and lights about
    Extinct, then time thy flame were out;
       Io Hymen Hymenaeus.

SAMUEL SHEPPARD (*c.* 1586?–after 1653)

Sheppard began his literary career about 1606 as Ben Jonson's amanuensis, but seems not to have written anything himself until some forty years later, when he began to publish a series of satires, ballads, farces

---

61.72 *Lucina* goddess of childbirth. Her name is derived from *lux* ('light').
61.78 *mought* may

and romances. He was an ardent royalist and in the early 1650s was twice imprisoned for his views.

Sheppard is known to have plagiarized some of his works, and some scholars have suggested that he took the selection below from an unknown poet. His text contains some obvious errors that are best explained as results of hasty copying from a poorly understood model (see especially on 23–4). His slightly abbreviated translation of *Carmen* 61.1–40 appears as the epithalamium of the title characters in a romance modestly entitled: *The Loves of Amandus and Sophronia Historically Narrated: A Piece of rare Contexture, Inriched with many pleasing Odes and Sonnets, occasioned by the Jocular, or Tragicall occurrences, happening in the progresse of the Historie.*

From *The Loves of Amandus and Sophronia* (1650).

Carmen 61.1–40

Epithalamium

Heavenly faire *Urania's* Son,
Thou that dwel'st on *Hellicon*;
Hymen, ô thy brows empale,
To the Bride, the Bridegroome hale,
Take thy Saffron Robe, and come
With sweet flowred Marjorum;
Yellow socks of woollen weare,
With a smiling look appeare:
Shrill *Epithalamiums* sing,
10   Let this day with pleasure spring:
Nimbly dance: the flaming Tree
Only dedicate to thee
Take in that fair hand of thine,
Let good *Auguries* combine,

61.11 *the flaming Tree* pine torch, a regular feature of Roman weddings

> For the paire that now are Wed,
> Let their joyes be nourished,
> Lik a Myrtle ever green,
> Owned by the Cyprian Queen,
> Who fosters it with Rosie dew,
20 Where her Nimphs their Sports pursue.
> Leave th' *Aonian Cave* behind,
> (Come, ô come with willing mind)
> And the *Thespian* Rocks, whence chill
> *Aganippe's* waters spill.
> Chastest Virgins, you that are
> Either for to make, or marre,
> Make the ayre with *Hymen* ring,
> *Hymen*, *Hymenaeus* sing.

ROBERT HERRICK (1591–1674)

Herrick, described by James Russell Lowell as 'the most Catullian of poets', in fact seems to have taken Horace and Martial as his principal classical models. Herrick enjoyed court life and the society of Jonson and his circle in London before taking up a living at Dean Priory in Devonshire in 1630. He lost his position in 1647 for being a royalist, but was restored to it in 1660 after spending the intervening years in London, where he published his *Hesperides*, a collection of short poems and epigrams modelled on the *Greek Anthology* and Martial's epigram books. In the selection below he has made an epigram from

---

61.18 *the Cyprian Queen* Venus
61.21 *Aonian Cave* cave of the Muses, whose sacred mountain, Helicon, was in Aonia
61.23 *Thespian Rocks* rocks of poetic power (Thespis was the traditional father of tragedy)
61.23–4 *chill Aganippe's* Sheppard's text reads *drill Aganippe*

Carmen 22 by translating only its last two lines, perhaps from a commonplace book.

From *Hesperides* (1648).

Carmen 22.20–21

Our own sinnes unseen

Other mens sins wee ever beare in mind;
   None sees the fardell of his faults behind.

ANONYMOUS (1612)

This lute song, once attributed to Campion, is now regarded as anonymous. Its opening lines bear a close resemblance to Campion's 'My sweetest Lesbia', but the poet further pares down his model, treating only the theme of censorious old men, and abandoning Catullus' musings on human mortality along with his demands for kisses.

From William Corkine's *Second Booke of Ayres* (1612).

Carmen 5

My deerest Mistrisse, let us live and love,
And care not what old doting fooles reprove.
Let us not feare their sensures, nor esteeme
What they of us and of our loves shall deeme.

22.2 *fardell* bundle, pack

Old ages critticke and sensorious brow
Cannot of youthfull dalliance alow,
Nor never could endure that wee should tast
Of those delights which they themselves are past.

RICHARD CRASHAW (1613?–49)

Crashaw, although of Puritan stock, converted to Roman Catholicism during the Civil War, and left England for Paris and Rome. He died in Italy after serving briefly in the entourage of a cardinal. Much of his poetry is religious and devotional; he has been described with both admiration and disdain as baroque, mystic and metaphysical.

Crashaw's poem (probably written in the 1630s during his student days at Cambridge) is the earliest full and close translation of *Carmen* 5. But the punning conceit in lines 6–7 ('But if we darke sons of sorrow / Set') adds a new element of Christianity and metaphysical wit to Catullus.

From *The Delights of the Muses* (1646).

Carmen 5

Out of Catullus

Come and let us live my Deare,
Let us love and never feare,
What the sowrest Fathers say:
Brightest *Sol* that dyes to day
Lives againe as blith to morrow,
But if we darke sons of sorrow
Set; ô then, how long a Night
Shuts the Eyes of our short light!
Then let amorous kisses dwell
10   On our lips, begin and tell

A Thousand, and a Hundred, score
An Hundred, and a Thousand more,
Till another Thousand smother
That, and that wipe of another.
Thus at last when we have numbered
Many a Thousand, many a Hundred:
Wee'l confound the reckoning quite,
And lose our selves in wild delight:
While our joyes so multiply
20   As shall mocke the envious eye.

RICHARD LOVELACE (1618–57)

Lovelace, generally regarded as the quintessential Cavalier poet, produced a slender *oeuvre* celebrating his lost cause. Although Lovelace seems to have done little actual fighting, he spent most of his fortune defending his king and was imprisoned as a Royalist in 1643 and again in 1648–9. Once famous for his elegant beauty ('the handsomest man of his time', according to one contemporary), he is said to have died in rags in a London doss-house. His brother, Dudley Posthumus, used lines from Catullus to preface a second edition of his poetry (*Lucasta: Posthume Poems*, 1659): *Nunquam ego te, vita frater amabilior, / Adspiciam posthac? At certe semper amabo* ('Shall I never see you again, brother dearer than life? But I will always love you', *Carmen* 65.10–11).

Lovelace translated thirteen of Catullus' poems, many more than had been undertaken by any previous translator; only one, *Carmen* 70, had been translated before. For the most part he translates very literally, and, except in *Carmen* 49, he even keeps to the same number of lines as Catullus. He places *Carmen* 85 at the end of *Carmen* 72 to form a single poem.

From *Lucasta: Posthume Poems* (1659).

Carmen 13

Ad Fabullum, Englished

Fabullus I will treat you handsomely
Shortly, if the kind gods will favour thee.
If thou dost bring with thee a del'cate messe,
An *Olio* or so, a pretty Lass,
Brisk wine, sharp tales, all sorts of Drollery,
These if thou bringst (I say) along with thee
You shall feed highly friend, for know the ebbs
Of my lank purse are full of Spiders webs,
But then again you shall recieve clear love
10   Or what more grateful or more sweet may prove,
For with an ointment I will favour thee,
My *Venus's* and *Cupids* gave to me,
Of which once smelt, the gods thou wilt implore
Fabullus that they'd make thee nose all ore.

Carmen 48

To Juvencius

Juvencius, thy fair sweet Eyes,
If to my fill that I may kisse,
Three hundred thousand times I'de kisse,
Nor future age should cloy this Blisse;
No not if thicker than ripe ears,
The harvest of our kisses bears.

---

13. 4 *Olio* a stew

Carmen 49

To Marcus T. Cicero
In an English Pentastick

Tully to thee *Rome's* eloquent Sole Heir,
The best of all that are, shall be, and were:
I the worst Poet send my best thanks and pray'r,
Ev'n by how much the worst of Poets I,
By so much you the best of Patrones be.

Carmen 69

To Rufus

That no fair woman will, wonder not why,
Clap (*Rufus*) under thine her tender thigh;
Not a silk gown shall once melt one of them,
Nor the delights of a transparent gemme.
A scurvy story kills thee, which doth tell
That in thine armpits a fierce goat doth dwell.
Him they all fear full of an ugly stinch,
Nor'st 't fit he should lye with a handsome wench;
Wherefore this Noses cursed plague first crush,
Or cease to wonder why they fly you thus.

---

title *Pentastick* a poem in five lines

Carmen 70

Female Inconstancy

My Mistresse sayes she'll marry none but me,
No not if *Jove* himself a Suitor be:
She sayes so; but what women say to kind
Lovers, we write in rapid streams and wind.

Carmina 72 and 85

Ad Lesbiam, Englished

That me alone you lov'd you once did say,
Nor should I to the King of gods give way,
Then I lov'd thee not as a common dear,
But as a Father doth his children chear;
Now thee I know, more bitterly I smart,
Yet thou to me more light and cheaper art.
What pow'r is this? that such a wrong should press
Me to love more, yet wish thee well much lesse.
I hate and love, wouldst thou the reason know?
I know not, but I burn and feel it so.

---

72 and 85.4 *chear* cherish

Carmen 75

In Lesbiam, Englished

By thy fault is my mind brought to that pass,
That it it's Office quite forgotten has;
For be'est thou best, I cannot wish thee well,
And be'est thou worst, yet must I love thee still.

Carmen 82

To Quintius

Quintius if you'll endear *Catullus* eyes,
Or what he dearer than his eyes doth prize,
Ravish not what is dearer than his eyes,
Or what he dearer than his eyes doth prize.

Carmen 86

De Quintia et Lesbia, Englished

Quintia is handsome, fair, tall, straight, all these
Very particulars I grant with ease:
But she all ore's not handsome; here's her fault,
In all that bulk, there's not one corne of salt,
Whilst *Lesbia* fair and handsome too all ore
All graces and all wit from all hath bore.

82.1 *endear* put in your debt, place under an obligation

Carmen 87

De Suo in Lesbiam amore, Englished

No one can boast her self so much belov'd,
Truely as *Lesbia* my affections prov'd;
No faith was ere with such a firm knot bound
As in my love on my part I have found.

Carmen 103

Ad Sylonem, Englished

Sylo pray pay me my ten *Sesterces*,
Then rant and roar as much as you shall please,
Or if that mony takes you, pray give ore
To be a pimp, or else to rant and roar.

Carmen 106

De Puero et Praecone, Englished

With a fair boy a Cryer we behold.
What should we think? but he would not be sold.

103.3 *takes* delights
106.2 *but he would not be* except that he wants to be

ABRAHAM COWLEY (1618–67)

Cowley launched his literary career at the age of ten with a poem in thirty-five stanzas on 'The Tragicall Historie of Pyramus and Thisbe' and published a collection of verse at fifteen (*Poetical Blossoms*, 1633). He was a friend of Crashaw and a supporter of the Royalist cause, serving the exiled court in Paris for nearly a decade. Cowley's poetry was so highly regarded by his contemporaries that he was buried near Chaucer and Spenser in Westminster Abbey, but his reputation soon declined and he was criticized as a 'metaphysical poet' by Samuel Johnson in *Lives of the English Poets* (1781).

Cowley's version of *Carmen* 45 exemplifies the method of translation he describes in the preface to *Pindarique Odes*: 'I have . . . taken, left out, and added what I please; nor make it so much my aim to let the Reader know precisely what he spoke, as what was his *way* and *manner* of speaking.' His poem, twice as long as Catullus', adds many baroque details. His God of Love sneezes because he is 'tickled by the sound' of the lovers' protestations, and he is accompanied by a chorus of 'little Loves' not in Catullus. Cowley has also added the last stanza, transforming Catullus' Septimius and Acme (a lover and his Greek mistress) into models of an ideal marriage. The translation was reprinted anonymously in *The Adventures of Catullus* (see Introduction) and became a popular song in a setting by John Blow. His translation of *Carmen* 85, like the translations of Ralegh and Gwinne, appears as an illustration in an essay.

Both selections were first published posthumously in *The Works of Mr. Abraham Cowley* (1668). *Carmen* 45 appeared in *Occasional Verses* and *Carmen* 85 in the essay, *Of Solitude*.

Carmen 45

Ode
Acme and Septimius out of Catullus
Acmen Septimius suos Amores Tenens in gremio, etc.

Whilst on *Septimius* panting Brest,
(Meaning nothing less than Rest)
Acme lean'd her loving head,
Thus the pleas'd *Septimius* said,

My dearest *Acme*, if I be
Once alive, and love not thee,
With a Passion far above
All that e're was called Love,
In a *Lybian* desert may
I become some Lion's prey;
Let him, *Acme*, let him tear
My Brest, when *Acme* is not there.

The God of Love, who stood to hear him,
(The God of Love was always near him)
Pleas'd and tickl'd with the sound,
Sneez'd aloud; and all around
The little Loves, that waited by,
Bow'd and blest the Augurie.

Acme, enflam'd with what he said,
Rear'd her gently-bending head,
And her purple mouth with joy,
Stretching to the delicious Boy,
Twice (and twice could scarce suffice)
She kist his drunken, rowling eyes.

My little Life, my All (said she)
So may we ever servants be
To this blest God; and ne'r retain
Our hated Liberty again;
So may thy passion last for me,
30 As I a Passion have for thee,
Greater and fiercer much than can
Be conceiv'd by Thee a Man.
Into my Marrow is it gone,
Fix'd and setled in the Bone,
It reigns not only in my Heart,
But runs, like Life, through ev'ry part.

She spoke; the God of Love aloud
Sneez'd again, and all the crowd
Of little Loves, that waited by,
40 Bow'd, and blest the Augurie.

This good Omen thus from Heaven
Like a happy signal given,
Their Loves and Lives (all four) embrace,
And hand in hand run all the race.
To poor *Septimius* (who did now
Nothing else but *Acme* grow)
Acme's bosome was alone,
The whole world's Imperial Throne,
And to faithful *Acme's* mind
50 *Septimius* was all Human kind.

If the Gods would please to be
But advis'd for once by me,
I'd advise 'em when they spie,
Any illustrious Piety,
To reward Her, if it be she;
To reward Him, if it be He;
With such a Husband, such a Wife,
With *Acme's* and *Septimius'* Life.

Carmen 85

It is very fantastical and contradictory in humane Nature, that Men should love themselves above all the rest of the world, and yet never endure to be with themselves. When they are in love with a Mistriss, all other persons are importunate and burdensome to them. . . . They would live and dye with her alone. . . . And yet our Dear Self is so wearisome to us, that we can scarcely support its conversation for an hour together. This is such an odd temper of mind as Catullus expresses towards one of his Mistresses, whom we may suppose to have been of a very unsociable humour.

I Hate, and yet I Love thee too;
How can that be? I know not how;
Only that so it is I know,
And feel with Torment that 'tis so.

It is a deplorable condition, this, and drives a man sometimes to pittiful shifts in seeking how to avoid Himself.

NAHUM TATE (1652–1715)

Tate, born to a Puritan family in Dublin, achieved popular success and rose to become Poet Laureate (1692), although he was derided by poets in the next generation. He was best known as a translator and dramatist. The works he translated alone or in collaboration include Ovid's *Ars Amatoria* and *Heroides*, the Psalms, Lucian and Juvenal's *Satires*. He wrote the libretto for Purcell's *Dido and Aeneas* as well as a version of *King Lear* with a happy ending that was produced well into the nineteenth century.

Carmen 3, Catullus' famous poem on the death of Lesbia's sparrow, had inspired many English imitations on the deaths of birds and other pets (see Introduction), but Tate's version seems to be the earliest published translation. Catullus' poem is all sentiment and charm, whereas Tate aims for brittle wit. He changes Catullus' 'honey-sweet' sparrow into an 'educated Bird . . . so slick and clean', and ends with a metaphysical conceit on Lesbia's tears. Catullus' two poems on his fruitless search for his friend Camerius (*Carmen* 55 and the fragmentary *Carmen* 58b) were often joined in early editions, and Tate obviously considered them a single poem. He has injected a note of English magic: the missing playboy Camerius is a 'Graceless Elf', and the poet imagines seeking him, not mounted on Pegasus as Catullus had done, but as a witch on a 'liquer'd Switch'.

From *Poems Written on Several Occasions. The Second Edition Enlarged* (1684).

Carmen 3

Catullus. Epigr. II
De passere mortuo Lesbiae

Weep, *Venus*, weep, bid all the Race
Of laughing Loves weep now apace;
Let Mortal's sorrow be as deep;
Bid the nobler Mortals weep:
All that have the soul or Sense
For Fate of such a Consequence.
Never was such Cause to moan,
Lesbia's Sparrow's dead and gone.
The Darling she was wont to prize
10   Above the Conquests of her Eyes.
That educated Bird, I mean
He that was so slick and clean;
Whose Wit and Judgment did excell;
For he my *Lesbia* knew as well

---

title *Epigr. II* i.e., *Carmen* 3 in modern editions

As she her own dear Mother knew,
And to her Arms as fondly flew.
No more Alas, shall he do so!
But wanders through the Shades below,
His Everlasting Residence;
20 For never Soul escapt from thence.
You have him Fates, and we allow
Your Groves the Seats of Pleasure now,
My *Lesbia*'s Bird has made them so.
But ours, as if their Soul were fled,
Are wither'd all since he is dead.
Clouds of Tears o'er-cast the Skies;
I mean the Heav'n of *Lesbia*'s Eyes.

Carmina 55 and 58b

To his Friend that absconded
Catullus, Epigr. 56

Now if thou hast one dram of Grace,
Save a Friends Life, and shew thy Face.
From me before thou ne're wast hid,
I saw thee tho the Sun ne're did.
Come forth I say thou sculking Elf,
Save a Friends Life and shew thy self.
For thee I've search'd, and search'd again
Park, Tavern, Play-house, but in vain;
All these thou long hast left i'th lurch,
10 I might as well have search'd a Church.
Distracted now I scour the street,
And seize all Females that I meet;

---

title *Epigr. 56* i.e., *Carmina* 55 and 58b in modern editions

Where's my Friend aloud I cry,
Naughty Creatures, speak or die,
One, making bare her snowy Breasts,
Cry'd – Seek no further, here he rests.
I'm tired with this *Herculean* work,
'Tis worse than tugging for the Turk.
Y'are in intrigue you'l say – be't so!
20   With Quality – That may be too;
Come tell your Conquest then say I,
That's Pleasure – T'other's Drudgery.
Mischief take Thee Graceless Elf.
Where canst thou thus conceal thy self?
I think (I'll swear) should I turn Witch,
To ride upon a liquer'd Switch,
Mount Lightning, and out-fly the Wind,
This Sculker I shall never find.

JOHN OLDHAM (1653–83)

Oldham, the son of a Presbyterian minister, tried for most of his short life to make a living from his writing, but was repeatedly thrown back on schoolmastering and tutoring for his livelihood. He established a reputation as an English satirist and wrote successful translations of Horace and Juvenal's satires, but his career was cut short by smallpox when he was at the height of his powers.

Although Oldham substituted London for Rome in translating ancient satire, he did not bring his own British world into the imitation of *Carmen* 7 as Campion and Jonson had done when they used features of the English landscape to count (or fail to count) the lover's kisses. Instead of Campion's 'Osiers of the *Temmes* / Or *Goodwins* Sands' or Jonson's 'grass that *Rumney* yeelds, / Or the sands in *Chelsey* fields', Oldham's counting moves from the particularity of human desires to the vastness of the universe.

From *Poems and Translations* (1683).

Carmen 7

Catullus, Epigr. VII
Imitated

Nay, *Lesbia* never ask me this,
How many Kisses will suffice?
Faith, 'tis a question hard to tell,
Exceeding hard; for you as well
May ask what sums of Gold suffice
The greedy Miser's boundless Wish:
Think what drops the Ocean store,
With all the Sands, that make its Shore:
Think what Spangles deck the Skies,
10   When Heaven looks with all its Eyes:
Or think how many Atoms came
To compose this mighty Frame:
Let all these the Counters be,
To tell how oft I'm kiss'd by thee:
Till no malicious Spy can guess
To what vast height the Scores arise;
Till weak Arithmetick grow scant,
And numbers for the reck'ning want;
All these will hardly be enough
20   For me stark staring mad with Love.

7.12 *Frame* the fabric or structure of the world

WILLIAM WALSH (1663–1708)

Walsh, a poet and critic, was fashionable in his dress and described himself as burdened with an 'amorous heart'. He is best known as a literary adviser of the young Alexander Pope and for his *Dialogue concerning Women, being a Defence of the Sex* (1691).

From *Letters and Poems, Amorous and Gallant* (1692).

Carmen 72

To his false Mistress

Thou saidst that I alone thy Heart cou'd move,
And that for me thou wou'dst abandon *Jove*.
I lov'd thee then, not with a Love defil'd,
But as a Father loves his only Child.
I know thee now, and tho' I fiercelier burn,
Thou art become the Object of my Scorn.
See what thy Falshood gets; I must confess
I love thee more, but I esteem the less.

Carmen 76

The Petition
(In imitation of Catullus)

Is there a pious pleasure, that proceeds
From contemplation of our vertuous Deeds?
That all mean, sordid Actions we despise,
And scorn to gain a Throne by Cheats and Lyes?

>   *Thyrsis*, thou hast sure Blessings laid in store,
>   From thy just dealing in this curst Amour.
>   What Honour can in Words or Deeds be shown,
>   Which to the Fair thou hast not said and done?
>   On her false Heart they all are thrown away;
> 10 She only swears, more eas'ly to betray.
>   Ye Powers! that know the many Vows she broke,
>   Free my just Soul from this unequal Yoke!
>   My Love boils up, and, like a raging Flood,
>   Runs through my Veins, and taints my Vital Blood.
>   I do not vainly beg she may grow chaste,
>   Or with an equal Passion burn at last;
>   The one she cannot practise, tho' she wou'd,
>   And I contemn the other, tho' she shou'd.
>   Nor ask I Vengeance on the perjur'd Jilt:
> 20 'Tis punishment enough to have her Guilt.
>   I beg but Balsam for my bleeding Breast,
>   Cure for my Wounds, and from my Labours rest.

TOM BROWN (1663–1704)

Tom Brown was an impecunious, facetious and hard-working hack, known in his own day for his feuds and licentious way of life, and famous to posterity for his immortal lines on Dr Fell (a translation of Martial 1.32):

> I do not love thee, Dr Fell,
> The reason why I cannot tell;
> But this I know, and know full well,
> I do not love thee, Dr Fell.

76.5 *Thyrsis* Walsh's name for himself, taken from one of Virgil's shepherds in *Eclogue* 7

He was a prolific polemicist and satirist, but made his living as a translator, turning his hand to French and Italian writers as well as to such diverse Greek and Latin authors as Lucian, Lucretius, Horace, Martial and Erasmus.

Brown's translation of *Carmen* 92 expands Catullus' four lines to twelve, but keeps the two-part structure in which Catullus' actions and feelings in the second half of the epigram mirror Lesbia's in the first. This version probably influenced Swift, who also makes his Lesbia 'rail' and rhymes 'sincerely' and 'dearly'. It was reprinted anonymously in *The Adventures of Catullus* (see Introduction).

From *A Collection of Miscellany Poems, Letters, etc.* (1699).

Carmen 92

A Translation of Lesbia, Mi dicit semper male
Out of Catullus

I

Each moment of the long-liv'd day,
Lesbia for me does backward pray,
    And rails at me sincerely;
Yet I dare pawn my life, my eyes,
My soul, and all that Mortals prize,
    That *Lesbia* loves me dearly.

II

Why shou'd you thus conclude, you'll say,
Faith 'tis my own beloved way,
    And thus I hourly prove her;
10 Yet let me all those curses share
That heav'n can give, or man can bear,
    If I don't strangely love her.

JOHN GLANVILL (1664?–1735)

Glanvill lost his chance of a fellowship and was expelled from his Oxford college 'because he would be drunk and swear', but went on to a career in the law and died a rich man. He wrote panegyrics on the king, imitated Horace's *Odes*, and translated excerpts from various Latin poets, including Virgil, Tibullus, Seneca and Lucan as well as Catullus. His purpose, he declares, is to give pleasure: 'I always write to entertain myself; and what I publish is with some Hopes I may a little entertain others.'

From *Poems: Consisting of Originals and Translations* (1725).

Carmen 83

Epig. LXXXIV
Lesbia mi praesente viro mala plurima dicit

Lesbia before her Husband's Face
Says all she can to my Disgrace;
Despises, hates me, curses, rails,
All that vex'd Woman never fails.
This tickles the Fool's easy Ear,
And he's o'er joy'd, as all were clear.
Blind *Mulus*, thou dost nothing see;
Did she not speak one Word of me,
She might forget me, and be well:
10 Now when she wishes me in Hell,
And urges all this Obloquy,
Not only she still thinks of me;

---

title *Epig. LXXXIV* i.e. *Carmen* 83 in modern editions

But, what is worse for both of you,
She thinks of me with Anger too;
That is, (whatever she would shew)
She loves me, and she tells thee so.

JONATHAN SWIFT (1667–1745)

Swift, a master of irony and polemic, is best known for satirical prose works (*The Tale of a Tub, A Modest Proposal* and *Gulliver's Travels*), but he began as a poet and wrote poetry throughout his life. Although he was born, educated and ordained in Dublin, he went to England at the earliest opportunity and for many years returned to Ireland only intermittently. He at last returned to Ireland in 1714 and took up permanent residence in Dublin as Dean of St Patrick's Cathedral. Swift translates *Carmen* 92 into octosyllabic couplets, a verse that neatly conveys the conversational flavour and couplet form of Catullus' epigram. His version is probably influenced by that of Tom Brown.

From Swift's autograph transcribed by Harold Williams, *The Poems of Jonathan Swift* (1958). First published in *The Works of Jonathan Swift D. D.* (1746).

Carmen 92

To Lesbia From Catullus
Jul. 18th 1736

Lesbia for ever on me rails;
    To talk on me she never fails:
Yet, hang me, but for all her Art;
    I find that I have gain'd her Heart:
My proof is this: I plainly see
    The Case is just the same with me:
I curse her ev'ry hour sincerely;
    Yet, hang me, but I love her dearly.

SAMUEL SAY (1676–1743)

Say was a prominent dissenting minister with few connections or pretensions to the literary world. His poetry, which was published two years after his death, is characterized by the *Dictionary of National Biography* as 'youthful rubbish'. Say would perhaps not disagree with the characterization, at least for his amatory poems, for they appear in a section headed 'Love Verses Chiefly Written in the Year 1701. *Semel insanivimus Omnes* [we've all been crazy once]'. The first selection is a translation of *Carmen* 76, the second Say's own retraction.

From *Poems on Several Occasions* (1745).

Carmen 76

The Complaint: From Catullus

I

If There be Pleasure to a Virtuous Man,
    When he reflects upon his Actions past;
His Piety, his Truth, and All that can
    Approve to Heaven: Just, Holy, Sober, Chaste;

II

Then many Joys are yet laid up in Store
    For Thee, my Soul, tho' wretched now in Love:
And She, perhaps, her Falseness shall deplore,
    And feel from Others what for Her I prove.

III

All that a Friend or faithful Lover may,
    That Thou hast done to Serve her, or to Please;
All which forgetful Winds bear swift away;
    And thy Barque founders in the flattering Seas.

IV

Why then shou'd'st thou torment thy-self, my Mind,
   And not with Equal Obstinacy strive
Some stubborn Cure for hopeless Love to find?
   Heaven will assist, and kindly bids thee live.

V

'Tis hard indeed long Passion soon to quell;
   A Task severe; but think it must be done:
Be bold the mighty Mischief to expell;
   The Work is half-perform'd that's well begun.

VI

Ye Pow'rs! (for wretched Man is still *Your* Care,
   And human Miseries *Your* Pity move)
Oh! ease the bitter Anguish of Despair,
   And free my Soul from this distracting Love.

VII

I ask not she shou'd Love for Love return,
   Or her Inconstant Thoughts to One confine;
But quench the raging Fire in which I burn,
   And since *her* Flames are dead, extinguish *mine*.

Say's Retraction

Haec Illa una – lachrymula OMNIA diluebat: et Ego cecini hanc Palinodiam:
[She washed away every word of this with a single tiny tear, and I sang this palinode]

The RETRACTATION

I

Thus good CATULLUS wou'd, of old, relieve
   Th' uneasy Tumults of his troubled Breast;
And strove with Verse his Sorrows to deceive,
   And charm the Cares, that charm'd yet know no Rest.

II

Too false *his* LESBIA, and his Love too strong,
   That still pursu'd in vain the treacherous Maid,
To whom nor Love nor goodness did belong,
   But with Inconstancy his Truth repaid.

III

Forgive my Folly, if th' afflicted Muse,
   Not led by Hate, but tortur'd with Despair,
Too rashly did *thy* purer faith accuse,
   And thought *my* LESBIA cou'd like *his* forswear.

JOHN GAY (1685?–1732)

Gay, a friend of Pope and Swift, is best known for his comic masterpiece, *The Beggar's Opera*, but he also wrote the libretto for Handel's *Acis and Galatea*, as well as other dramatic works and several volumes of verse.

The selection below is a parody of one of the objections to marriage sung by the chorus of maidens in Catullus' wedding-song. (See Jonson above both for a more literal version of these lines and for the youths' response.) Polly Peachum sings the air to reassure her father that she will not throw her virginity away on Macheath.

From *The Beggar's Opera* (1728), Act I, Air vi.

Carmen 62.39–48

I know as well as any of the fine Ladies how to make the most of my self and of my Man too. A Woman knows how to be mercenary, though she hath never been in a Court or at an Assembly. We have it in our Natures, Papa. If I allow Captain Macheath some trifling Liberties, I have this Watch and other visible Marks of his Favour to show for it. A Girl who cannot grant some Things, and refuse what is most material, will make but a poor hand of her beauty, and soon be thrown upon the Common.

Virgins are like the fair Flower in its Lustre,
    Which in the Garden enamels the Ground;
Near it the Bees in Play flutter and cluster,
    And gaudy Butterflies frolick around.
But, when once pluck'd, 'tis no longer alluring,
    To *Covent-Garden* 'tis sent, (as yet sweet,)
There fades, and shrinks, and grows past all enduring,
    Rots, stinks, and dies, and is trod under feet.

ANONYMOUS IN *THE GENTLEMAN'S JOURNAL*
(1692 and 1693)

The selections below were printed anonymously in *The Gentleman's Journal*. The first appears in an essay on love and marriage and is perhaps to be attributed to the journal's editor, Pierre Motteux. The translator of the second is described as 'a Gentleman, whose late Poetical Productions

---

62.6 *Covent-Garden* a *double entendre* since Covent Garden was both a vegetable and flower market and a haunt of prostitutes

have been much admired'. The editor's comments accompanying the
translations are printed in italics.

Carmen 3 is from The Gentleman's Journal: or the Monthly Miscellany, *March 1693. Carmen 5 is from* The Gentleman's Journal, *October 1692.*

Carmen 3

Whatever may be said against Love or Marriage, doubtless both have their Bliss, when they are the result of a well-made choice. Constancy also makes many languish long, who think themselves over-paid at last for all their amorous Grief; yet many loving Wretches are still more unhappy, and die unregarded and unlamented, while the loss of the little Dog or Bird is attended with floods of Tears. See how Catullus joins with his Lesbia in her grief for the death of a Sparrow.

Lesbia's Sparrow, paraphras'd

Oh! a thousand weeping Eyes,
Tender Sighs, and mournful Cryes!
Beauteous Nymphs, whose gentle Hearts
Ever felt Love's flaming Darts!
Smiling Graces! Wanton Loves!
Venus Sparrows, and her Doves!
Oh! one tear for Pity shed,
Lesbia's Love her Sparrow's dead.
    Death hath seiz'd what she did prize
10 Dearer than her lovely Eyes:
Oh! 'twas sweet, 'twas neat and pretty,
Gentle, active, brisk and witty:
Never Twins yet lov'd each other
Better, never Child its Mother.
    From my *Lesbia's* Bosom none
Could seduce it to be gone;

But it hopp'd now here, now there,
Waiting silently to hear
Her bewitching Tunes, and then
20 Sweetly chirp'd her Notes again.
    But the little Soul is flown
Now from us alas! 'tis gone
Down the dark and dismal way
Whence none e're returned, they say.
    Now may endless Curses dwell
With that ugly place call'd Hell;
Nothing lovely, nothing fair,
Those ill-natur'd Fiends can spare.
All my *Lesbia's* Joys are fled,
30 All with the sweet Creature's dead;
All the Glories of her Eyes
Are eclips'd, and now she cryes,
Since her darling Sparrow fell,
Till her ruddy Eye-lids swell.

Carmen 5

Vivamus, mea Lesbia &c.

Let us live on, my *Lesbia*, let us live,
And love, for Love is all that Life can give:
No matter what the Grave and Aged say,
Their sullen Night is envious of our Day.
The setting Sun, which leaves the World to mourn
In Clouds his absence, will again return:
But oh! when those much fairer Suns, thy Eyes,
Shall once be set they never more will rise;
Perpetual Night will overcast thy Charms,
10 And jealous Death will lock thee in his Arms.
Give me a thousand Kisses then in haste,
O let us not one precious moment waste,

But give a hundred next, and then a thousand more,
Another hundred now, for yet I'm poor;
A thousand next; quickly our Lips let's ply,
We cannot kiss so fast as Time will fly:
And after thousand thousands more, we'll then,
With other thousands, kiss out those again:
So shall we lose th' Accompt, and never know
A stint of what we to each other owe:
So shall not Envy reach, nor Malice guess
Our countless Kisses, unknown Happiness.

Indeed it must be granted, that many times Vertue has a less share than Envy, in the grave Lectures of decay'd sinners to the amorous Young.

ANONYMOUS (1693)

These selections appear in Dryden's *Examen Poeticum*, and for many years the first was attributed to Dryden himself. Both poems have also been assigned to Matthew Prior, but Prior's recent editors consider the attribution unlikely.

The treatment of *Carmen* 22 is a translation, that of *Carmen* 35 an imitation that alters and simplifies the premise of Catullus' poem. Both *Carmen* 35 and its imitation invite a friend to leave his mistress and join the poet, but Catullus obliquely teases the friend for neglecting his poetry, while the imitation is a straightforward invitation to leave the city for country pleasures.

From John Dryden, *Examen Poeticum: Being the Third Part of Miscellany Poems, Containing a Variety of New Translations of the Ancient Poets Together with Many Original Copies by the Most Eminent Hands* (1693).

5.20 *stint* a fixed amount or limit

Carmen 22

Catullus, Epig. 19
Suffenus iste, Vare, quem probe nosti

SUFFENUS whom you know, the Witty,
The Gay, the Talkative, and Pretty;
And, all his Wonders to rehearse,
The *THING* which makes a World of Verse,
I'm certain I shou'd not bely him,
To say he has several thousands by him,
Yet none deform'd with Critick Blot,
Or wrote on Vellom to rub out.
Royal Paper! Scarlet Strings!
Gilded Backs! And such fine things!
But – When you read 'em, then the Witty,
The Gay *Suffenus*, and the Pretty:
Is the dullest, heaviest Clown,
So alter'd, he can scarce be known.
This is strange! That he who now
Cou'd so Flatter, Laugh, and Bow,
So much Wit, such Breeding show,
Shou'd be so ungenteel a Wight,
Whenever he attempts to write,
And yet the Wretch is ne're so pleas'd,
As when he's with this madness seiz'd.

    Faith, Sir, w'are all deceiv'd alike,
All Labour in the same mistake,
Nor is the best of Men so clear
From every Folly, but somewhere
Still the *Suffenus* will appear.
Quickly we others Errors find,
But see not our own Load behind.

---

title *Epig. 19* i.e., *Carmen* 22 in modern editions
22.18 *Wight* person, creature

Carmen 35

*Invitation into the Country
In Imitation of the 34th Epig. Of Catullus*

Go – for I'm impatient grown,
Bid him leave the noisie Town,
Charge him he no longer stay,
But with haste devour the way.
Tho' a thousand times he's staid
By that fond, bewitching Maid:
Tho' she summon all her Charms,
Kiss him, press him in her Arms.
Let him not the *Syren* mind,
10 Tears are Water, Sighs are Wind.
Tell him how kind Nature here,
Dresses up the Youthful Year,
Strowing on the thoughtless Hours,
Opening *Buds*, and new-born Flow'rs;
Tell him underneath this Shade,
Innocence and Mirth are laid;
Not without forbidden Claret,
Books or Musick, if he'll hear it.
See the Lawrel, and the Vine,
20 Round about that *Arbour* twine,
So we Wit, and Pleasure joyn;
So *Horace*, and *Anacreon* meet
The Jolly God, within that Seat.
Thus from Noise and Care set free,
The snares of *Beauty* we defie.
Let him then no longer stay,
But with haste devour the way.

---

title *34th Epig.* i.e., *Carmen* 35 in modern editions

NICHOLAS AMHURST (1697–1742)

Amhurst was expelled from Oxford either for his Whig principles (his explanation) or for libertinism and misconduct (the university's explanation) and spent the rest of his life in London as a professional writer and pamphleteer. He died in poverty.

His translations from Catullus, published a year after his expulsion from the university, present the poet in the character of a young man about town. In *Carmen* 58, like the anonymous translator in *The Adventures of Catullus*, he transports the scene of Lesbia's debauchery from Rome to London. In *Carmen* 83 he makes his Lesbia rail, not against the poet as in Catullus, but against the immorality of London society, and presents her railing as a sign of her own prurient nature – not of her love for the poet.

From *Poems on Several Occasions* (1720).

Carmen 58

Catullus Imitated, Ep. 58

Cloe, dear Jack, that once victorious name,
Cloe, the object of my raging flame,
Whom I did more than life or friendship prize,
In *Fleetstreet* now, a common strumpet, plies,
Turns up to every puppy in the town,
And claps the *Temple* rake for half a crown.

58.6 *claps* infects with clap, i.e., gonorrhea

Carmen 83

Catullus Imitated, Ep. 81

Before her husband LESBIA calls me names,
And at the lewdness of the Town exclaims;
This tickles the poor Cuckold to the life,
And he thanks heav'n for such a virtuous Wife.
Contented fool! – indeed you reason wrong.
If she were virtuous, she would hold her tongue;
Scandal and noise her virtue do not prove,
But are the marks of unextinguish'd love.
Still, in her veins, the wanton itch prevails,
And in the madness of her lust, she rails.

ANONYMOUS (1702)

This selection appears without attribution in a collection of poems by various authors, including the Earls of Roscommon, Rochester and Orrery, Sir Robert Howard and John Dryden.

From *A Collection of Poems: viz. the Temple of Death by the Marquis of Normanby . . . with Several Original Poems Never before Printed* (1702).

Carmen 62

An Epithalamium from Catullus

YOUTHS
Rise Youths, the Evening's come, and her bright Star
With long expected light flames from afar:
'Tis time to rise, 'tis time the Feast to leave,

---

title *Ep. 81* i.e., *Carmen* 83 in modern editions

To sing the Nuptials, and the Bride receive.
>   *Come*, Hymen, *God of marriage come, and shed*
>   *Thy sacred influence on the Nuptial Bed.*

VIRGINS

See, see they 'dvance, and *Hesperus* above
On *Oeta's* top now lights the Lamp of Love:
What Life, what vigour in their Mien appears!
And sprightly joy assures the Triumph theirs.
>   *Come*, Hymen, *God of marriage come, and shed*
>   *Thy sacred influence on the Nuptial Bed.*

YOUTHS

For us, no light, no easy Task's prepar'd,
Doubtful's the Strife, and to Subdue is hard.
See with what studious care the Virgin Train
Employ their Thoughts, nor will employ in vain;
'Tis Care and Labour must the Victory gain.
Whilst we ignobly by our sloth betray'd
Shall fall, and be an easy Conquest made.
Let this a vig'rous emulation raise,
And as *They sing*, let *Us return* their Lays.
>   *Come*, Hymen, *God of marriage come, and shed*
>   *Thy sacred influence on the Nuptial Bed.*

VIRGINS

O *Hesperus*! what more *malignant* light
Glares in the *dusky forehead* of the Night?
Thou, *Cruel* thou, dost from the bosom tear
Of her Fond Mother the unwilling Fair;
And giv'st her up with all her Virgin Charms,
Expos'd to th' fury of a Lovers Arms.
What greater Cruelty than this is shown
By Lawless Conquerors in a taken Town?
>   *Come*, Hymen, *God of marriage come, and shed*
>   *Thy sacred influence on the Nuptial Bed.*

YOUTHS

No Star, like thee, with such a *Chearful* light,
Smiles on the *sober face of silent* Night.
You, *kindly* you, when your glad beams arise,
Ripen the Parents hopes, and Lovers joys;
Which, both with strong desire inflam'd, delay
Till thy bright Star has clos'd the tedious Day.
What greater Bliss can be bestow'd by *Jove*,
Than the soft Minute of transporting Love?
   Come, Hymen, *God of marriage come, and shed*
   Thy sacred influence on the Nuptial Bed.

VIRGINS

Thou under covert of the treach'rous Night,
Hast snatch'd our dear Companion from our Sight:
At thy approach the watchful Guards are set,
And Night led on by Thee affords retreat
To Thieves and Robbers; till again you rise
With kindlier Beams, to gild the *Eastern* Skies,
And whom the Evening hid, thy Morning Rays surprize.
   Come, Hymen, *God of marriage come, and shed*
   Thy sacred influence on the Nuptial Bed.

YOUTHS

Let the Chaste Virgins modestly complain
With well-dissembled Rage, and false disdain:
They at the *Joys thou giv'st* will ne'er repine,
And nature softly pleads thy cause within.
   Come, Hymen, *God of marriage come, and shed*
   Thy sacred influence on the Nuptial Bed.

VIRGINS

As some fair Plant that's in a Garden rear'd,
Safe from the piercing Plough, and trampling herd,
Whilst yet the Sun's mild Rays, and gentle Show'rs,
With fanning Winds refresh its op'ning flow'rs,

The *eyes* of ev'ry *Youth*, and ev'ry *Maid* allures.
Torn from the Stalk, the tender Blossoms fade,
Despis'd by every *Youth*, and every *Maid*.
So while her Virgin Bloom adorns the Fair,
By all she's Courted, and to all is Dear;
But when her faded Chastity is gone,
By none she's Courted, is Belov'd by none.
70   *Come*, Hymen, *God of marriage come, and shed*
    Thy sacred influence on the Nuptial Bed.

YOUTHS
As the Wild Vine, that in the Desart grows,
And bears no fruitful Blossoms on its Boughs,
Which, by their weight bent downwards, all unbound,
Spread their neglected Tendrils on the ground,
Despis'd and scorn'd, can no assistance find,
Or from the Peasant, or the labouring Hind.
But if the Elm be Wedded to the Vine,
And round his Waste her clasping Branches twine,
80 Her loaded Arms, which a full Vintage bear,
Tempt and reward the Hinds and Peasants care.
So the Unmarry'd Virgin's *drooping Charms*,
Receive fresh Vigour from a Lovers Arms.
Dear to her Husband still new Joys she gives,
And in her Aged Sire past Youth revives.

Be not, Fair Virgin, with reluctance led
To the chaste transports of the Nuptial Bed:
Let thee, the will of thy kind Parents move,
And be not deaf to Duty as to Love.
90 Your self's not wholly yours, one third is due
To either Parent, and one third to you;
And since both these to *Him* their Right convey,
If *Love perswades* not, *Reason bids* obey.
Come, Hymen, *God of marriage come, and shed*
Thy sacred influence on the Nuptial Bed.

THOMAS COOKE (1703–56)

Cooke, nicknamed 'Hesiod Cooke' for his translation of Hesiod (1728), was a hard-working writer and translator, who never managed to make ends meet and finally died in poverty. His translations from Catullus show a particular interest in themes of unfaithfulness and betrayal, whether of friends or lovers.

From *Mr. Cooke's Original Poems, with Imitations and Translations* (1742).

Carmen 8

To Himself

Catullus, give your Follys o'er
And wretched seek what's loss'd no more:
Propitious Days 'e'rwhile were thine,
When I could call the fair one mine,
When eager of the Chace I view'd
Her Steps with Joy, and quick pursu'd:
Such was my Love, and such my Pain,
As none shall ever cause again.
Too swiftly did the Moments glide
In sports you sought, nor she deny'd.
Propitious Days were truly thine,
When I could call the fair one mine.
No more in vain your Hours employ;
The Nymph to all you wish is coy;
No longer watch her Steps in vain,
Nor make your Life a Life of Pain;
Resolve to act the manly Part,
And drive the Poyson from your Heart.
Farewell my Love, here ends your Reign,
Catullus is himself again;

With his Consent unsought you fly;
He'll ask no more what you'd deny;
But think, now thou art false to me,
What sorrow is reserv'd for thee.
What Gallant will receive you now?
Or who prefer of Love the Vow?
Who now shall court the treach'rous Kiss,
That leaves the Token of the Bliss?
Catullus, act the manly Part,
30 And keep the Poyson from your Heart.

Carmen 30

To Alphenus

Alphenus, say can you a Friend deceive,
And him, tho true, without Reluctance leave?
Tell me, perfidious man, *Alphenus*, say,
Can you a Friend forsake, and then betray?
Have not the Pangs of Guilt your bosom seiz'd?
Think not with impious Acts the Gods are pleas'd;
But these are Thoughts which never plagu'd thy breast,
Who basely left me, and when much distress'd.
What can we do amidst a Race unjust,
10 Where find a Man regardful of his Trust?
The Heart of Friendship you seduc'd from me,
As if no Danger could arise from thee;
But now, a Traytor to the social Ty,
Your Actions give your former Vows the Ly;
Nor Words, nor Deeds, retracted longer bind,
Your Words retracted, and your Deeds, are Wind.

8.26 *prefer* proffer, present

You may forget, and live a Wretch abhor'd,
But know the Gods remember, and record;
Faith well remembers, rev'rend Deity,
20   Who will exact due Penitence from thee.

Carmen 64.143–8

From the Epithalamium on the Nuptials of Thetis and Peleus

Ye Fair attend not with a faithful Ear,
Nor hope the Words of Man can be sincere;
He vows, he swears, and begs to be believ'd;
And ye too easy trust, and are deceiv'd;
He in the Gust of Love will Truth defy,
Will promise all he can, and dread no Ly,
Till he has slak'd the Raging of his Mind;
When that is over all his Vows are Wind.

Carmen 109

To Lesbia

You wish, my Life, in the soft Hours of Love,
Our Flame may constant burn, and mutual prove;
Ye Gods, if from her Heart her Wishes came,
Grant it to end but with our vital Flame.

THE ADVENTURES OF CATULLUS (1707)

The Adventures of Catullus is an anonymous translation of a novel entitled *Les Amours de Catulle* (Paris, 1680) by Jean de Lachapelle (1655–1725), a French diplomat and dramatist who specialized in tragedies on classical themes. The novel, a fanciful history constructed from hints in Catullus' poetry, contained translations of over forty poems, and was written to rescue Catullus from the pedantry of scholars, as Lachapelle notes in his preface:

> I had a long time lamented the want of Skill, in most of those, that have undertaken to explain the Gallant Poets of Antiquity. They give us long and tiresome Dissertations upon every Verse, which might be explained with less pains, and much more pleasure to those that wou'd understand these fine wits ... I had a mind then, to give the Sense of Catullus, in a manner, that shou'd not smell of the School, or the Commentary: And in Reading over his Works with some Thought and Application, I have endeavour'd to give a Guess at all his Intrigues and Galantries. Perhaps I have hit right; however it be, I have found out a Link, and by it a certain Chain of Adventures, which gives a very fair connexion to all the amorous Sonnets, that lie scatter'd without order or design, amidst his other Works.

The Adventures of Catullus, like its French original, treats Catullus and his friends as if they were characters in a novel of seventeenth-century courtiers and their ladies. Its translations, all presented without attribution, are from various sources, including Cowley for *Carmen* 45 and Tom Brown for *Carmen* 92. In most cases the anonymity of the translators is both impenetrable and well deserved. The work is most interesting, however, for its frank translations of invective and pederastic poems that were largely avoided until late in the twentieth century. In the selection below we find Catullus threatening to force *fellatio* on Aurelius (*Carmen* 21), attacking the dried up and constipated Furius

(*Carmen* 23), showering scorn on Caesar and his lover Mamurra (*Carmina* 29 and 57), characterizing his Lesbia as a common prostitute (*Carmen* 58) and addressing a charming kiss poem to the boy Juventius (*Carmen* 48). In the case of Juventius, however, Lachapelle inventively avoids attributing homosexual affection to Catullus himself. Juventius, he claims, was a pseudonym for a certain Crastinia (a character he invents for the purpose). It seems that there *was* indeed a beautiful youth named Juventius, whom fair Crastinia much resembled:

> All agreed that there was a great Resemblance, and from that day, *Catullus* call'd her nothing but the *Lovely Juventius*. The Verses that he made upon her were inscribed to *Juventius*, and there were but very few that understood the Mystery.

From *The Adventures of Catullus and History of his Amours with Lesbia Intermixt with Translations of the Choicest Poems by Several Hands* (1707).

Carmen 21

Aurelius, you the Chief, and Head,
Of those who Niggard Tables spread,
And are with next to nothing fed –
Not only those who breath this Air
But all that are to come, and were –
You'd feign Debauch my pritty Boy,
That is his Master's Love and Joy.
Nor do you hide your base design,
But with him in discourses join;
10   All Ways and Means in publick try'd
As you stick closely to his side.
But all attempts in vain shall be;
The Snares you lay for him and me,
Thou Villain, shall entangle thee.

21.6 *feign* i.e., *fain*, 'gladly'

Not but I'd see't, and hold my tongue;
Did you make Love, well fed and strong.
Now for him I with Grief cou'd burst,
Lest he from you shou'd learn to *Thirst*;
Lest he, poor Boy, shou'd know the way
20   Of feeding upon *Air* all Day.
Wherefore I Counsel you decline,
While you well are, this Leud design.
But you'll ne'er cease to seize the Youth,
'Till I have drench'd your nasty Mouth.

Carmen 23

Furius, whose Dwelling's not possess'd
Of either Fire, or Slave, or Chest;
Who'st not enough in all thy House,
To entertain one single Mouse.
But Father, and Step-mother in't,
So rav'nous they cou'd eat a Flint;
Yet you, your Mother, and your Sire,
Cohabit to your Hearts desire.
No wonder, for your all in Health
10   Without the Cares attend on Wealth.
No risques of dreadful Fires you run,
Nor fear to be by Fraud undone.
No secret Poison need you dread,
Nor other Dangers hanging o're your Head:
Besides, your Body's hard and dry,
Defie the most inclement Sky;
Which is a Blessing will be lasting,
And comes from Heats, and Colds, and Fasting.
Why shou'd thou then perplex your Mind
20   Who these Conveniencies find?

No Sweat, nor Spittle from you flows;
Nor Liquor issues from your Nose.
To this, we add, tho' 'tis obscene,
Another cleanliness as clean.
Your Fundaments, in such a Case,
As Salt-sellers that Tables grace;
That newly scour'd upon 'em shine,
And give a Lustre when we dine.
Not ten times in a Year you Vent
30 That nasty thing call'd Excrement;
And when you do, it is so hard,
It rather seems a Stone than T—
Which if it in your Fingers stands,
Tho' rub'd, cannot defile your Hands.
With these Advantages you'r born:
These Advantages don't scorn.
But cease to wish for an Estate,
For thou art but too happy in thy Fate.

Carmen 26

Furius you to me often cry,
For *which Wind* best does our House *lie*?
I answer *none*, nor East nor West,
Nor Southern, nor for Northern Blast.
It *lies* with its adjacent Grounds,
In Pawn *for several Thousand Pounds*.
O horrid and Tempestuous Wind!
Worse than those Four, together join'd!

Carmen 29

Who can bear this, or on it tamely look?
Unless a Letcher, Spend-thrift, or a Rook;
To see *Mamurra* cloath'd with all the Spoils
Caesar brought home from *Gaul*, and *Britain's* Isles?
   On this can you, O Caesar, *tamely look*?
   Caesar's *a Letcher, Spend-thrift,* and *a Rook*.
Shall he, blown up with Wealth, and Ease and Pride,
Insult the Chastities of all beside;
Walk o'er the Beds of such as he approves
10 For *Catamites*, or Bill, like one of *Venus* Doves?
   On this can you, O Caesar, *tamely look*?
   Caesar's *a Letcher, Spend-thrift,* and *a Rook*.
Wast thou for this the first of Emperors nam'd?
When Savage *Britains* by our Troops were tamed.
Britains, that in remotest Regions lie,
Distant from *Rome*, and from the *Roman* Eye?
That this your Stallion should profusely waste
Three hundred thousand *Sesterces* at last;
What is it? or is this destructive Grant,
20 A Sum, that's thought proportion'd to his want:
Or has he on his Lust but little spent?
But little to give Gluttony content?
First, went his Fathers Chattles, and his Lands.
From all their dirtiness he wash'd his Hands.
Next were consum'd the spoils from Pontus brought;
And last the Wealth of *Spain*, for which we fought.
Yet *Gauls* and *Britains* do this Spend-thrift fear,
Why do ye hold your own Destruction dear?
Or what can he for *Gauls* or *Britains* do,
30 But his Voluptuous Course of Life persue,
And glibly swallow down Estates a-new?

29.2 *Rook* cheat, scoundrel

O First of Chiefs, whom we an Emperor call,
For this did you, and *Pompey*, ruin all?
For this o'erturn in most unnatural Broils
The *Roman* State, that he might have the Spoils?

Carmen 48

Juventius, might I kiss those Eyes,
    That such becoming sweetness dart,
The Numbers might to thousands rise,
    Yet be too few to satisfie my Heart.
A Heart no Surfeit wou'd allow
    Ev'n though the Harvest of our Kisses were,
More thick than what succeeds the Plough,
    And speaks the Blessings of a fruitful Year.

Carmen 57

No two Male Harlots e'er agreed,
More perfectly in Thought and Deed,
Than *Caesar* and *Mamurra*, who
The same ill Courses both pursue.
No wonder, both alike inclin'd,
Have the same Vices of the Mind.
Which on it still impress'd shall stay,
Hopeless of being wash'd away.
One Bed has always both contain'd,
Both have a little Learning gain'd.
Nor is one's Lust more hot than t'others,
The two *He whores* are mere Twin-Brothers
Joint Rivals of the Lady's grown,
And to their Sex prefer their own.
No two Male Harlots e'er agreed,
So perfectly in Thought and Deed.

Carmen 58

That *Lesbia*, *Caelius*, that dear faithless she;
That *Lesbia*, who was all in all to me;
That *Lesbia*, whom alone *Catullus* priz'd
Above himself, and Friends, for whom he all despis'd;
False to her Vows, to her attested Flame,
Forgetful of her Love, and of her Fame,
Now upon Bulks, in every Alley, lies,
And in the Arms of Brawny Porters dies.

Carmen 93

Caesar, so little I regard thy sight,
I care not if thou't *Black*, or if thou't *White*;
But this I know, and dare this knowledge tell;
Thy Lust, and Course of Life's as *Black* as Hell.

ANONYMOUS (1717)

The following translations of *Carmina* 4 and 31, printed in *Pope's Miscellany*, are sometimes attributed to Pope himself, but are probably by an unknown hand.

Catullus' *Carmen* 4 purports to be the self-description of a yacht retired from service and musing on its life, from its origins as a leafy forest on Mt Cytorus on the Black Sea to its long journey to a final safe haven, where it dedicates itself to Castor and Pollux, patrons of seafaring. The boat supposedly tells its story to Catullus, who in turn relates it to

---

58.7 *Bulks* frameworks or stalls projecting from fronts of shops, notoriously frequented by prostitutes and thieves
58.8 *dies* experiences sexual climax

us ('this boat you see, my friends, says it was the swiftest of ships'). The anonymous translator keeps the poem's three essential themes (the boat's transformation from tree to ship, its journey and its well-deserved retirement), but he abandons Catullus' narrative device. By simply telling the story himself he has lived up to his claim to have paraphrased 'in the manner of Cowley', for like Cowley, he has 'left out what he pleased'. (For Cowley's own bold imitation of *Carmen* 4, see Appendix.) The imitation of *Carmen* 31 is still farther from its model, substituting a generalized celebration of homecoming for Catullus' specific return to Sirmio, 'gem of peninsulas and islands'. Stanza IV has no parallel in Catullus.

From *Pope's Own Miscellany Being a reprint of Poems on Several Occasions* (1717).

Carmen 4

The Fourth Ode of Catullus
Paraphras'd in the manner of Cowley
Phasellus ille, &c.
On the Boat that carried him into his own Countrey

I

This racer of the watry plain,
Cou'd once outstrip the fleetest sail;
With oary finns to swim the main,
Or wing'd with canvass, fly before the gale!

II

On *Pontus* streams she freely rides,
Whom roots once fasten'd to the shore;
And turn'd a tenant of the tides,
Reviews the mountains where she grew before:

III

Where once she stood a living shade,
And (veil'd in clouds) her head did rear,
Her verdant tresses round her play'd,
Sung to the wind, and danc'd in open air.

IV

Of old, *Cytorus* top she crown'd;
And, at his bottom while she moves,
Renews acquaintance with the ground,
Her kindred trees, and her coeval groves.

V

Here, where she tempted first the tides,
And crept on unexperienc'd oars;
On bounding billows tost she rides,
Secure on surges, as of old on shoars.

VI

Whether when hov'ring in the sky,
The wandring winds did loosely blow;
Or sweeping from all quarters fly,
When *Jove* abroad on all their wings would go.

VII

At last she left the stormy seas,
But to no gods her vows did make,
Till now her vessel, laid at ease,
Sleeps on the bosom of the gentle lake.

VIII

Here her old age its rest obtains,
Secure from all the watry war;
And consecrates its last remains,
To thee, bright *Castor*, and thy Brother Star!

Carmen 31

CATULLUS
Ad Peninsulam Sirmionem

I

    Fair soil, thou brightest of all isles;
        Of earths sweet face thou charming eye,
    On whom the dimpled ocean smiles,
While in his glass thou dost thy beauty spy.

II

    Though round all lands he throws his arms,
        He most prefers thy lov'd embrace,
    Returns, and dwells upon thy charms,
And bears to thee the spoils of ev'ry place.

III

    Oh happy he! that freed from care,
        Lays by his load; and, weary grown,
    Whence first he wander'd, settles there;
And on his native earth lies softly down!

IV

    Gentle and soft, as tender sheep
        On their own easy fleeces fall;
    His silent life drops fast asleep,
Forgets all toils, or only dreams of all.

V

    Hail land, that all diversion yields!
        Rejoice and laugh, thou flow'ry soil!
    Shine in your gaudy dress, my fields,
And ev'ry sporting wave put on a smile!

CHRISTOPHER SMART (1722–71)

Smart was a prolific professional writer who fought a life-long battle against poverty, madness and drink and died in debtor's prison. He wrote plays, composed both amatory and devotional poetry, and translated Horace and the Psalms.

Carmen 49 is generally taken today as a backhanded or at best ambiguous compliment to Cicero, 'most eloquent of Romulus' descendants'. Smart's compliment, however, is evidently sincere. His imitation honours William Murray (1705–93), who took an early interest in Smart's poetic career and was also the brother-in-law of Smart's patron, the Duchess of Cleveland. Smart's use of the title 'Mr.' for Murray places the composition of the poem not later than 1756, when Murray became Lord Chief Justice.

From *Poems on Several Occasions* (1763).

Carmen 49

Disertissime Romuli Nepotum,
Imitated after Dining with Mr. Murray

O Thou, of British Orators the chief
That *were*, or are in *being*, or belief;
All eminence and goodness as thou art,
Accept the gratitude of POET SMART,
The meanest of the tuneful train as far,
As thou transcend'st the brightest at the bar.

ROBERT LLOYD (1733–64)

Lloyd, son of a prominent schoolmaster and churchman, started to follow in his father's footsteps but soon gave up teaching in favour of dissipation and a writer's career. He lived as a literary drudge in London, and died in debtors' prison.

Lloyd's translation of *Carmen* 92 is modelled on Brown's and invites comparison with it. Using Brown's stanzas and rhyme scheme, he makes the poet's feelings in the second stanza exceed the girl's in the first – not mirror them as in Brown.

From *Poems by Robert Lloyd* (1762).

Carmen 92

From Catullus

Chloe, that dear bewitching prude,
Still calls me saucy, pert, and rude,
   And sometimes almost strikes me;
And yet, I swear, I can't tell how,
Spite of the knitting of her brow,
   I'm very sure she likes me.

Ask you me, why I fancy thus?
Why, I have call'd her jilt, and puss,
   And thought myself above her;
10 And yet I feel it, to my cost,
That when I rail against her most,
   I'm very sure I love her.

JOHN NOTT (1751–1825)

Nott, a physician and classical scholar, moved in aristocratic circles and travelled extensively in both Europe and Asia. He wrote scientific works, produced anthologies of English poets, and translated Italian, Persian and Latin poetry into English verse. In 1795 he published the first complete English translation of Catullus. This two-volume work, printed anonymously, is both scholarly and literary, for Nott includes parallel passages from contemporary English poetry and notes on points of Latin style and Roman custom. He presents his translations and Catullus' Latin text on facing pages. Nott intends his work for a sophisticated audience and claims to have given 'the whole of Catullus without reserve', undeterred by the poet's 'indecencies'. 'The chaste reader might think them best omitted,' he admits, 'but the inquisitive scholar might wish to be acquainted even with the ribaldry, and broad lampoon of Roman times.' He regards 'a clean well-pointed satire' as Catullus' forte; and, not surprisingly, is at his best in translating the poems of invective. He was harshly treated by contemporary reviewers both for translating the indecent poems and for false rhymes and harshness of style.

The selections below include attacks on napkin thieves (*Carmina* 12 and 25), on the constipated Furius (*Carmen* 23), on Caesar and his effeminate henchman Mamurra (*Carmina* 29 and 93–4), on the young charmer with a pimp (*Carmen* 106), and on a depraved 'great man' (*Carmen* 112), as well as Catullus' dedication (*Carmen* 1), and a rebuke of a lover for wiping off his kiss (*Carmen* 99). For the most part Nott translates frankly but without obscenity, endeavouring, as he says, 'to convey our poet's meaning in its fullest extent, without overstepping the modesty of language'. In both *Carmen* 99 and *Carmen* 106, however, he fails to reveal that the lovers in question are boys.

From *The Poems of Caius Valerius Catullus in English Verse* (1795).

Carmen 1

Poem I
Or the Dedication

With pumice dry just polish'd fine,
To whom present this book of mine;
This little volume smart, and new? —
Cornelius, I will give it you:
For then you oft were wont to say
Some trifling merit had my lay;
When, chief of Italy's learn'd train,
You dar'd in three small tracts explain,
Gods! how laborious and how sage,
10 The history of ev'ry age.
Whatever then its value be,
Accept this little book from me;
And, o protecting Virgin, deign
It may for centuries remain!

Carmen 12

To Asinius

When, Asinius, with mirth, and good wine, you're elate;
You employ your left hand with a freedom too great;
For let any one careless his head turn away,
In a trice on his napkin your fingers you lay.

1.4 *Cornelius* Cornelius Nepos, Roman biographer and historian. The synopsis of universal history Catullus mentions in lines 8–10 is lost.
1.13 *Virgin* the Muse

Do you think this is wit? – silly boy, not to know
How unworthy this trick, how indecently low!
You doubt me? if so, trust to Pollio your brother;
Who, could he but shift your mean frauds to another,
Would bestow in exchange a whole talent at least:
10   Yet what youth better knows how to laugh, or to jest?
Then without further trouble my napkin restore,
Or expect me to send you lampoons by the score.
Not on worth that's intrinsic its merit depends,
But a keep-sake it was from some intimate friends;
For Fabullus, Verannius, in Spain having met:
Of Setabian fine napkins they sent me a set:
Then of course highly valued the present must be;
As Verannius, Fabullus are valued by me.

Carmen 23

To Furius

   Nor menial slave, nor coffer strong,
Nor blazing hearth to thee belong;
Not e'en a spider, or a louse,
Can live within thy famish'd house;
Yet does my Furius, to his cost,
A father, and a stepdame boast;
So hungry, so extremely thin,
Their teeth a very flint would skin;
And, such thy sire, so lean his wife,
10   You needs must lead a pleasant life:

12.7 *Pollio* probably the historian and orator Asinius Pollio, a friend of Virgil and Horace
12.16 *Setabian* from Saetaba, the centre of the Spanish linen industry

What wonder? when, beyond a question
You all are blest with good digestion;
Have nought to fear, nor fire, nor losses,
Nor impious deeds, nor pois'nous doses;
Nor all the dangers, which await
The wretchedness of human state.

    Your harden'd bodies drier are
Than horn, or ought that's drier far;
And, nurs'd by hunger, cold, and heat,
20 How can your bliss but be compleat?
From you no sweat, no spittle flows;
No rheum, no snivel from your nose:
Besides; one cleanliness superior
To all you boast; that your posterior
Is so exceeding trim, and sweet;
A saltcellar's not half so neat:
Scarce ten times in the year you vent
Your indurated excrement;
So indurated ne'er was known
30 Or shrivell'd bean, or hardest stone;
Which, rubb'd, and crumbled o'er and o'er,
Would leave the finger as before.

    Then hold not cheap, nor yet despise
Blessings, my Furius, you should prize;
Nor, as you're wont, ask more of heav'n;
To thee enough's already giv'n!

Carmen 25

To Thallus

    Voluptuous Thallus; soft, I own,
    As rabbit's fur, as cygnet's down;
    Soft as the tip of softest ear;
As flimsy age, or spider's silken snare!

> Yet more rapacious than the sea,
>   Which, vex'd with storms, sweeps all away;
>   Whilst boding birds, with dismal cry,
> O'er the tempestuous, wintry billows fly.
>
>   My cloak thou shalt return, I vow!
>   My fine Setabian napkin too;
>   My tablets, from the Thynian coast;
> All which, as lineal wealth, vain fool, you boast!
>
>   Unglue thy hands, my things restore!
>   Lest thy soft breech, and sides made sore
>   With unaccustom'd stripes, you rave;
> Lash'd, like some skiff that dares wild ocean's wave.

Carmen 29

To Caesar, On Mamurra

> Shall utmost Britain, fine-hair'd Gaul,
>   Mamurra's be, with wealth replete?
> He, who views this unmov'd, is all
>   That's squand'ring, lewd, extortionate:
> This, vicious Caesar, wilt thou see, and bear?
> O lewd, o squandering, extortioner!
>
> Shall he extravagant, and vain,
>   From bed to bed licentious rove;
> Like the white dove of Paphos' queen,
>   Or young Adonis form'd for love:
> This, vicious Caesar, wilt thou see, and bear?
> O lewd, o squandering, extortioner!

29.9 *Paphos' queen* Venus, who had a famous temple in Paphos on Cyprus

Say, chief of monarchs, did thy sword
    Visit the last of Western isles;
That thy drain'd minion might afford
    To riot in excess of spoils?
Wert thou for this so prodigal; that he,
Nurs'd by thy lust, might sate his gluttony?

First thy own private funds he spent,
    Then the lewd gains of Pontic lands,
Next all Iberia's treasures went,
    And Tagus with its golden sands:
Now trembling Gaul beholds the plund'rer near,
And Britain's destin'd land now shakes with fear!

Then to thy fost'ring breast why lay
    That wretch, who but devours the state?
Thou first of emperors, o say,
    Was it for this thou wert made great?
That you, and Pompey, in contention, hurl'd
Distress, and ruin o'er th'affrighted world?

Carmina 93–4

To Caesar

So little I for Caesar care,
    Whatever his complexion be;
That whether dark, or whether fair,
    I vow 'tis all the same to me!

29.14 *the last of Western isles* Britain
29.15 *drain'd* sexually exhausted

His favourite so debauch'd is got,
    Yes, so debauch'd is his rank blood
Folks say, he's like a kitchen pot
    That's cramm'd with ev'ry dainty food.

Carmen 99

To his Favourite

It happen'd in sport, I remember it well,
    As together we pleasingly strove;
I chanc'd from your lips the sweet nectar to steal;
    It was sweet as the nectar of Jove!

But to punish my theft, a full hour or more
    On the rack of despair I was laid;
In vain did I weep, and protest, and implore;
    'Twas in vain to thy pity to plead.

Nay, scarce had I touch'd that dear mouth, when behold,
    Lest one atom of mine should remain,
With water as much as each hand could well hold
    How you wash'd it again, and again!

Had some nasty wanton bedaub'd you with slime,
    Sure you could not have shewn more affright:
O, cruel, why punish for ever my crime?
    Why for ever my passion thus slight?

Sweet kiss of ambrosia, how alter'd, how lost!
    Not more bitter sad hellebore now;
But since thou such trouble, such anguish hast cost,
    I will ne'er steal another, I vow!

Carmen 106

On an Auctioneer

When along with a sly auctioneer
    Such a dainty, young thing we behold;
To the world it must surely appear,
    That its beauty is meant to be sold.

Carmen 112

To Naso

Does greatness to that man belong,
    (And in thy own esteem, I know,
Thou'rt counted great) who in lust's throng
    Descends to all that's vile, and low? –
Naso, it does: for we behold in thee
    Greatness, combin'd with lustful infamy.

JOHN HOOKHAM FRERE
(1769–1846)

Frere, a diplomat and man of letters, was known as a wit and composer of humorous verse. He helped found and write for the short-lived but politically important *Anti-Jacobin* weekly journal (1797–8) and a few years later served as British envoy to Portugal and Spain. After retiring in 1809 he devoted himself to literary studies, most notably to the translation of Aristophanes and Theocritus. His translations of Catullus are probably to be dated 1800–1810.

Frere's translation of *Carmen* 10 catches Catullus' urbanity and conversational flavour, while softening his characterization of Varus' troublesome girlfriend as 'a little tart, but not without her charms' (*scortillum . . . / non sane illepidum neque invenustum, Carmen* 10.3–4) His version of *Carmen* 39, on the Spaniard Egnatius and his disgusting smile, is dated 1810, intriguingly close to the time of his embassy to Spain, which ended in 1809. In *Carmen* 91, the least offensive of Catullus' attacks on the incestuous Gellius, he uses seventeen lines to Catullus' ten, but again catches Catullus' tone, here of moral outrage. He also follows Catullus' structure: a very long periodic sentence followed by a short punch line.

From *The Works of the Right Honourable John Hookham Frere in Verse and Prose* (1874).

Carmen 10

Varus me meus, &c.

Varus, whom I chanced to meet
The other evening in the street,
Engaged me there, upon the spot
To see a mistress he had got.
She seem'd, as far as I can gather,
Lively and smart, and handsome rather.
There, as we rested from our walk,
We enter'd into different talk –
As, how much might Bithynia bring?
10 And had I found it a good thing?
I answered, as was the fact,
The province had been stript and sack'd;
That there was nothing for the praetors,
And still less for us wretched creatures,
His poor companions and toad-eaters.

10.9 *Bithynia* a rich Roman province in Asia Minor, where Catullus had been on the governor's staff   **10.13** *praetors* governors

'At least,' says she,'you brought some fellows
To bear your litter; for they tell us,
Our only good ones come from there.'
I chose to give myself an air;
20 'Why, truly, with my poor estate,
The difference wasn't quite so great
Betwixt a province, good or bad,
That where a purchase could be had,
Eight lusty fellows, straight and tall,
I shouldn't find the wherewithal
To buy them.' But it was a lie:
For not a single wretch had I –
No single cripple fit to bear
A broken bedstead or a chair.
30 She, like a strumpet, pert and knowing,
Said – 'Dear Catullus, I am going
To worship at Serapis' shrine –
Do lend me, pray, those slaves of thine!'
I answer'd – 'It was idly said, –
They were a purchase Cinna made
(Caius Cinna, my good friend) –
It was the same thing in the end,
Whether a purchase or a loan –
I always used them as my own;
40 Only the phrase was inexact –
He bought them for himself, in fact.
But you have caught the general vice
Of being too correct and nice,
Over curious and precise;
And seizing with precipitation
The slight neglects of conversation.'

10.32 *Serapis' shrine* an appropriate destination, since the worship of Isis and Serapis was much favoured by prostitutes

Carmen 39

Egnatius quod candidos, &c.

Egnatius has a certain pride that centres
In his white teeth; he smiles at all adventures:
He goes, like other people, to attend
And countenance the trial of a friend:
The orator insists and perseveres;
The audience and judges are in tears;
When in the midst of his pathetic style,
Egnatius sympathises with a smile.
Following a widow to the funeral pile
10 Of her last child, he cannot choose but smile:
Without a thought of person, time, or place,
He wears a constant smile upon his face:
In business, in distress, in haste, in sadness,
It looks like a disease, a kind of madness:
(Though not a witty madness or refined) –
A madness in degree, though not in kind,
And therefore all his friends must speak their mind.
– My dear Egnatius, if your birth had been
At Tiber, Rome, or in the space between;
20 Were you a Susian fat or Umbrian poor,
A Volscian, or a Lanuvinian boor,
Sharp-tooth'd and eager at your meals and labours:
Or a Cisalpine, like my friends and neighbours;
Of any nation, tribe, or race, in short,
That scour their teeth and gums in cleanly sort,
I still should disapprove that constant smile,
It shows a silly, poor, affected style. –

> But in his native Celtiberian land,
> Your Celtiberian, as we understand,
> 30 Time out of mind cleanseth his jaws and bone,
> Each for himself, with urine of his own,
> Reserved and hoarded from the day before;
> And therefore calculated on that score,
> The whiteness of your teeth seems to imply
> A steady, copious use of chamber-lye.

Carmen 91

Non ideo Gelli, &c.

> Gellius, it never once was my design,
> In all that wretched, tedious love of mine,
> To treat you as a worthy man or just,
> Alive to shame, susceptible of trust,
> In word or act true, faithful, or sincere;
> But since that idol which my heart held dear
> Was not your sister, niece, or near of kin,
> The slight inducement of so small a sin
> As broken faith to a confiding friend,
> 10 Would scarce, methought, allure you to descend
> From those proud heights of wickedness sublime –
> Giant ambition that aspires to climb
> The topmost pinnacles of human guilt: –
> – To make the mistress of your friend a jilt
> Appear'd too poor a triumph. I was blind
> To that perpetual relish which you find
> In crimes of all degrees and every kind.

39.28 *Celtiberian land* Spain

SAMUEL TAYLOR COLERIDGE (1772–1834)

Coleridge was one of the giants of the English romantic movement. The selection below was written in the same period as *The Rime of the Ancient Mariner*, *Kubla Khan* and *Christabel*. Catullus' poem treats three themes: censorious old men, the shortness of human life, and kisses. Unlike most previous translators, Coleridge virtually omits the first, leaving the lovers alone in a perpetual kissing that defies the laws of time.

First published in *The Morning Post*, 1798. The text below is from *The Complete Poetical Works* (1912).

Carmen 5

Lines imitated from Catullus

My Lesbia, let us love and live,
And to the winds, my Lesbia, give
Each cold restraint, each boding fear
Of age and all her saws severe.
Yon sun now posting to the main
Will set, – but 'tis to rise again; –
But we, when once our mortal light
Is set, must sleep in endless night!
Then come, with whom alone I'll live,
10   A thousand kisses take and give!
Another thousand! to the store
Add hundreds – then a thousand more!
And when they to a million mount,
Let confusion take the account, –
That you, the number never knowing,
May continue still bestowing –
That I for joys may never pine,
Which never can again be mine!

WALTER SAVAGE LANDOR
(1775–1864)

Landor, famous for being irascible, opinionated and quarrelsome, spent much of his long life in Italy and died in Florence. Although he is best known as an elegant prose stylist, he also wrote dramas and poetry. Catullus was Landor's favourite ancient poet (even though he criticized him for 'uncleanly wit'); and he translated, imitated and made pronouncements about him throughout his career, never hesitating to abridge or rewrite his poetry in accordance with his own taste and notions of propriety.

Landor's own remarks are the best commentary on his translations. On *Carmen* 10, he says: 'Instead of expatiating on this, which contains, in truth, some rather coarse expressions, but is witty and characteristical, we will subjoin a paraphrase, with a few defalcations.' He omits Catullus' last two lines (for which see Frere's translation, lines 42–6), 'because they injure the poem', commenting, 'this, if said at all, ought not to be said to the lady.' On *Carmen* 22: 'this may be advantageously contracted in a paraphrase'. On *Carmen* 64.269–75 (which he compares to a description of morning in Milton): 'A more beautiful description, a sentence on the whole more harmonious, or one in which every verse is better adapted to its peculiar office, is neither to be found nor conceived.' On *Carmina* 87 and 75, which he found in his Latin text as a single poem: 'Here are eight verses, the rhythm of which plunges from the ear into the heart. Our attempt to render them in English is feeble and vain.' '*Carmen* 20', to Priapus, the god of gardens, was printed in Landor's text, but is not attributed to Catullus by modern editors.

Carmina 2 and 3 were first published in *Poems of Walter Savage Landor* (1795); *Carmen* 10 in T*he Monthly Repository*, October 1837; the other selections in *The Foreign Quarterly Review*, July 1842. The text of *Carmina* 2 and 3 is from *The Poetical Works of Walter Savage Landor* (1937).

Carmen 2

To the Sparrow of Lesbia

Sparrow! Lesbia's lively guest,
Cherish'd ever in her breast!
Whom with tantalizing jokes
Oft to peck her she provokes:
Thus in pretty playful wiles
Love and absence she beguiles.

Oft, like her, to ease my pain,
I thy little fondness gain.
Dear to me as, bards have told,
Was the apple's orb of gold
To the Nymph whose long-tied zone
That could loose, and *that* alone.

Carmen 3

On the Death of Lesbia's Sparrow

Venus! Cupid! Beaux! deplore –
Lesbia's sparrow is no more!
That which she was wont to prize
Dearer than her lovely eyes.
Like a child, her voice it knew,
'Twittering here and there it flew:
Cunningly her breast it loved,
Whence it very seldom moved.

2.11 *Nymph* Atalanta, who swore to wed only the man who could beat her in a foot-race, remained unbeaten until Hippomenes won her by distracting her with golden apples he tossed on the race track; *zone* belt, symbolic of her virginity

Now, alas! 'tis in the bourn
Whence it never may return.
Cruel shades! that round it lour!
All that's pretty ye devour.
Lesbia's sparrow ye have ta'en! —
Cause of unabating pain!
Little bird! now thou art fled,
Lesbia's weeping eyes are red.

Carmen 10

De Varri scorto

Varrus would take me t'other day
   To see a little girl he knew,
Pretty and witty in her way,
   With impudence enough for two.

Scarce are we seated, ere she chatters
   (As pretty girls are wont to do)
About all persons, places, matters —
   'And pray, what has been done for *you*?'

'Bithynia, lady!' I replied,
   'Is a fine province for a pretor,
For none (I promise you) beside,
   And least of all am I her debtor'.

   'Sorry for that!' said she. 'However
   You have brought with you, I dare say,
Some litter bearers: none so clever
   In any other part as they.

10.9, 10 and 31 *Bithynia, pretor* and *Serapis* see notes on Frere's translation of *Carmen* 10

'Bithynia is the very place
   For all that's steady, tall, and straight;
It is the nature of the race.
   Could you not lend me six or eight?'

'Why, six or eight of them or so',
   Said I, determined to be grand,
'My fortune is not quite so low
   But these are still at my command'.

'You'll send them?' 'Willingly', I told her,
   Altho' I had not here or there
One who could carry on his shoulder
   The leg of an old broken chair.

'Catullus! what a charming hap is
   Our meeting in this sort of way!
I would be carried to Serapis
   To-morrow'. 'Stay, fair lady, stay!

'You overvalue my intention.
   Yes, there *are* eight – there may be nine . . .
I merely had forgot to mention
   That they are Cinna's, and not mine.'

Carmen 13.1–8

Ad Fabullum

With me, Fabullus, you shall dine,
   And gaudily, I promise you,
If you will only bring the wine,
   The dinner, and some beauty too.

With all your frolic, all your fun,
   I have some little of my own;
And nothing else: the spiders run
   Throughout my purse, now theirs alone.

Carmen 22

Ad Varrum

Suffenus, whom so well you know,
My Varrus, as a wit and beau,
Of smart address and smirking smile,
Will write you verses by the mile,
You can not meet with daintier fare
Than title-page and binding are;
But when you once begin to read
You find it sorry stuff indeed,
And you are ready to cry out
Upon this beau, *Ah! what a lout!*
No man on earth so proud as he
Of his own precious poetry,
Or knows such perfect bliss as when
He takes in hand that nibbled pen.
   Have we not all some faults like these?
Are we not all Suffenuses?
In others the defect we find,
But can not see our sack behind.

Carmen 64.269–75

As, by the Zephyr wakened, underneath
The sun's expansive gaze the waves move on
Slowly and placidly, with gentle plash
Against each other, and light laugh; but soon,
The breezes freshening, rough and huge they swell,
Afar refulgent in the crimson east.

Carmina 87 and 75

Ad Lesbiam

None could ever say that she,
Lesbia! was so loved by me,
Never all the world around
Faith so true as mine was found:
If no longer it endures
(Would it did!) the fault is yours.
I can never think again
Well of you: I try in vain:
But . . . be false . . . do what you will . . .
10   Lesbia! I must love you still.

'Carmen 20'.5–14

In spring the many-colour'd crown,
The sheafs in summer, ruddy-brown,
The autumn's twisting tendrils green,
With nectar-gushing grapes between,
Some pink, some purple, some bright gold,
Then shrivel'd olive, blue with cold,

        Are all for me: for me the goat
        Comes with her milk from hills remote,
        And fatted lamb, and calf pursued
10   By moaning mother, sheds her blood.

CHARLES ABRAHAM ELTON
(1778–1853)

Elton, an English gentleman, went to Eton, joined a regiment and inherited a baronetcy. He devoted much of his early life to poetry and translations from Greek and Latin, attaining some reputation for his three-volume work, *Specimens of the Classic Poets* (1814), which presented a sampling of ancient poets 'from Homer to Tryphiodorus' in English verse.

Unlike Landor, Elton disapproved of rewriting or improving on the works he translated. 'Taste is a capricious and variable standard', he asserts in his preface: 'the fit standard of a translator is fidelity'. Although he is generally faithful, in *Carmen* 45 he turns Septimius' Greek mistress into his 'bride', making a marriage out of a liaison, just as the freely translating Cowley had done before him. He uses blank verse for the story of Ariadne from *Carmen* 64, Catullus' miniature epic.

From *Specimens of the Classic Poets* (1814).

Carmen 2

To Lesbia's Sparrow

Sparrow! my nymph's delicious pleasure!
Who with thee, her pretty treasure,
Fanciful in frolic, plays
Thousand, thousand wanton ways;

And, flutt'ring lays to panting rest
On the soft orbings of her breast;
Thy beak with finger-tip incites,
And dallies with thy becks and bites;
When my beauty, my desire,
10 Feels her darling whim inspire,
With nameless triflings, such as these,
To snatch, I trow, a tiny ease
For some keen fever of the breast,
While passion toys itself to rest;
I would that happy lady be,
And so in pastime sport with thee,
And lighten love's soft agony.
The sweet resource were bliss untold,
Dear as that apple of ripe gold,
20 Which, by the nimble virgin found,
Unloos'd the zone that had so fast been bound.

Carmen 3

Elegy on the Sparrow

Each Love, each Venus, mourn with me!
Mourn, every son of gallantry!
The sparrow, my own nymph's delight,
The joy and apple of her sight;
The honey-bird, the darling dies,
To Lesbia dearer than her eyes.
As the fair-one knew her mother,
So he knew her from another.
With his gentle lady wrestling;
10 In her snowy bosom nestling;

2.20 *nimble virgin* Atalanta. See note on Landor's translation of *Carmen 2*.

With a flutter, and a bound,
Quiv'ring round her and around;
Chirping, twitt'ring, ever near,
Notes meant only for her ear.
Now he skims the shadowy way,
Whence none return to cheerful day.
Beshrew the shades! that thus devour
All that's pretty in an hour.
The pretty Sparrow, thus, is dead;
20   The tiny fugitive is fled.
Deed of spite! poor bird! – ah! see,
For thy dear sake, alas! for me! –
My nymph with brimful eyes appears,
Red from the flushing of her tears.

Carmen 45

Acme and Septimius

On Septimius' lap entwining,
While his Acme sank reclining;
'If I love thee not', he cried,
'Oh my Acme! oh my bride!
Even to perdition love thee,
And shall feel thy beauties move me,
As the rapid years roll by,
Like men, who love distractedly;
Then, where Afric sands are spread,
10   Or India's sun flames over-head,
May a lion cross me there,
With his green-eyed angry glare'.
    Love stood listening in delight,
    And sneezed his auspice on the right.

Acme, as her lover said,
Lightly bending back her head,
And with lips of ruby skimming
His tipsy eyes in pleasure swimming;
'Septimillus! darling mine!
So may we thus ever twine,
Victims vow'd at Cupid's shrine,
As, with still more keen requitals,
Thou art felt within my vitals!'
   Love stood listening in delight,
   And sneezed his auspice on the right.

In the heavenly omen blest,
They love, caressing and carest;
The poor youth would lightlier prize
Syria's groves than Acme's eyes;
Acme centres in the boy
All her longings, all her joy;
Who more bless'd has mortals seen?
When has a kinder passion been?

Carmen 64.38–277

Ariadne
From the Nuptials of Peleus and Thetis

No peasant tills the fields: the steers are eased
Of the neck-galling yoke; no bull upturns
With downward-sloping share the mouldering glebe;
Discolouring rust soils the deserted plough;
Nor the bent rake clears from the creeping vine
The crumbling earth; nor he that prunes the bough
Lops with his lightening hook the leafy tree.
The palace, through its inner space discern'd
Of long-receding halls, shone gorgeously
With gold, and burnish'd silver; couches gleam'd

Whitening with ivory; tables glitter'd thick
With goblets; all the splendid mansion laugh'd
With regal opulence. The couch, prepared
In the mid-chamber for the goddess-bride,
Rose high with plumy cushions. It was carved
From teeth of Indic elephants, and spread
With the shell-purple's crimson of the sea.
The tapestried covering, wrought with antique forms
Of men, display'd heroic lore, in threads
20 Of wond'rous art. For there upon the shore
Long-echoing to the flowing sound of waves,
Stood Ariadne: casting a far look
On Theseus, as in rapid bark he pass'd
Away; and pangs of furious wild despair
Master'd her throbbing heart. Nor yet believed
That she was Ariadne; while, scarce waked
From her deceiving sleep, she saw herself
Left wretched on the solitary sands.
The youth, who could forget her, flying, beat
30 The billows with his oars, and left his vows
Light-scatter'd to the winds and to the storms.
Him when the princess from the weedy shore
Discern'd remote, she bent her straining eyes,
In posture like the statue of a nymph
Madding in Bacchic orgies: troubled thoughts
Rush'd on her soul, like waves; nor suffer'd she
The slender mitre on her yellow hair;
Or the transparent scarf, that o'er her breast
Spread light its covering; or the girdle's grasp
40 Gainst which her bosom's struggling orbs rebell'd;
But all torn wildly off from all her form

64.22 *Ariadne* The Cretan princess Ariadne gave Theseus a ball of string to guide him through the labyrinth to kill her half-brother, the Minotaur. Theseus and Ariadne fled to escape her father's wrath, but when they reached the deserted island of Naxos Theseus sailed away abandoning Ariadne as she slept.
64.37 *mitre* headband

Lay strewn on every side, and the salt seas,
White-foaming at her feet, broke over them.
She nor her mitre, nor her floating zone,
Regarded aught: on thee, oh Theseus! – still
On thee she dwelt with heart, and mind, and soul,
Distracted. Ah! unhappy one! how grief,
And senseless frenzy seized her! and what thorns
Of anguish Venus planted in her breast!
50 In that heroic age did Theseus leave
Piraeus' winding bay, and visited
The Cretan walls of that inhuman king.
For legends tell that Athens, erst constrained
By cruel pestilence, atoned the death
Of slain Androgeos; and a tribute sent
Of chosen youths, and maids in beauty's flower,
To glut the monstrous Minotaur: When thus
The noble city underneath its curse
Groan'd heavily, the gallant Theseus chose
60 To perish self-devoted, in behalf
Of his dear Athens; rather than these maids
Find graves in Crete, yet need a funeral rite.
So, in light bark, with gentle breeze he sail'd
To awful Minos, and his stately court.
When on the stranger fell the eager gaze
Of that same royal virgin, who reposed
Within her mother's arms, on pillow chaste
That breathed sweet perfumes, like the myrtle buds
On green Eurotas' river-banks, or breath
70 Of the Spring-gale, that draws the colours forth
From all the streaky flowers. No sooner then
The gazing maid withdrew her glowing eyes,

64.51 *Piraeus* the port of Athens   **64.52** *inhuman king* Minos
64.55 *Androgeos* a son of Minos, killed by Theseus' father Aegeus
64.69 *Eurotas* famous river near Sparta

And bent them on the floor, than all her breast
Conceived a flame, and all her vitals burn'd.
   Oh sacred Boy! that merciless of heart,
Troublest, alas! how cruelly! the soul
With passion's fury, yet with human griefs
Minglest delights; and thou, oh Venus! queen
Of Golgos, and Idalia's leafy lawns;
80 With what a sea of troubles did ye toss
The maiden's heart; with what a flame consume!
When for the stranger of the yellow locks
She drew full many a sigh. How languish'd she
In heart-struck terrors! how her cheek grew pale
With yellowing tinge, like the wan shine of gold,
When Theseus, match'd against the monster, sought
Death, or the palm of glory! Nor to Heaven
Vow'd she unpleasing offerings, though to her
Fruitless: nor vainly on her silent lips
90 Whisper'd suspended hopes. For as the blast
Of irresistible whirlwind, with a rush
Of sudden eddy shakes a branching oak
On the mount Taurus; or cone-rustling pine
Dropping with gums; and smites the knotted trunk:
Wrench'd from the roots the tree falls headlong down,
And crushes all beneath it: with such force
Did Theseus quell the savage, prostrated
In dust, and beating with his horns the wind.
Then, in his glory, he secure retraced
100 His footsteps, governing with silken skein
His wandering feet; lest, measuring forth his way
From windings of the labyrinth, he should err,

64.75 *sacred Boy* Cupid
64.79 *Golgos* a town in Cyprus famous for the worship of Aphrodite (Venus); *Idalia* so called from Idalium, a mountain in Cyprus sacred to Aphrodite
64.93 *mount Taurus* in Asia; but the name is chosen to pun with *taurus* ('bull'), i.e., the Minotaur

>   Foil'd by the cunning edifice, that spread
>   Its undiscoverable maze around.
>   But why, thus starting from my theme, recount
>   Superfluous tales? how Ariadne left
>   Her father's aspect, and her sister's kiss,
>   And mother's folding arms: who, wretched made,
>   Should with flush'd weeping mourn her daughter lost?
> 110   But Theseus' love was dearer than them all.
>   Or how the ship was wafted to the shore
>   Of Naxos' foaming isle; or how, when closed
>   Her heavy eyes in that disastrous sleep,
>   Ingrate he fled, and left her? – Oft, they say,
>   With burning indignation she pour'd forth
>   Shrill outcries from the bottom of her heart:
>   Climb'd sad the steepy mountains; and threw out
>   A long glance o'er the vast and foamy deep:
>   Or on the flat shore ran amidst the waves,
> 120   That swell'd their rippling surface opposite;
>   From her bared leg lifting the drapery light:
>   Then, in extremity of anguish, spoke
>   These wild upbraidings; with her cheek all bathed
>   In tears, while shivering sobs confused her words:
>   'And is it thus, perfidious man! led far
>   From my own country, thou forsakest me now,
>   Perfidious Theseus! on a desert shore?
>   And dost thou then depart, of watchful Gods
>   Heedless, and ah! bear with thee to thy home
> 130   Those vows, accursed by me? Could nothing turn
>   Thy cruel purpose? did no sudden thought
>   Of pity cross thee? did thy hard heart feel
>   No soft, compunctious visitings for me?
>   Not such thy utter'd promises; not these
>   The hopes thy lips convey'd to me undone:
>   But wedding joys, and wishes all fulfill'd
>   Of marriage love: now to the winds of air
>   Blown and dispers'd! Let never woman trust

The oath of man: let never woman hope
140 Faith in his tender speeches. He, while aught
Inflames his ardour to possess, will fear
No oath; will spare no promise. But when once
His gust is sated, fears not what he spoke;
Heeds not his perjured promise. Yet 'twas I
That from death's whirlpool snatch'd thee, and resolved
To sacrifice my brother Minotaur,
That I might spend with thee life's latest hour.
Deceiver as thou art! – and 'tis for this
That forest beasts must tear me; birds of prey
150 Dismember; and no heap of friendly earth
Be scatter'd o'er my corse! – What lioness
In wilderness of rocks first brought thee forth?
What sea conceiv'd thee in its roaring depths,
And from its foaming billows cast thee out?
Syrt, Scylla, or Charybdis, which, or what
Art thou? that for the sweets of life bestow'd
Mak'st this return? but, if thy heart repell'd
Union with me; and if to thee seem stern
The laws of marriage which old Cecrops framed,
160 Thou could'st, at least, have brought me to thy home;
That I, with pleasant labour, might have been
Thy handmaid: tenderly thy snowy feet
Laving in limpid waters, or thy couch
Spreading with purple coverings. Ah! what boots
This frenzy of misfortune? why complain
To the unconscious air, that neither hears
My utter'd speech, nor can in words reply?
He, now, has nearly past the middle seas;
And not one solitary mortal meets
170 My gaze, along the ocean's weedy shore:

64.155 *Syrt* Syrtis, a famous sandbank off the coast of Africa
64.159 *old Cecrops* a legendary king of Athens

And Fate, insulting even my dying hour,
Envious denies the blessing of complaint
To listening ears. O mighty Jupiter!
Would that, in time long past, no ships had touch'd
From Athens on our coast; no mariner
With dreadful tribute to the bull, had loosed
His cable, and, perfidious, sail'd for Crete!
Nor ere that stranger, masking in sweet form
His cruel purpose, rested in my home!
180 Whither shall I betake me? On what hope
Lean for support? say, shall I seek again
The hills of Cretan Ide? ah me! the deep
Rolls broad its severing flood, and cruel forms
Of the wide seas a gulph impassable.
Or might I hope my father's succouring hand?
I, who could leave him; following this stern youth
While reeking with my brother's sprinkled blood?
Shall I console my sorrows with the love
Of that so faithful spouse, while now his oars
190 Bend pliant in the billows, as he flies?
Shall I pass inland, and forsake the shore?
No dwelling has this lone, unpeopled isle.
There is no egress hence; the sea-waves roll
A girdle round; no plan, no hope of flight;
All solitary, silent, desolate;
A prospect of inevitable death.
But let not yet my dying eyes grow dim,
Nor sense my faint limbs leave, ere thus betray'd,
I ask the Gods for vengeance, and attest
200 With my last breath the holy faith of Heaven.
Ye, then, that with retributive revenge
Visit the deeds of men; whose forehead, twined
With snaky hair, waves with th' avenging wrath
Of my expiring breast, arise and hear!
Come to my side; come listen the complaints
Which, oh me miserable! I perforce

>   Now from my inmost vitals breathe, thus lost,
>   Burning, and blind with my delirious rage.
>   Since from the very bottom of my heart
> 210 I heave this plaintive voice, o suffer not
>   My tears and groans to vanish on the winds!
>   But in the spirit, that within him wrought,
>   When he forsook me on the desert shore,
>   In that same spirit, deadly to himself,
>   And to his kindred, let him stain his house
>   With horror and pollution.' When she, thus,
>   Had given her sorrows utterance, and had call'd,
>   In her distraction, heavenly vengeance down
>   On Theseus' cruel deed, Heaven's Ruler bow'd
> 220 His head: and at his unresisted nod
>   Earth and sea trembled, and the firmament
>   Rock'd its bright orbs. But Theseus, dark of mind,
>   Dismiss'd from memory all injunctions past,
>   Though long with heed retain'd: nor lifted up
>   The gladdening symbol, that he safe return'd
>   To his own country's harbours, in the eyes
>   Of his long-sorrowing father. Story tells,
>   That when old Aegeus trusted to the winds
>   His son, who bent his galley's sails to leave
> 230 Minerva's towers, he clasp'd him in his arms,
>   And gave this mandate: 'Oh, my only son!
>   More pleasant in mine eyes than length of life:
>   My son! whom I, perforce, dismiss to cope
>   With doubtful perils; son! so lately lent
>   Again to these fond arms, in the last stage
>   Of feeble years: since now my mournful hap
>   And thy own fervid valour tear thee hence
>   From these unwilling eyes, whose languid orbs
>   Still gaze unsated on my son's dear face;

64.230 *Minerva's towers* Athens

240   Not glad I send thee hence; nor shalt thou bear
      Symbols of prosperous Fortune. I will ease
      My bosom of complaint, and soil in dust
      My hoary locks; and on thy flitting mast
      Suspend discolour'd sails: that this my grief
      And soul-inflaming anguish may be read
      In thy Iberian canvas, while its folds
      Are tinged with dusky blue. If she, who dwells
      In blest Itonus, Pallas, who defends
      Our race and city, grant, that in the blood
250   Of that half-human bull thy hand be red;
      Then bury these injunctions in thy heart:
      Let them take growth, and flourish, so that time
      May never root them out. Soon as thine eyes
      Behold our hills again, straight let thy crew
      The dismal canvas on the yard-arm furl,
      And hoist with ropes the sails of snowy white:
      That, seeing, I may recognize the joy
      Of that blest moment, when auspicious time
      Returns thee present to mine eyes again.'
260   These mandates which, before, with constant mind
      He cherish'd, now from Theseus' memory fled,
      Like mists from airy ridge of snowy Alp
      Swept by the whirlwind. Still the father bent
      From a high turret's top his straining eyes,
      Anxious, and dim with weeping. When he saw
      The sable-swelling sails, from the steep rocks
      He cast himself down headlong; deeming then
      His Theseus lost by an inhuman death.
      So Theseus, glorying in the monster slain,
270   Enter'd beneath his father's roof, now changed
      With funeral horror; and himself now felt
      A portion of that anguish, which, ingrate
      Of soul, he fix'd in Ariadne's breast:
      When, wounded to the heart, a thousand griefs
      Roll'd in her bosom, while she pensive bent

On the receding ship her lengthening gaze.
   But in another part, Iacchus, flush'd
With bloom of youth, came flying from above
With choirs of Satyrs, and Sileni, born
280 In Indian Nyse: seeking thee he came,
Oh Ariadne! with thy love inflamed.
They, blithe, from every side came revelling on,
Distraught with jocund madness: with a burst
Of Bacchic outcries, and with tossing heads.
Some shook their ivy-shrouded spears; and some
From hand to hand, in wild and fitful feast,
Snatch'd a torn heifer's limbs: some girt themselves
With twisted serpents: others bore along,
In hollow arks, the mysteries of the God:
290 Mysteries to uninitiated ear
In silence wrapt. On timbrels others smote
With tapering hands, or from smooth orbs of brass
Clank'd shrill a tinkling sound; and many blew
The horn's hoarse blare, and the barbaric pipe
Bray'd harsh upon the ear its dinning tune.
   Thus gorgeously with colour'd figures wrought
The drapery spread its mantling folds, and veil'd
With arras coverlet the wedding couch.
   When now the throng of Thessaly had gazed
300 Their eager fill, they rev'rently gave place
To step of Gods approaching. As the gale,
Ruffling the calm sea with its murm'ring breeze,
Stirs the sloped waves, at rising of the dawn,
Beneath the flitting lustre of the sun:
They, forward driven with gentle blast, roll on
Slowly, and as with sounds of laughter shrill
Dash their soft echo; till the growing wind
Freshens, and more and more in heaving swell
They float far-glittering in the purple light:
310 So from the palace vestibule the throng
Flow'd gradual forth, and wander'd wide away.

Carmen 96

To Calvus,
On the Death of his Quintilia

If ere in human grief there breathe a spell
    To charm the silent tomb, and soothe the dead;
When soft regrets on past affections dwell,
    And o'er fond friendships lost, our tears are shed;
Sure, a less pang must touch Quintilia's shade,
    While hov'ring o'er her sad, untimely bier;
Than keen-felt joy that spirit pure pervade,
    To witness that her Calvus held her dear.

THOMAS MOORE (1779–1852)

Moore, often called the national lyrist of Ireland for his *Irish Melodies*, was one of the most popular song-writers and poets of his day. He was a friend of George Lamb, and on good enough terms with Hunt to visit him in prison, although he later attacked him for his quarrel with Byron, whom he greatly admired. He published (and expurgated) Byron's memoirs.

Moore's lines from *Carmen* 7 appear in a footnote in the metrical translation of Anacreon that he completed as a student at Trinity College, Dublin. Omitting the first half of Catullus' poem, he presents in a few short strokes the night stars, the embracing lovers and their kisses, and intimations of mortality ('so many kisses ere I slumber'). As his asterisks indicate, Moore has also dispensed with the first half of *Carmen* 11, in which Catullus enumerates the far-away places to which his willing friends would accompany him. Catullus' poem moves both from the ends of the earth (and the Roman empire) to the flower on the edge of a meadow, and from imperial dreams to private grief.

Moore's, shorn of geographical and historical particularity, is a simple, timeless plea to unnamed friends. But he does not always omit and condense. Song-writer that he is, he has turned the eight-line epigram of Catullus' *Carmen* 72 into a sixteen-verse lyric in stanzas.

Carmen 7.7–12 is from *Odes of Anacreon* (1800). The other selections are from *The Poetical Works of Thomas Moore* (1841).

Carmen 7.7–12

As many stellar eyes of light,
As through the silent waste of night,
Gazing upon the world of shade,
Witness some secret youth and maid,
Who fair as thou, and fond as I,
In stolen joys enamour'd lie!
So many kisses ere I slumber,
Upon these dew-bright lips I'll number,
So many vermil, honied kisses,
10   Envy can never count our blisses:
No tongue shall tell the sum but mine;
No lips shall fascinate, but thine!

Carmen 11

* * * * * *

Comrades and friends! with whom, where'er
    The fates have will'd through life I've rov'd,
Now speed ye home, and with you bear
    These bitter words to her I've lov'd.

7.9 *vermil* rosy, glowing

Tell her from fool to fool to run,
    Where'er her vain caprice may call;
Of all her dupes not loving one,
    But ruining and maddening all.

Bid her forget – what now is past –
    Our once dear love, whose ruin lies
Like a fair flower, the meadow's last,
    Which feels the ploughshare's edge, and dies!

Carmen 72

To Lesbia

Thou told'st me, in our days of love,
    That I had all that heart of thine;
That, ev'n to share the couch of Jove,
    Thou would'st not, Lesbia, part from mine.

How purely wert thou worshipp'd then!
    Not with the vague and vulgar fires
Which Beauty wakes in soulless men, –
    But lov'd, as children by their sires.

That flattering dream, alas, is o'er; –
    I know thee now – and though these eyes
Doat on thee wildly as before,
    Yet, ev'n in doating, I despise.

Yes, sorceress – mad as it may seem –
    With all thy craft, such spells adorn thee,
That passion ev'n outlives esteem,
    And I at once, adore – and scorn thee.

LEIGH HUNT (1784–1859)

Hunt, a prolific journalist, poet, essayist and critic, was always impecunious and sometimes destitute. He edited and wrote for a series of papers, notably *The Examiner*, a liberal weekly that he founded in partnership with his brother John. Many of his poems and translations first appeared in *The Examiner*, as did a sharp criticism of the Prince Regent which won him two years in prison (1812), and an essay on 'Young Poets' (1816) that was among the first to recognize the talents of Keats and Shelley.

The selections below were all favourite Catullan poems in the early nineteenth century. *Carmen* 63 especially was greatly admired (see Introduction). The poem is the sole complete ancient example of the metre called galliambic, after the *Galli*, castrated priests of the goddess Cybele. Hunt imitates its effect with his own metrical pyrotechnics. He relates Attis' madness with a rushing trochaic/iambic octameter (1–17), shifting to anapaestic dimeter (18–33) and back to iambic octameter (34–43). He moderates into iambic hexameter (44–5) for the sudden sleep of Attis, and relates his sane regret in a contemplative iambic pentameter (46–115).

Carmina 31, 38 and 45 are from *The Feast of the Poets* (1814). All were first published in *The Examiner* (21 August 1808, 4 October and 13 September 1812). *Carmen* 63 (first published in *The Reflector*, 1810) is from *Foliage* (1818).

Carmen 31

Catullus' Return Home to the Peninsula of Sirmio

O best of all the scatter'd spots that lie
In sea or lake, – apple of landscape's eye, –
How gladly do I drop within thy nest,
With what a sigh of full, contented rest,
Scarce able to believe my journey o'er,
And that these eyes behold thee safe once more!

Oh where's the luxury like a loosened heart,
When the mind, breathing, lays its load apart, –
When we come home again, tir'd out, and spread
The greedy limbs o'er all the wish'd for bed!
This, this alone is worth an age of toil.
Hail, lovely Sirmio! Hail, paternal soil!
Joy, my bright waters, joy: your master's come!
Laugh every dimple on the cheek of home!

Carmen 38

Catullus to Cornificius

Sick, Cornificius, is thy friend,
Sick to the heart; and sees no end
Of wretched thoughts, that gath'ring fast
Threaten to wear him out at last.
And yet you never come and bring –
Though 't were the least and easiest thing –
A comfort in that talk of thine: –
You vex me: – this, to love like mine?
Prithee, a little talk, for ease, for ease,
Full as the tears of poor Simonides.

Carmen 45

Acme and Septimius, or the Entire Affection

'Oh, Acme, love!' Septimius cried,
As on his lap he held his bride, –
'If all my heart is not for thee,
And doats not on thee desperately,

38.10 *Simonides* a Greek poet famous for his lyric laments and dirges

And if it doat not more and more,
As desperate heart ne'er did before,
May I be doom'd, on desert ground
To meet the lion in his round!'
    He said; and Love, on tiptoe near him,
    Kind at last, and come to cheer him,
    Clapp'd his little hands to hear him.

But Acme to the bending youth
Just dropping back that rosy mouth,
Kiss'd his reeling, hovering eyes,
And 'O my life, my love!' replies,
'So may our constant service be
To this one only Deity,
As with a transport doubly true
He thrills your Acme's being through!'
    She said; and Love, on tiptoe near her,
    Kind at last, and come to cheer her,
    Clapp'd his little hands to hear her.

Favour'd thus by heav'n above,
Their lives are one return of love;
For he, poor fellow, so possessed,
Is richer than with East and West, –
And she, in her enamour'd boy,
Finds all that she can frame of joy.
Now who has seen, in Love's subjection,
    Two more blest in their connection,
    Or a more entire affection?

Carmen 63

Atys

Atys o'er the distant waters, driving in his rapid bark,
Soon with foot of wild impatience touch'd the Phrygian forest dark,
Where amid the awful shades possess'd by mighty Cybele,
In his zealous frenzy blind,
And wand'ring in his hapless mind,
With flinty knife he gave to earth the weights that stamp virility.
Then as the widow'd being saw its wretched limbs bereft of man,
And the unaccustomed blood that on the ground polluting ran,
With snowy hand it snatch'd in haste the timbrel's airy round on high,
10 That opens with the trumpet's blast, thy rites, Maternal Mystery;
And upon its whirling fingers, while the hollow parchment rung,
Thus in outcry tremulous to its wild companions sung: –
Now come along, come along with me,
Worshippers of Cybele,
To the lofty groves of the deity!
Ye vagabond herds that bear the name
Of the Dindymenian dame!
Who seeking strange lands, like the banished of home,
With Atys, with Atys distractedly roam;
20 Who your limbs have unmann'd in a desperate hour,
With a frantic disdain of the Cyprian pow'r;

63.17 *Dindymenian dame* Cybele, so called from Mt Dindymus in her native Phrygia
63.21 *Cyprian* of Venus

Who have carried my sect through the dreadful salt sea,
Rouse, rouse your wild spirits careeringly!
No delay, no delay,
But together away,
And follow me up to the Dame all-compelling,
To her high Phrygian groves, and her dark Phrygian dwelling,
Where the cymbals they clash, and the drums they resound,
And the Phrygian's curv'd pipe pours its moanings around;
Where the ivy-crown'd priestesses toss with their brows,
And send the shrill howl through the deity's house;
Where they shriek, and they scour, and they madden about, –
'Tis there we go bounding in mystical rout.

No sooner had spoken
This voice half-broken,
When suddenly from quiv'ring tongues arose the universal cry.
The timbrels with a boom resound, the cymbals with a clash reply,
And up the verdant Ida with a quicken'd step the chorus flew,
While Atys with the timbrels' smite the terrible procession drew;
Raging, panting, wild, and witless, through the sullen shades it broke,
Like the fierce, unconquered heifer bursting from her galling yoke;
And on pursue the sacred crew, till at the door of Cybele,
Faint and fasting, down they sink, in pale immovability;
The heavy sleep – the heavy sleep – grows o'er their failing eyes,
And lock'd in dead repose the rabid frenzy lies.

But when the Sun look'd out with eyes of light
Round the firm earth, wild seas, and skies of morning white,
Scaring the ling'ring shades
With echo-footed steeds,

50 Sleep took his flight from Atys, hurrying
    To his Pasithea's arms on tremulous wing;
    And the poor dreamer woke, oppress'd with sadness,
    To memory woke, and to collected madness. −
    Struck with its loss, with what it was, and where,
    Back trod the wretched being in despair
    To the sea-shore, and stretching forth its eye
    O'er the wide waste of waters and of sky,
    Thus to its country cried with tears of misery: −

    My country, oh my country, parent state,
60 Whom like a very slave and runagate,
    Wretch that I am, I left for wilds like these,
    This wilderness of snows and matted trees,
    To house with shiv'ring beasts and learn their wants,
    A fierce intruder on their sullen haunts, −
    Where shall I fancy thee? Where cheat mine eye
    With tricking out thy quarter in the sky?
    Fain, while my wits a little space are free,
    Would my poor eyeballs strain their points on thee!
    Am I then torn from home and far away?
70 Doom'd through these woods to trample day by day,
    Far from my kindred, friends, and native soil,
    The mall, the race, and wrestlers bright with oil?
    Ah wretch, bewail, bewail; and think for this
    On all thy past variety of bliss!
    I was the charm of life, the social spring,
    First in the race, and brightest in the ring:
    Warm with the stir of welcome was my home;
    And when I rose betimes, my friends would come
    Smiling and pressing in officious scores,
80 Thick as the flow'rs that hang at lovers' doors: −

63.51 *Pasithea* the bride of Sleep

And shall I then a minist'ring madman be
To angry gods? A howling devotee? —
A slave to bear what never senses can, —
Half of myself, sexless, — a sterile man?
And must I feel, with never-varied woes,
The o'erhanging winter of these mountain snows,
Skulking through ghastly woods for evermore,
Like the lean stag, or the brute vagrant boar?
Ah me! ah me! Already I repent;
E'en now, e'en now I feel my shame and punishment!

As thus with rosy lips the wretch grew loud,
Startling the ears of heav'n's imperial crowd,
The Mighty Mistress o'er her lion yoke
Bow'd in her wrath, — and loos'ning as she spoke
The left-hand savage, scatterer of herds,
Rous'd his fell nature with impetuous words: —

Fly, ruffian, fly, indignant and amain,
And scare this being, who resists my reign,
Back to the horror-breathing woods again!
Lash thee, and fly, and shake with sinewy might
Thine ireful hair, and as at dead of night
Fill the wild echoes with rebellowing fright!

Threat'ning she spoke, and loos'd the vengeance dire,
Who gath'ring all his rage, and glaring fire,
Starts with a roar, and scours beneath her eyes,
Scatt'ring the splinter'd bushes as he flies:
Down by the sea he spies the wretch at last,
And springs precipitous: — the wretch as fast,
Flies raving back into his living grave,
And there for ever dwells, a savage and a slave.

> O Goddess! Mistress! Cybele! dread name!
> O mighty Pow'r! O Dindymenian dame!
> Far from my home thy visitations be:
> Drive others mad, not me:
> Drive others into impulse wild, and fierce insanity!

GEORGE LAMB (1784–1834)

Lamb, although acknowledged as the youngest son of Viscount Melbourne, was in fact the illegitimate son of the Prince of Wales. He was an early writer for the *Edinburgh Review*, but his great interest seems to have been the theatre in all its aspects. He also adapted Shakespeare's *Timon of Athens* in a bowdlerized version (1816) that he described as 'an attempt to restore Shakespeare to the stage, with no other omissions than such as the refinement of manners has rendered necessary'. His translation of Catullus is considered his most important literary work.

Lamb regarded Catullus' poems as expressions of sincere emotion: 'his friendship, gratitude, advice, indignation, ridicule, and hatred, all speak in poetry; for this reason his compositions breathe a warmth and truth that still powerfully carry our feelings'. He omitted over twenty poems that he considered offensive, and rewrote many others, incurring severe criticism from contemporary reviewers. He almost turns Catullus' obscene invitation to Ipsitilla (*Carmen* 32) into an invitation to tea. (For his treatment of Juventius in *Carmina* 48 and 99 see Introduction.) Like Landor, he translates as genuine the non-Catullan '*Carmen* 20', in which the wooden garden god Priapus warns off potential thieves from his master's garden.

From *The Poems of Caius Valerius Catullus* (1821).

Carmen 32

The Rendezvous
To Hypsithilla

Kind of heart, of beauty bright,
Pleasure's soul, and love's delight,
None by nature graced above thee,
Hypsithilla, let me love thee.

Tell me then, that I shall be
Welcome when I come to thee;
And at noon's inspiring tide
Close thy gate to all beside.
Let no idle wish to roam
10 Steal thy thought from joys at home;
But prepare thy charms to aid
Every frolic love e'er play'd.
Speed thy message. Day goes fast.
Now's the hour; the banquet's past:
Mid-day suns and goblets flowing
Set my frame with passion glowing.

Speed thee, wanton, fair and free!
Tell me I must haste to thee.

Carmen 36

To 'the Annals',
A Poem, by Volusius

Volusius' Annals – worthless lay!
   E'en than thy writer's self more stupid;
'Tis thou, my damsel's vow must pay
   To sacred Venus, and to Cupid.

She vow'd, that, should my soften'd heart
    Be reconciled to her again;
And at her I should cease to dart
    My cross and keen Iambic strain;

That she would give to him, the lame
    Grim God, whom yet Jove's anger curses,
To be consumed by evil flame,
    The chosen worst of all bad verses.

No fruitful tree must form the pyre,
    Which heaven protects and man loves well;
Ill-omen'd wood shall feed the fire,
    Dear only to the Gods of Hell.

Thou art the Poem, all declare,
    Fore-destined by her frolic oath;
Then, oh, thou goddess bright and fair,
    Form'd of the azure Ocean's froth;

Goddess of Syria's open meads,
    Of sacred woods, Idalia's boast,
Cnidus, where grow the poet's reeds,
    Amathus, and Ancona's coast,

Of Golgos, and Dyrrachium's port,
    The market of the Adrian main;
Accept the vow, nor deem our sport
    That taste should shun, or wit disdain.

Then come, ye pointless rugged lays,
    Into the fire; 'tis there you're due.
Then, whether Venus blame or praise,
    We shall at least get rid of you.

36.9–10 *the lame Grim God* Vulcan, the god of fire, lamed when the angry Jupiter cast him down from heaven

Carmen 41

On Mamurra's Mistress

Can that hackney'd jade be sane?
   She, whom dirt and vice surrounds,
Spendthrift Formian's mistress plain
   Asks me for two hundred pounds.

Neighbours, quick, physicians have in,
   All her friends and kinsmen summon.
Doubt not she is mad; she's raving,
   Thinks herself a pretty woman.

Carmen 42

On a Courtezan,
Who Kept his Tablets from Him

Come, Verses, come at my request;
   Nor, Satyre, now thy coarseness lack;
Yon filthy wench makes me her jest,
   And will not give your tablets back.

If ye can bear the task, with me
   Come claim them, worry, teaze, and bait.
Ask ye of whom? – Of her ye see
   Who struts with yon affected gait;

Who gapes with stunning laughter wide
   As is the Gallic beagle's grin,
Come, Satyre, come, demand, and chide,
   And persecute with ceaseless din.

Restore them, wench of vilest trade!
   Restore the tablets, wretch accurst!
Dost thou not heed? Oh filth! oh jade!
   Oh, all that's lowest, basest, worst!

And will not this abuse prevail?
   At least, however rare, let's place
One blush, if in all else we fail,
   Upon the strumpet's iron face.

Shout then, in terms more loud and keen,
   'Drab, harlot! give them back again!
Give back the tablets, filthy quean!'
   Yet she's not moved, and all is vain.

Ah! we must breathe a softer tale.
   Then, 'Chaste and modest maid, restore
Our tablets, pray!' – That must prevail,
   For that she never heard before.

Carmen 46

To Himself
On the Approach of Spring

Spring returns, and blended meet
Winter's cold, and Summer's heat.
Zephyr's soothing airs assuage
Heaven's equinoctial rage.
Leave, Catullus, Phrygia's plains,
Leave Nicaea's rich domains;
And to Asia take thy flight
Where her splendid towns invite.

42.23 *quean* harlot, strumpet

All my mind's for travel fired;
Hope has all my limbs inspired:
Loved society, farewell,
Friends with whom I've joy'd to dwell;
From our happy jovial home
Now we all together roam;
Very soon how far and wide
Various paths shall all divide.

Carmen 54

To Caesar, on his Companions

Oh thou to taste, to feeling dead!
If neither Otho's dwarfish head,
   Nor Libo's filthy gibe,
Nor Vettius' unwash'd feet; if these
Thee nor Fuffecius can displease,
   Thine old and hackney'd scribe,

Then, mighty emperor, once again
I'll pour forth my Iambic strain
   Uncourtly, bold, and free:
Again shalt thou my truth condemn;
And he, who will be friend to them,
   Shall still be foe to me.

Carmen 70

On the Inconstancy of Woman's Love

My Fair says, she no spouse but me
Would wed, though Jove himself were he.
   She says it: But I deem
That what the fair to lovers swear
Should be inscribed upon the air,
   Or in the running stream.

'Carmen 20'

The Garden God's Threat

Form'd from the season'd poplar's heart
By the unskilful rustic's art,
From every foe and danger free,
I guard the little spot you see;
And save from theft and rapine's hand
My humble Master's cot and land.

To me the flowery chaplet, Spring,
The deep brown ear doth Summer bring:
Autumn the luscious grape bestows,
10 The pale-green olive, Winter snows.
The she-goat bears from my rich down
Dugs swol'n with milk to yonder town.
The lamb that's fatten'd in my fold
Sends back its owner chinking gold.
The tender heifer hence that goes,
While here the frantic mother lows,
Oft pours its gushing blood to stain
The threshold of the richest fane.

Then, Trav'ller, view this God with fear,
20   And check all thirst for plunder here.
'Twere well thou didst; for I can be
Quick means of punishment to thee.
Say'st thou, 'Come on', and scorn'st advice?
Behold the Cotter in a trice;
And, if he please thy sides to drub,
Myself will serve him for a club.

GEORGE GORDON, LORD BYRON (1788–1824)

Byron, the quintessential romantic poet, lived a glamorous, rakish and tragic life, worthy of one of his own Byronic heroes, and died of a fever in Missolonghi while he was trying to help the Greeks in their war to gain independence from the Turks.

Byron's Catullus' translations are all from his first published work, *Fugitive Pieces*, which he had privately printed in 1806 at the age of eighteen. His imitation of *Carmen* 48 is sometimes wrongly said to be based on *Carmen* 5 or 7, no doubt because *Carmen* 48 is addressed not to a woman but to the boy Juventius. It is perhaps in keeping with his philandering nature that Byron dedicated it first 'to Anna' but retitled it 'to Ellen' in the next edition. Like many other translators and critics, he omits the last stanza of *Carmen* 51. (For the complete poem see Gladstone and Symons below.)

First printed in *Fugitive Pieces* (1806). The text is from *Lord Byron. The Complete Poetical Works* (1980).

20.24 *Cotter* cottager

Carmen 3

Translation from Catullus
'Luctus de morte Passeris'

Ye Cupids, droop each little head,
Nor let your wings with joy be spread,
My Lesbia's fav'rite bird is dead,
    Whom dearer than her eyes she lov'd:
For he was gentle, and so true,
Obedient to her call he flew,
No fear, no wild alarm he knew,
    But lightly o'er her bosom mov'd:

And softly fluttering here and there,
He never sought to cleave the air;
But chirrup'd oft, and free from care,
    Tun'd to her ear his grateful strain.
Now having pass'd the gloomy bourn,
From whence he never can return,
His death, and Lesbia's grief, I mourn,
    Who sighs, alas! but sighs in vain.

Oh! curst be thou, devouring grave!
Whose jaws eternal victims crave,
From whom no early power can save,
    For thou hast ta'en the bird away:
From thee, my Lesbia's eyes o'erflow,
Her swollen cheeks, with weeping, glow;
Thou art the cause of all her woe,
    Receptacle of life's decay.

Carmen 48

Imitated from Catullus
To Ellen

Oh! might I kiss those eyes of fire,
A million scarce would quench desire;
Still, would I steep my lips in bliss,
And dwell an age on every kiss;
Nor then my soul should sated be,
Still, would I kiss, and cling to thee;
Nought should my kiss from thine dissever,
Still, would we kiss, and kiss for ever;
E'en though the number did exceed
10   The yellow harvest's countless seed;
To part would be a vain endeavour,
Could I desist? – ah! never – never.

Carmen 51

Translation from Catullus
'Ad Lesbiam'

Equal to Jove, that youth must be,
Greater than Jove, he seems to me,
Who, free from Jealousy's alarms,
Securely, views thy matchless charms;
That cheek, which ever dimpling glows,
That mouth, from whence such music flows,
To him, alike, are always known,
Reserv'd for him, and him alone.
Ah! Lesbia! though 'tis death to me,
10   I cannot choose but look on thee;

But, at the sight, my senses fly;
I needs must gaze, but gazing die;
Whilst trembling with a thousand fears,
Parch'd to the throat, my tongue adheres,
My pulse beats quick, my breath heaves short,
My limbs deny their slight support;
Cold dews my pallid face o'erspread,
With deadly languor droops my head,
My ears with tingling echoes ring,
And life itself is on the wing;
My eyes refuse the cheering light,
Their orbs are veil'd in starless night;
Such pangs my nature sinks beneath,
And feels a temporary death.

THE RIGHT HON. W. E. GLADSTONE (1809–98)

Gladstone was actively involved in most of the major historical crises of his century, whether as an MP, a member of the Cabinet or as Prime Minister. At the same time he wrote numerous works not only on political and historical subjects, but also on theology, contemporary poetry and classics (in which he had gained a first at Oxford). He wrote several books on Homer, and completed his translation of Horace's *Odes* on the day of his retirement from Parliament in 1894.

Gladstone's sole translation of Catullus appears in a work written with his brother-in-law Lord Lyttelton (the two friends married sisters on the same day in 1839). Their book of translations was undertaken as a means of distracting Lyttelton from his grief on the death of his wife in 1857, and it is dedicated to the memory of their two weddings.

From *Translations*, with Lord Lyttelton (1861).

Carmen 51

Catullus to Lesbia
Carm. LI

Him rival to the gods I place,
   Him loftier yet, if loftier be,
Who, Lesbia, sits before thy face,
   Who listens and who looks on thee;

Thee smiling soft. Yet this delight
   Doth all my sense consign to death;
For when thou dawnest on my sight,
   Ah wretched! flits my labouring breath.

My tongue is palsied. Subtly hid
   Fire creeps me through from limb to limb:
My loud ears tingle all unbid:
   Twin clouds of night mine eyes bedim.

Ease is thy plague; ease makes thee void,
   Catullus, with these vacant hours,
And wanton: ease, that hath destroyed
   Great kings, and states with all their powers.

1859

WILLIAM JAMES LINTON
(1812–97)

Linton, a wood-engraver, printer, reformer and poet, was born in England and moved to the United States in 1866. He produced engravings for the *Illustrated London News* and the American *Illustrated News*, as well as for many English and American books. In the early 1870s he established the Appledore Press in Hamden, Connecticut, and began to issue limited editions. The selections below were printed by Linton's press and have been ascribed to him, although the work is unsigned. The volume, printed in only twenty-five copies, contains *Carmen* 70 in Latin and thirty-two 'variations' on it in English quatrains. (For close translations see Sidney, Lovelace and Lamb above.)

From *In Dispraise of a Woman – Catullus with Variations* (1886).

Carmen 70

VII

With none, that woman tells me, would she wed
    Except with me: No! Not with Jove himself.
Believe her? Take a summer wind to bed;
    Or keep your running water on a shelf!

XII

She loved me more than any:
    With the wind so went the stream.
    Did ever wavelet dream
It was not One of many?

XIII

Of course you are first, you'll bet!
    By Jove, it's always so:
When wind and water met,
    Where did the bubble go?

XXXI

Sweet to be told that I am loved the best,
    Sweet in a pleasant haven to abide:
But winds must veer, and water hateth rest,
    And Venus is but sea-foam deified.

CHARLES BADHAM (1813–84)

Badham, although a distinguished text critic and classical scholar, never achieved a position worthy of his talents in England and finally moved to Australia in 1867 to become professor of classics and logic at the University of Sydney. His works include editions of Euripides and Plato. The selection below was published by his friend Sir Theodore Martin along with his own translations of Catullus.

From Theodore Martin, *The Poems of Catullus Translated into English Verse* (1861).

Carmen 17

On a Stupid Husband

Colonia, dear,
That wouldst fain on thy pier
Be dancing,
And prancing,
And standest all ready,
But shrinkest through fear,
Lest of timbers unsteady
The crazy erection
Come down with a crash,
10   And a smash,
And a splash,
And repose in the wash
Past all resurrection!
May Jupiter grant
Such a bridge as you want
To stand e'en the motions
Of Jumpers' devotions,

17.17 *Jumpers* the *Salii*, 'leaping' priests who performed elaborate ritual dances

If from thence I may meet
With the exquisite treat
20   Of beholding a certain superlative ass,
Who's a man of my town,
Taken clean off his feet,
And like rubbish shot down,
To congenial ooze in the stinking morass.
The inanimate gaby
Knows less than a baby,
Sufficiently old
For its daddy to hold
In the utmost alarm,
30   While it sleeps on his arm.
There's a bride
That is tied
To this nincompoop fellow;
A neat little thing
In her bloomiest spring,
As soft as a kid,
To be guarded and hid
Like grapes that are mellow.
But he's blind to the risk,
40   Lets her gambol and frisk,
And cares not a groat,
In his helplessness sunk,
Like a half-rotten trunk,
Lying felled in a moat.
If she didn't exist,
She'd be just as much miss'd;
For the lout's deaf and blind,
Hasn't made up his mind,
Who himself is, or what,
50   Or whether, in fact, he be or be not.

I should like from your bridge just to cant off the log,
For the chance that his rapid descent to the bog
    Might his lethargy jog,

    And the sloth of his mind
    Being left there behind,
    In the quagmire should stay,
As the mule leaves his shoe in the glutinous clay.

SIR THEODORE MARTIN
(1816–1909)

Martin was both a successful parliamentary solicitor and a versatile man of letters. His many works include writings for and about the stage, comic verse and parodies of contemporary poets (his *Bon Gaultier Ballads* ran to sixteen editions), a five-volume biography of the Prince Consort, and translations from German, Danish and Italian poets as well as from Virgil, Horace and Catullus. Martin, like Lamb, omitted many of Catullus' poems he considered obscene or offensive. He reordered the poems to follow the ups and downs of the affair with Lesbia, but reverted to the traditional arrangement in his second edition (1875), which he dedicated to his friend Charles Badham.

From *The Poems of Catullus Translated into English Verse* (1861).

Carmen 14

To Calvus

Thee did I not more dearly prize,
Most pleasant Calvus, than mine eyes,
I'd hate thee with Vatinian hate
For sending what thou didst of late!
What had I done, what said, to be
Belaboured so remorselessly

14.3 *Vatinian hate* i.e., with the hatred that Vatinius, Calvus' legal adversary, bears against him. Vatinius appears again in *Carmen* 53.

With such a mass of maudlin verse?
May Jove with countless mischiefs curse
The client, who on thee bestow'd
Of fustian rascals such a load!
But if, as shrewdly I surmise,
That pedant Sylla sent this prize
Of new and most recondite stuff,
I can't feel gratitude enough,
That all thy toil in his defence
Has had such fitting recompense.

    Gods! what a book! and this you send
To your Catullus, to your friend,
His comfort wholly to undo,
Upon the Saturnalia, too,
Of all our holidays the day,
One most relies on to be gay.
A harmless jest, you say? But no,
I shan't so lightly let you go;
For by the peep of sunrise I
To all the booksellers will fly,
And gathering into one vile hash
Suffenus' versicles, the trash,
Rank poison all, indited by
The Caesii and Aquinii,
With these I'll quit you, throe for throe,
The pangs you've made me undergo.

    But you, ye wretched sons of rhyme,
The plagues and vermin of the time,
Hence to that grim infernal haunt,
From which ye sprang! Hence, hence, avaunt!

Carmen 26

The Mortgage

Dear friend, your little country seat
   Lies in a famous shelter,
That keeps it snug, though tempests beat
   Around it helter-skelter.

But there's a mortgage, I've been told,
   About it wound so neatly,
That, ere this new moon shall be old,
   'Twill sweep it off completely.

Carmen 28

To Verannius and Fabullus

Come tell me, lads, who went to Spain,
To make a purse in Piso's train,
Verannius, best of friends, and you,
My excellent Fabullus, too,
Your looks are lean, your luggage light!
What cheer, what cheer? Has all gone right?

Or have you had of cold enough,
And hunger, with that wretched chuff;
And have you netted, – worse than worst, –
A good deal less than you disbursed?
Like me, who, following about
My praetor, was – in fact – clean'd out.

28.2 *Piso* probably L. Calpurnius Piso Caesonius, consul in 58 BC

O Memmius, by your scurvy spite
You placed me in an evil plight!
And you, my friends, for aught I see,
Have suffer'd very much like me;
For knave as Memmius was, I fear,
That he in Piso had his peer.

And so a fool's tale fitly ends!
This comes of courting noble friends.
But you, ye praetor scum, the shame
Of all that bear the Roman name,
May every god and goddess shower
Disasters on you hour by hour!

Carmen 44

To his Farm

Whate'er thou be, o farm of mine,
Of Sabine soil or Tiburtine,
(For Tiburtine they say thou art,
Who have Catullus' peace at heart,
While those, who like to give him pain,
That thou art Sabine will maintain);
But whether Sabine soil thou be,
Or Tiburtine, most sweet to me
Thy villa was, where I shook off
A most abominable cough
My stomach caused me t'other day, —
And right it served me, I must say,
For loving with too keen a zest
Luxurious dinners highly dressed.

With Sextianus I *would* dine –
They said his dinners were divine; –
But, oh! that dinner cost me dear,
For he insisted I should hear
His speech 'gainst Antius; such a hash
20 Of pestilent and poisonous trash,
An ague seized me as he read!
I sneezed, I cough'd, until I fled,
And cured within thy cosy breast
Myself with nettle-juice and rest.

Wherefore, my pristine health renew'd,
Accept my warmest gratitude,
That thou hast not avenged on me
My epicure propensity.
And when again I'm doom'd, if e'er
30 The Fates such doom for me prepare,
To hear the wretched rubbish writ
By Sextianus' freezing wit,
Oh! may the chill his comfort mar
With shivering ague and catarrh,
Not mine, whom he alone invites
To hear the rubbish that he writes!

Carmen 103

To Silo

You, Silo, rude and surly? Zounds!
Deliver back my fifty pounds,
And then you may, for aught I care,
Be rude and surly – if you dare!

But, pray, while pimping is your trade,
Remember, sir, for what you're paid,
And keep, whate'er may lurk beneath,
A civil tongue within your teeth!

Carmen 113

To Cinna

When Pompey was Rome's consul first,
'Twas with but two adulterers cursed.
When next he did the office fill,
These two remained to cuckold still;
But they had managed so to teach,
That myriads more had sprung from each:
So fast it breeds and breeds again,
The taste for wives of other men.

SIR RICHARD BURTON (1821–90)

Burton was a famous explorer and traveller, and well known (if not notorious) for his translations of works like the *Arabian Nights* and *Kama Sutra*.

In the late 1880s he entered into collaboration with Leonard Smithers, a promoter and publisher of erotica, to produce an unexpurgated translation of the *Priapeia*, a collection of explicit, largely pederastic, poems on the fertility god Priapus. Smithers provided prose translations and annotations, and Burton wrote verse translations for the work, published in 1889. Soon they made the same arrangement for Catullus. Burton was already in poor health at the outset of the project, and lived just long enough to complete his translations, which are explicit, severely literal and presented in an archaizing, often unreadable, English of his own creation. Smithers had the work privately printed, mendaciously advertising it as the first complete English translation of Catullus even as he pirated the Blake engraving of Catullus that had adorned the frontispiece of Nott's complete translation. For the verse translations he used a typescript from Burton's wife, who seems to have removed (but not replaced) her husband's frankest obscenities. Smithers indicated the omissions by dots, as in the first and last lines of *Carmen* 16 below.

From *The Carmina of Gaius Valerius Catullus* (1894).

Carmen 16

To Aurelius and Furius in Defence of His Muse's Honesty

I'll . . . you twain and . . .
Pathic Aurélius! Fúrius, libertines!
Who durst determine from my versicles
Which seem o'er softy, that I'm scant of shame.
For pious poet it behoves be chaste
Himself; no chastity his verses need;
Nay, gain they finally more salt of wit
When over softy and of scanty shame,
Apt for exciting somewhat prurient,
10   In boys, I say not, but in bearded men
Who fail of movements in their hardened loins.
Ye who so many thousand kisses sung
Have read, deny male masculant I be?
You twain I'll . . . and . . .

Carmen 43

To Mamurra's Mistress

Hail, girl who neither nose of minim size
Owns, nor a pretty foot, nor jetty eyes,
Nor thin long fingers, nor mouth dry of slaver,
Nor yet too graceful tongue of pleasant flavour.
Leman to Formian that rake-a-hell.
What, can the Province boast of thee as belle?
Thee with my Lesbia durst it make compare?
O Age insipid, of all humour bare!

Carmen 46

His Adieux to Bithynia

Now Spring his cooly mildness brings us back,
Now th' equinoctial heaven's rage and wrack
Hushes at hest of Zephyr's bonny breeze.
Far left (Catullus!) be the Phrygian leas
And summery Nicaea's fertile downs:
Fly we to Asia's fame-illumined towns.
Now lust my fluttering thoughts for wayfare long,
Now my glad eager feet grow steady, strong.
O fare ye well, my comrades, pleasant throng,
10 Ye who together far from homesteads flying,
By many various ways come homewards hieing.

Carmen 54.1–5

To Julius Caesar (?)

The head of Otho, puniest of pates

* * * *

The rustic, half-washt shanks of Nerius
and Libo's subtle silent fizzling-farts.

* * * *

I wish that leastwise these should breed disgust
In thee and old Fuficius, rogue twice-cookt.

JAMES CRANSTOUN (1837–1901)

Cranstoun was Rector of Kirkcudbright Grammar School in Scotland. Like Nott, he translated all of Catullus. Perhaps thinking of the many poems omitted by Lamb, he argued that no translator should suppress part of an author's works 'merely to give him a more respectable appearance', and that such omissions would be particularly damaging to Catullus. None the less, he does soften Catullus' obscenities, and, like Lamb, he transforms Juventius into a woman in *Carmen* 99.

From *The Poems of Valerius Catullus Translated into English Verse* (1867).

Carmen 6

To Flavius

Flavius! unless your cherish'd flame
    Were graceless and ungainly,
From me you could not keep her name,
    You'd wish to tell me plainly;
Some hackney'd jade, I'll take my oath upon it,
Has crazed your head, and you're ashamed to own it.

Your bed, ah! Vainly mute! with flowers
    And Syrian unguents scented;
Your cushion in the midnight hours,
10   All here and there indented;
Its crazy frame – the ambling and the creaking –
Reveal a tale, the truth too plainly speaking.

While these are there, you're mute in vain;
    And why so lean, unless it
Be true you're with such follies ta'en?
    Come – good or bad – confess it.
You and your love – I wish in song to blaze you,
And to the stars in sprightly verse to raise you.

Carmen 13

To Fabullus
Invitation to Dinner

If the gods will, Fabullus mine,
With me right heartily you'll dine,
Bring but good cheer – that chance is thine

> Some days hereafter;
> Mind a fair girl, too, wit, and wine,
> > And merry laughter.

> Bring these – you'll feast on kingly fare –
> But bring them – for my purse – I swear
> The spiders have been weaving there;
> > But thee I'll favour
> With a pure love, or what's more rare,
> > More sweet of savour,

> An unguent I'll before you lay
> The Loves and Graces t'other day
> Gave to my girl – smell it – you'll pray
> > The gods, Fabullus,
> To make you turn all nose straightway.
> > Yours aye, Catullus.

10

Carmen 27

To his Cupbearer

> Young server of old Falern! ho!
> > Pour drier cups for me,
> Our queen Postumia wills it so,
> > Be sacred her decree.

> For as the tipsy grape-stone sips
> > The juice that round it rolls,
> So revel gay Postumia's lips
> > In nectar-brimming bowls.

27.1 *Falern* Falernian, an excellent wine
27.3 *queen Postumia* as *magister bibendi* ('master of the drinking') Postumia will determine how much, if any, water is to be mixed with the wine – a role ordinarily played by men.

Then, water, hence where'er ye will,
    Thou bane of rosy wine!
Go, seek the sober: here we swill
    Thyonian juice divine.

Carmen 79

Lesbius is fair: why not? in Lesbia's love,
Catullus! thee and all thy race above:
Yet me and all my kindred let him sell
If he but find three *men* to wish him well.

Carmen 89

On Gellius

Gellius is thin: and what wonder? when he
    Has so blithe and so buxom a mother,
And a sister as lovely as maiden can be,
    Sooth! 'twould beat you to find such another.

And then he's an uncle so good and so green,
    And of she-cousins such a bright bevy,
'Twould rather be strange if he were not so lean,
    Their demands on him *must* be so heavy.

For although he *should never* a woman embrace
    Save the very same ones he *should never*,
You'll find good enough reason, I trow, why his face
    Should be lean and still leaner than ever.

27.12 *Thyonian juice* the drink of Bacchus (Thyoneus) himself

Carmen 94

On Mamurra

Mamurra sins: Mamurra is a sot:
The proverb's true: Herbs grow to fill the pot.

Carmen 99

The Kiss – To a Beauty

Fair honey'd maid! the while you play'd
    I stole a little kiss,
And sweet ambrosia could not match
    The sweetness of my bliss.

For that fond raid I dearly paid,
    For hourly more and more,
What pains the cross-nail'd wretch endures,
    Such agonies I bore.

I pleaded love – in vain I strove:
10   No grief, no tears of mine
Could drive away one jot of that
    Hard-heartedness of thine.

Whene'er 'twas done, too cruel one!
    Thy little lips were rinsed,
And by each finger of thy hand
    With every effort cleansed,

Till not a trace on thy sweet face
    From lip of mine remain'd,
As if some vicious profligate
20   Its purity had stain'd.

Nay more: thy spite 'tis thy delight
    In every way to vent,
And never hast thou ceased my heart
    To torture and torment,

That this wee kiss might smack of bliss
    Ambrosian never more,
But be more bitter to my soul
    Than bitter hellebore.

Since such the pains thy heart ordains
30   To my sad love, I swear,
I'll never steal a kiss again,
    Nor tamper with the fair.

Carmen 104

On Lesbia

What! I my love, my very life malign,
    Who's dearer far to me than both mine eyes?
No: that could never be with love like mine,
    But you with Tappo frame a world of lies.

Carmen 112

To Naso

Naso, thou'rt great, as greatness goes with thee:
Naso, thou'rt great in lust and infamy.

THOMAS HARDY (1840–1928)

Hardy trained and worked as an architect and attained a lasting reputation for his novels, but poetry was his first and greatest love. The selection below commemorates an incident from his extended visit to Italy in 1887, but may have been written some years after the fact. In *Carmen* 31 Catullus rejoices in his return to his home, the peninsula Sirmione on Lake Garda, and closes with an invitation to the place and its waters 'to rejoice in their rejoicing master'. Hardy omits this invitation with its suggestion of mutual pleasure in order to focus entirely on the emotions of the modern poet – an 'old friend' from 'stranger lands' – as he passes the home of the ancient poet he had read in his youth.

From *Poems of the Past and the Present* (1902).

Carmen 31

Catullus XXXI
(After passing Sirmione, April 1887)

Sirmio, thou dearest dear of strands
That Neptune strokes in lake and sea,
With what high joy from stranger lands
Doth thy old friend set foot on thee!
Yea, barely seems it true to me
That no Bithynia holds me now,
But calmly and assuringly
Around me stretchest homely Thou.

Is there a scene more sweet than when
10   Our clinging cares are undercast,
And, worn by alien moils and men,

The long untrodden sill repassed,
We press the pined for couch at last,
And find a full repayment there?
Then hail, sweet Sirmio; thou that wast,
And art, mine own unrivalled Fair!

G. S. DAVIES (1845–1927)

Davies, a Scot, was Master of Charterhouse School. He wrote on subjects as diverse as St Paul, horseracing, the history of his school and European painting (he was perhaps best known for his biography of Frans Hals). His often reprinted translation of *Carmen* 3 into Scots dialect was praised as 'perfect' by his friends.

From *The Oxford Book of Latin Verse* (1912).

Carmen 3

Weep, weep, ye Loves and Cupids all,
And ilka Man o' decent feelin':
My lassie's lost her wee, wee bird,
And that's a loss, ye'll ken, past healin'.

The lassie lo'ed him like her een:
The darling wee thing lo'ed the ither,
And knew and nestled to her breast,
As ony bairnie to her mither.

Her bosom was his dear, dear haunt –
So dear, he cared na lang to leave it;
He'd nae but gang his ain sma' jaunt,
And flutter piping back bereavit.

> The wee thing's gane the shadowy road
> That's never travelled back by ony:
> Out on ye, Shades! ye're greedy aye
> To grab at aught that's brave and bonny.
>
> Puir, foolish, fondling, bonnie bird,
> Ye little ken what wark ye're leavin':
> Ye've gar'd my lassie's een grow red,
> 20 Those bonnie een grow red wi' grievin'.

EUGENE FIELD (1850–95)

Field, a journalist and poet, edited newspapers in St Louis, Kansas City and Denver, before moving in 1883 to the *Chicago Morning News*, where he gained a wide reputation for his column, 'Sharps and Flats', a miscellany of comment, satire and verse. His verse treats a number of themes: the selection below appears in a volume containing translations of Virgil's *First Eclogue*, Moschus, Bion and Horace, as well as a poem entitled 'At Cheyenne' that begins:

> Young Lochinvar came in from the west,
> With fringe on his trousers and fur on his vest;
> The width of his hat brim could nowhere be beat,
> His No. 10 brogans were chock full of feet.

Not surprisingly, Field's rendition of *Carmen* 5 is colloquial and cheerful – far from the tone of Campion, Crashaw and Coleridge – to say nothing of Catullus himself.

From *Second Book of Verse* (1892).

Carmen 5

Catullus to Lesbia

Come my Lesbia, no repining;
    Let us love while yet we may!
Suns go on forever shining;
    But when we have had our day,
Sleep perpetual shall o'ertake us,
    And no morrow's dawn awake us.

Come, in yonder nook reclining
    Where the honeysuckle climbs,
Let us mock at Fate's designing,
10   Let us kiss a thousand times!
And if they shall prove too few, dear,
    When they're kissed, we'll start anew, dear!

And should any chance to see us,
    Goodness, how they'll agonize!
How they'll wish that they could be us,
    Kissing in such liberal wise!
Never mind their envious whining;
    Come, my Lesbia, no repining!

HUGH MACNAGHTEN
(1862–1929)

Macnaghten taught for many years at his Alma Mater, Eton College, and became its Vice-Provost in 1920. He was greatly interested in Catullus throughout his career, especially in the 'story' of his life and romance with Lesbia, and he read the poems as exact reflections of the biography and emotional state of their author. His earliest translations appeared in *The Story of Catullus* (1899), a biographical narrative interspersed with translations of about a third of the poems. He published a more complete but bowdlerized translation in 1925. For the most part he translates very literally, but in the selection from *Carmen* 61 he has made a poem ('the Wish') from a single stanza of Catullus' epithalamium.

Except for *Carmen* 61.209–13 (from *Verse Ancient and Modern*, 1911), the selections below are from *The Poems of Catullus Done into English Verse* (1925). *Carmina* 9, 46 and 93 first appeared in *The Story of Catullus* (1899).

Carmen 9

The joy of Catullus at the return of his bosom-friend from Spain

Is it you, my friend of friends, who come
Dearer to me than a million others,
Veranius, home to your hearth and home,
The aged mother, the loving brothers?
You have come! ah, joy, it is well, it is well!
I shall see you safe, I shall hear you tell
(You best know how) of Hiberian races
And the deeds they do, and the storied places,
And drawing your neck to my own the while,
10 I shall kiss the face and the eyes that smile.
Oh! hearts that are happy above the rest,
Is any so happy as I, so blest?

Carmen 14a

Fragment
Possibly an Introduction to one group of the poems

If you my readers anywhere
Finger perchance these leaves, and care
To read the trifles written there . . .

Carmen 27

A Bacchanalian song in real earnest

Bearer of old Falernian wine,
Good boy, a stronger glass be mine.
Mistress of toasts (as drunk as she
Not ev'n the drunken grape can be)
Postumia will have it so.
You, water, wine's destruction, go:
Away with you to folk austere:
The god of wine himself is here.

Carmen 46

Catullus, leaving Bithynia, 56 B.C., is to visit the famous cities of Asia, in the spring

Spring – and the warmth has thawed the cold;
Spring – and the March winds overbold,
Lulled to glad Zephyrs, rage no more.
Catullus, leave the Phrygian plain
And parched Nicaea rich in grain,
Take wing for Asia's famous shore.

　　　　Spring stirs the heart to roam at will,
　　　　Spring bids the feet exultant thrill.
　　　　Adieu sweet friends who fared from Rome
10　　　In fellowship – we part, to come
　　　　By many ways and wanderings home.

Carmen 61.209–13

A Wish
From Catullus

God send a little son
Stretching soft hands anon
From mother's lap, to greet
Father with infant-sweet
Glimmer of laughter fleet.

Carmen 93

The poet's contemptuous indifference to the master
of many legions

Not overmuch I care, Caesar, your friend to be;
You may be dark or fair, I never looked to see.

ARTHUR SYMONS (1865–1945)

Symons, most famous as the author of *The Symbolist Movement in Literature*, was a prolific man of letters – an editor, poet, translator and literary historian, whom Yeats called 'the best critic of his generation'. He was a prominent member of an avant-garde literary circle of the 1890s which included Wilde, Yeats and Beardsley, and he edited *The*

Savoy, the short-lived but influential journal that succeeded *The Yellow Book* after Wilde's disgrace.

Symons translated and imitated Catullus in his life as well as in his poetry, for he visualized his own relations with a series of London prostitutes as a re-enactment of Catullus' love-affair with Lesbia. 'Catullus loved passion for Passion's sake', he says in his *Memoirs*. 'I have loved Passion . . . as passionately as Catullus.'

From *Knave of Hearts. 1894–1908* (1913).

Carmen 8

Miserable Catullus, put an end to this folly:
Let all things dead be over and ended wholly.
Once the sun was bright and the light was fair,
And there was a woman to love, and she waited there,
And never a woman was better loved than she.
Surely the sun was bright and fair to see,
And merrily then the hours of love went by
When nothing that you desired would she deny.
Now the woman, desiring no more, denies:
10 You too, deny, nor follow her as she flies.
Be miserable no more, for all is vain:
Set your soul steadfast and harden your heart again.
Farewell: Catullus has hardened his heart again,
He will not follow nor cry to you now in vain.
No, it is you that shall weep, as you lie alone,
And no man cries at your gate, and the night goes on.
What shall remain to you then? who shall come to your call?
Who shall call you fair? nay, whom shall you love at all?
Who shall have you for his? whose lips shall you bite and kiss?
20 But you, Catullus, harden your heart at this.

Carmen 43

Hail, although of nose not neat,
Black of eyes nor trim of feet,
Long of fingers, dry of mouth,
Nor too dainty-tongued, forsooth,
Mistress of no better man
Than a bankrupt Formian.
Does your province not declare you
Beautiful? and even compare you
With my Lesbia? O disgraced
Age, incapable of taste!

Carmen 51

I liken him unto a god,
Or if so be it a higher thing,
Who sits and gazes on thy face,

Looking and listening
To thy sweet laughter. Whereas I,
With senses ravished if I come
So near as to behold thy face,
Swoon, and my tongue is numb,

And a thin fire through all my limbs
Races, and both my ears are stopped
With a great sound that rings, and dark
Is upon daylight dropped.

43.6 *bankrupt Formian* Caesar's henchman Mamurra, who was from the town of Formiae. He is also attacked in *Carmina* 29, 41, 94, 105, 114 and 115.

But thou, Catullus, know that ease
Wrongs thee: put off thy idleness.
Older and happier states and kings
Have perished for no less.

Carmen 60

Who gave you birth? a Libyan lioness
Or Scylla barking from her nether womb?
That thus you mock a suppliant in distress
Who cries to you from off the edge of doom?
O entire monster of hard-heartedness!

Carmen 86

Quintia is beautiful, many will tell you: to me
She is white, she is straight, she is tall: to all this I agree,
But does this make her beautiful? though she be found without fault,
Can you find in the whole of her body the least pinch of salt?
But Lesbia is beautiful: hers is the secret alone
To steal from all beauty its beauty, and make it her own.

Carmen 96

If living sorrows any boon
Unto the silent grave can give
When sad remembrances revive
Old loves and friendships fugitive,
She sorrows less she died so soon
Than joys your love is still alive.

Carmen 101

Wandering many waters and many lands,
I come, my brother, to do sad rites as of old;
See, I bring you the death-gift in my hands,
Hear, I speak to you, speak to the ashes cold.
All that fortune has left me in place of you,
Alas, poor brother, bereft of innocent breath!
Yet, as our sires before us have done, I do,
I bring the same sad gifts, an offering for death.
Take them, that they of a brother's tears may tell;
And now for all time, brother, hail and farewell.

Carmen 107

If a wished-for thing and a thing past hoping for
Should come to a man, will he welcome it not the more?
Therefore to me more welcome it is than gold
That Lesbia brings me back my desire of old,
My desire past hoping for, her own self, back.
O mark the day with white in the almanac!
What happier man is alive, or what can bring
To a man, whoever he be, a more wished-for thing?

AUBREY BEARDSLEY (1872–98)

Beardsley was an artist and illustrator whose works both dazzled and scandalized his contemporaries. He was considered decadent, brilliant, grotesque and pornographic – sometimes all at the same time. He

---

107.6 *white in the almanac* as we might say, 'a red-letter day'

illustrated Oscar Wilde's *Salome* and served as art editor of *The Yellow Book*. After Wilde's disgrace he worked with Symons on *The Savoy*. He died of tuberculosis at twenty-six.

Beardsley's translation of Carmen 101 appeared in *The Savoy* accompanied by a drawing of Catullus headed 'Ave atque Vale'. Even more than most of the poet's interpreters, Beardsley has pictured himself in Catullus, for the nude torso of Catullus in his drawing is outlined by black draperies that form a profile of Beardsley, his eye sketched in the navel and his characteristically beaky features and prominent nose outlined by the lower folds of the garment.

From *The Savoy* (1896).

Carmen 101

Carmen CI

By ways remote and distant waters sped,
Brother, to thy sad grave-side am I come,
That I may give the last gifts to the dead,
And vainly parley with thine ashes dumb;
Since she who now bestows and now denies
Hath ta'en thee, hapless brother, from mine eyes.

But lo! these gifts, the heirlooms of past years,
Are made sad things to grace thy coffin shell,
Take them, all drenchèd with a brother's tears,
10   And, brother, for all time, hail and farewell!

MAURICE BARING (1874–1945)

Baring, a cosmopolitan man of letters with a gift for languages, served in the British diplomatic service, worked as a newspaper correspondent in Manchuria, St Petersburg and Constantinople, and wrote in several genres, including literary history, novels, satire and poetry. He is best remembered for his last work, *Have You Anything to Declare?* (1937), a commonplace book of favourite passages from several languages, with translations and comments.

Baring brought Catullus into several of his works. He seems to have modelled the unhappy love-affair of Caryll and Leila in his early novel *C* (1924) on that of Catullus and Lesbia. One of the fictitious letters in *Dead Letters* (1910) purports to be from Lesbia complaining about *Carmen* 58 as '*quite, quite* impossible, with a *horrible* word in it'. *Carmen* 76 appears in *Have You Anything to Declare?* with the comment: 'It is in the Latin as close in utterance as the tightest of Shakespeare's sonnets, and gives one the impression of a man almost inarticulate, so much has he to say.'

From *Have You Anything to Declare?* (1937).

Carmen 76

If it can please a man to recollect
His deeds of kindness done, and to reflect
That he has shown true loyalty in act
And word unto his friends, nor in a pact
Misused the gods to cheat his fellow men,
Your unrequited love should earn you then,
Catullus, life-long joys in overflow;
For what of kindness man to man may show,
In word or deed was said and done by you:
10   All this was given to a heart untrue:
And it is lost: then wherefore, spirit-sore,
Torment yourself with anguish any more?
Nay, stand entrenched within your peace to be,
And doff, despite the gods, your misery.
'Tis hard to bid long-rooted love begone,
But must in this way or in that be done.

---

horrible word the word is *glubit* ('peels', 'pushes back the foreskin')

There alone safety lies! This, carry through:
This, if you can or cannot, you must do.
Ye gods, if mercy lives within your span,
20 If you have ever helped a dying man,
Look down upon me in my agony;
My life was clean, so take this plague from me.
Ah me! within my inmost bones a blight
Has crept, and in my heart killed all delight.
I ask no more that she be kind to me –
Nor become chaste, for that could never be;
Gods, from this festering wound give me release,
If I have ever served you, grant me peace.

MARY STEWART (c. 1877–1943)

Mary Stewart graduated from the University of Colorado in 1900, taught English and German in various high schools in Colorado, and in 1907 became Dean of Women and Instructor in Language at the University of Montana in Missoula. She later worked for the US Department of Labor. In addition to translating Catullus, she wrote papers for the Department of Labor, as well as religious tracts and books for children.

From *Selections from Catullus* (1915).

Carmen 1

To whom shall I offer this book, young and sprightly,
Neat, polished, wide-margined, and finished politely?
To you, my Cornelius, whose learning pedantic,
Has dared to set forth in three volumes gigantic
The history of ages – ye gods, what a labor! –
And still to enjoy the small wit of a neighbor.

A man who can be light and learned at once, sir,
By life's subtle logic is far from a dunce, sir,
So take my small book – if it meet with your favor,
10 The passing of years cannot dull its sweet savor.

Carmen 34

Goddess of the crescent moon,
Guardian of youth's radiant noon,
Hail to thee, Diana!
Maidens pure as lilies white,
Youths as spotless as the light,
Let us sing Diana!

Daughter of Latona's love,
Whiter than fair Venus' dove,
Better loved by mortals;
10 Chaste child of Saturnian Jove,
Cradled in an Olive grove
Near the Delian portals.

Born to be untouched and free,
Mistress of the wild-wood tree,
Goddess of the mountains,
Spirit, too, of light and shade,
Sunny slope and dusky glade,
Sprite of laughing fountains.

Tenderer tasks are also thine,
20 Goddess of the hill and pine,
Sweeter than all others:
Thou, with gentle look and mild,
Smilest on the new-born child,
Patron of young mothers.

By thy shining lunar light,
Thou dost mark the season's flight
For the farmer's pleasure;
Sendest, too, the quickening rain,
Fruitful vine, and golden grain,
30 Bountiful in measure.

Goddess of all kindliness,
By whatever name addressed,
Hail to thee, Diana!
Guard and save our ancient race,
By the favor of thy grace,
While we sing Diana.

Carmen 43

Pshaw, little girl, you're much too small,
You've scarcely any nose at all.
Your feet are shapeless, fingers, too,
Your eyes a dull and faded blue,
With lips as parched as last year's peas,
And silly tongue, untaught to please.
They say that Formian calls you fair,
And that they praise you everywhere.
A dull and worthless age, – ah me,
10 If they could Lesbia's beauty see!

Carmen 50

'Twas yesterday, Licinius mine,
While idling at our nuts and wine,
As gay young bloods think proper,
In sportive vein we teased the Muse
To scribble verses so profuse,
My faith, we scarce could stop her.

And when at last I left the place,
So fired with your rare wit and grace –
Or wine, you say – you dare it? –
I tossed upon my bed all night,
Impatient for the morning light
And you – by Jove, I swear it.

'Twas you I longed again to see,
To hear the clever repartee,
The thrust and answer ready.
I rose, my brain half dead for rest,
And scrawled these rhymes that might attest
My hand, at least, was steady.

Then speed the hour, sweet friend of mine,
When we shall meet at nuts and wine,
With wit and jest distracting.
And if you scorn a love like this,
Then, oh, beware of Nemesis,
A lady most exacting.

Carmen 73

Then cease to strive to win esteem,
Or think another fair;
The whole world's thankless, selfish, mean,
There's none who truly care.
Good deeds but weary, nay, far more,
They even oft offend;
No enemy so bitter quite,
As he who was a friend.

Carmen 102

If ever friend has trusted friend
Whose faith is tried and true,
Discretion proved, allegiance firm,
Cornelius, it is you.

My tongue is bound, as by an oath,
A secret to defend;
The very god of Silence I,
When once I've pledged a friend.

FRANKLIN P. ADAMS (1881–1960)

Adams was a New York newspaperman and radio personality. He gained a reputation for erudition and wit both through his long-running newspaper column and as a panellist on the popular radio programme 'Information Please' in the 1940s.
  From *Weights and Measures* (1917).

Carmen 23

To Furius, on Poverty
Catullus: Ode 23
'Furi, quoi neque servus est, neque arca'

Financial troubles irk thee not:
    No servants test thy strong endurance;
No germs infest thy simple cot;
    Thou hast no need for fire insurance.

How happy, Furius, is thy life
    Shared with thine estimable Popper
And his – excuse me – wooden wife!
    (I think those birds could lunch on copper!)

In utter health how happy thou,
    Fearing nor fire nor indigestion!
No fall in stocks can blanch thy brow
    Serene beyond all doubt or question.

Hay fever, rheumatiz, the grip,
    Malaria, gout, and such diseases
Elude thy frugal guardianship –
    Both when it's hot and when it freezes.

Cease then to pray the gods for wealth
    Not worth the pains to have amassed it!
I wonder if, with naught but health
    Thou knowest just how soft thou hast it?

JAMES ELROY FLECKER
(1884–1915)

Flecker began writing poetry as a child and continued to do so at Oxford and during his brief career in the British consular service. He published several volumes of verse and prose before his premature death of tuberculosis; other works (including his plays and Catullus translations) were published posthumously.

Flecker was a meticulous literary craftsman and devoted to the idea of art for art's sake – principles also espoused by Catullus, whom he began to translate when he was still at school. His translation of *Carmen* 4, written when he was only sixteen or seventeen, catches both the gentle humour and the self-conscious pedantry of Catullus' poem.

From *The Collected Poems of James Elroy Flecker* (1916).

Carmen 1

For whom this pretty pamphlet, polished new
With pumice-stone? Cornelius, for you:
For you were never unprepared to deem
My simple verses worthy of esteem,
Though you yourself – who else in Rome so bold? –
In volumes three have laboured to unfold
A 'Universal History of Man' –
Dear Jove! A learnèd and laborious plan!

Wherefore to you, my friend, I dedicate
This so indifferent bookling; yet I pray,
Poor as it is – O goddess of my fate,
Let it outlive the writer's transient day!

Carmen 4

Proud is Phaselus here, my friends, to tell
That once she was the swiftest craft afloat:
No vessel, were she winged with blade or sail
Could ever pass my boat.
Phaselus shunned to shun grim Adria's shore,
Or Cyclades, or Rhodes the wide renowned,
Or Bosphorus, where Thracian waters roar,
Or Pontus' eddying sound.
It was in Pontus once, unwrought, she stood,
10 And conversed, sighing, with her sister trees,
Amastris born, or where Cytorus' wood
Answers the mountain breeze.
Pontic Amastris, boxwood-clad Cytorus!
You, says Phaselus, are her closest kin:
Yours were the forests where she stood inglorious:
The waters yours wherein

She dipped her virgin blades; and from your strand
   She bore her master through the cringing straits,
   Nought caring were the wind on either hand,
20 Or whether kindly fates
   Filled both the straining sheets. Never a prayer
   For her was offered to the gods of haven,
   Till last she left the sea, hither to fare,
   And to be lightly laven
   By the cool ripple of the clear lagoon.

   .   .   .

   This too is past; at length she is allowed
   Long slumber through her life's long afternoon,
   To Castor and the twin of Castor vowed.

EZRA POUND (1885–1972)

Pound, one of the great poets of the twentieth century, was born in Idaho and educated at Hamilton College and the University of Pennsylvania. His sensibilities and intellectual formation, however, were more European than American, for he spent most of his long life abroad, living in London (1908–20), Paris (1920–24) and Rapallo, Italy (1924–45). During World War II he made pro-Fascist broadcasts to the United States over Italian radio. He was arrested after the war, but found unfit for trial and committed to a mental institution. He returned to Italy in 1958 after his release.

All his life Pound advocated and practised translation – not only from Greek and Latin, but from French, Italian, Anglo-Saxon, Chinese and Japanese. Since literal fidelity was of less interest to him than what Hugh Kenner has called 'the clairvoyant absorption of another world', he was often criticized for inaccuracy – especially in the case of his *Homage to Sextus Propertius*.

Pound used *Carmen* 1.1 as the epigraph of the dedication of *Lustra* (1916): *cui dono lepidum novum libellum?* ('to whom shall I give my charming, new little book?'). He greatly admired Catullus, placing him above both Horace and Virgil, and toyed with the idea of a full translation: 'there is no useful English version of Catullus', he says in 'How to Read' (1931). But he published only the three selections below, dating from the beginning and near the end of his poetic career. The earliest (*Carmen* 43) seems very close, but even here Pound veers from the literal in the way that was to enrage his critics, rendering Catullus' *decoctoris . . . Formiani* ('bankrupt of Formiae') as 'Formianus, the vendor of cosmetics'.

Carmen 26 was first printed in *Edge* (Melbourne) in May 1957 from an earlier version in *Furioso* (1940); *Carmen* 43 appeared first in *Poetry and Drama* II.1 (March 1914); *Carmen* 85 in Ezra Pound and Marcella Spann (eds.), *Confucius to Cummings: An Anthology of Poetry* (1964). The texts of all are from *The Translations of Ezra Pound* (1970).

Carmen 26

Catullus: XXVI

This villa is raked of winds from fore and aft,
All Boreas' sons in bluster and yet more
Against it is this TWO HUNDRED THOUSAND sesterces,
All out against it, oh my God:
      some draft.

Carmen 43

To Formianus' Young Lady Friend
After Valerius Catullus

All Hail; young lady with a nose
 by no means too small,
With a foot unbeautiful,
 and with eyes that are not black,

With fingers that are not long, and with a mouth undry,
And with a tongue by no means too elegant,
You are the friend of Formianus, the vendor of cosmetics,
And they call you beautiful in the province,
And you are even compared to Lesbia.

10 O most unfortunate age!

Carmen 85

Catullus: LXXXV

I hate and love. Why? You may ask but
It beats me. I feel it done to me, and ache.

F. L. LUCAS (1894–1967)

Lucas, a scholar, poet and critic, was described by T. E. Lawrence as 'a mental athlete'. He wrote plays, novels, poetry, translations and literary studies of authors as diverse as Euripides and Pirandello, as well as books attacking totalitarianism. A traditionalist, Lucas strongly attacked modernist poets and translators like Pound, and wrote close translations in familiar verse forms. In both selections below he translates Catullus' elegiacs into English couplets. He omits most of *Carmen* 76 and makes its last ten lines into a separate poem.

Carmen 76 is from *Poems, 1935* (1935). *Carmen* 101 is from F. Kinchin Smith and T. W. Melluish (eds.), *Catullus: Selections from the Poems* (1942).

Carmen 76.17–26

Last Reckoning

Ah, Heaven, if you know pity; if any ever,
    Sick unto death, through you has risen whole,
Look on my pain. If pure my life, oh sever
    This plague and desolation from my soul.
Gone all my gladness, in these thoughts that fetter
    Spirit and flesh with lifeless lethargy;
No more I ask that she might love me better,
    That she be faithful – that thing cannot be.
To be healed myself – that is my one last prayer.
10   I am innocent, O god! Hear my despair.

Carmen 101

Through many seas, my brother, and many a nation
    To this thy bitter burial I come,
Bringing thy death its debt of lamentation,
    My last vain call to thee whose dust is dumb.
Now, since a callous fortune has bereft us
    Each of the other, dear, unhappy head,
By that old custom that our fathers left us
    For the last mournful duties to the dead,
Wet with my weeping take these gifts of me:
10   Hail, brother, and Farewell – eternally!

HORACE GREGORY (1898–1982)

Gregory, a poet, translator and critic, studied classics at the University of Wisconsin before moving to New York and becoming a professional writer. Although many of his poems treat twentieth-century life and problems, Gregory maintained a life-long interest in Roman poetry and classical mythology. In addition to his early translation of Catullus, he also translated Ovid's *Metamorphoses* (1958) and *Love Poems* (1964).

Gregory greatly admired Pound's translations and conceived his own in the same spirit, rejecting traditional English verse forms and disdaining as clichés what he called 'Anglo-classical vocabularies'. Using unrhymed verse and trying to approximate the effect of Catullus' metres, he set out to reproduce 'the personal charm, the epigrammatic vigour and the rapid transition from lyrical beauty to outspoken grossness' of Catullus for the modern reader.

From *The Poems of Catullus* (1931).

Carmen 46

Now warm-smelling Spring has come
and here's our sweet weather,
and the gallant West wind
clears dark April skies.
Say good-bye, Catullus, to the plains of Asia Minor,
leave these spawning farmlands
and heat-sick Nicaea.
We shall sail, shall fly
to our fair Aegean cities.
10   Now my soul grows swift wings, look my feet are dancing,
they shall lead the way.
O my friends, good-bye,
good-bye my fellow exiles, many miles from Italy,
for our ways dissever,
each to his own pleasure,
each to his own home.

Carmen 47

Socration and Porcius,
two scrofulous
right hands of Consul Piso,
synonymous with greed and plague
devouring our country. The great god Priapus,
erect, has served your pleasure:
look, a banquet spread at noon,
you feed and spawn,
drunken in the sunlight.
10 And my friends, dear Fabullus
and my little Veranius, starve, forever walking
down city streets to find a meal,
gazing at banquets, wondering who
will take them in for dinner.

Carmen 74

There came a time when Gellius heard that his uncle, stern,
    pious, censorious,
issued an order: there was to be no talk of lechery in his
    house,
no fornication within its walls. So Gellius set to work,
slept with his uncle's wife and the doomed man could say
    nothing;
Gellius had changed him into an Egyptian god, carved out of
    stone and noted for his silence.
10 And now if Gellius were to practise nimble tricks of pede-
    rasty upon him,
the poor devil would not dare to say a word,
not even a whisper.

---

74. 8 *Egyptian god* Harpocrates, represented as a boy with his finger in his mouth

Carmen 90

Let them conceive a child, these two, Gellius and his mother,
from their dark sighs and kisses let them make a priest
out of their devilish love-making at all hours.
And if the legends about the Persians are true,
then let the child be born a Persian priest glib with holy
    soothsaying,
son of mother and son, torn from the womb, worshipping the
    gods,
melting the veil from his eyes and the spew of after-birth
10 in the flames of the altar.

Carmen 96

If anything can pierce impenetrable earth and echo in the
    silence
of the grave, my Calvus, it is our sad memory
of those we love. (Our longing for them makes them bloom
    again,
quickened with love and friendship,
even though they left us long ago, heavy with tears.)
Surely, your Quintilia now no longer cries against powerful
    death
10 (who had taken her away from you too soon and she was
    gone).
Look she is radiant, fixed in your mind, happy forever.

BASIL BUNTING (1900–1985)

Bunting lived in poverty most of his life and produced a slender but distinguished body of poetry. An Englishman, he was nevertheless closer in spirit to the American poets, Pound, Eliot and Zukofsky, than to his fellow countrymen. He became friendly with the three Americans in Europe in the 1920s and stayed with Pound for some time at Rapallo. Largely with the help of Pound and Eliot, he eked out a livelihood in the 1920s and '30s working and writing for various literary journals. His masterpiece, the autobiographical poem *Briggflatts*, appeared in 1966 after a long period of silence.

Like Pound, Bunting regarded translation as an essential part of his art. He translated from the Persian, as well as from Lucretius, Horace and Catullus. His poetry is conspicuously attentive to sound, metre and above all music, which he described as 'not the only thing' in poetry, 'but . . . the only *indispensable* thing'. His translation of *Carmen* 51 nearly reproduces the metre of Catullus' sapphic stanza but changes the poem's direction. Catullus ends with a picture of the lover's death, Bunting with an apotheosis that echoes the opening: 'O, it is godlike!' In *Carmen* 64 Bunting imitates the long epic line of Catullus' hexameters, reproduces his alliterations, sound effects and learned periphrases – exactly living up to his own standard for translation: 'A good translator intends to make the same impression on his readers as the original poet made on his.' All this for twenty lines, until he stops abruptly and bursts the balloon with a devastating aside.

From *The Complete Poems* (1994); first published in *Collected Poems* (1968).

Carmen 51

Ille mi par esse deo videtur

O, it is godlike to sit selfpossessed
when her chin rises and she turns to smile;
but my tongue thickens, my ears ring,
what I see is hazy.

I tremble. Walls sink in night, voices
unmeaning as wind. She only
a clear note, dazzle of light, fills
furlongs and hours

so that my limbs stir without will, lame,
10 I a ghost, powerless,
treading air, drowning, sucked
back into dark

unless, rafted on light or music,
drawn into her radiance, I dissolve
when her chin rises and she turns to smile.
O, it is godlike!

1965

Carmen 64.1–28

Once, so they say, pinetrees seeded on Pelion's peak swam
over the clear sea waves to the surf on the beaches of Phasis
when the gamesome fleece-filchers, pith of Argos, picked for a
    foray,
bearded the surge in a nimble ship, deal sweeps swirling the
    waters.

The Lady of Citadels shaped them a light hull for darting to windward
and laid the cutaway keel with her own hands and wedded the timbers.
That ship first daunted untamed Amphitrite. When her forefoot
scattered the fickle calm and oarwrenched waves kindled with spindrift
the mermaids rose from the dazzling sluices of the sound to gaze at the marvel.

10 Then, ah then! mortal eyes, and by day, had sight of the sea-girls
and marked their naked bodies stretched breasthigh out of the tiderace.
Forthwith, thus the tale runs, love of Thetis flamed up in Peleus
and Thetis took Peleus spite of the briefness of man's lifetime;
even her father himself deemed Peleus worthy of Thetis.

Health to you, heroes, brood of the gods, born in the prime season,
thoroughbreds sprung of thoroughbred dams, health to you aye, and again health!

I will talk to you often in my songs, but first I speak to you, bridegroom
acclaimed with many pinebrands, pillar of Thessaly, fool for luck, Peleus,
to whom Jove the godbegetter, Jove himself yielded his mistress,
20 for the sea's own child clung to you

– and why Catullus bothered to write pages and pages of this drivel mystifies me.

1933

64.5 *Lady of Citadels* Athena
64.7 *Amphitrite* i.e., the sea (Amphitrite was a sea-nymph)

JACK LINDSAY (1900–1990)

Lindsay, an Australian, wrote over 150 books in various genres, including poetry, novels, criticism and political and social commentary. He studied classics at university, translated a wide range of classical authors and used classical themes in much of his work. He took ancient Rome as the setting for several novels, three of which included Catullus and Lesbia as characters: *Rome for Sale* (1934), *Despoiling Venus* (1935) and *Brief Light* (1939), a fictional biography of Catullus.

Lindsay wrote two different complete translations of Catullus – an explicit version with illustrations for the Fanfrolico Press (1929) and a slightly less frank line-for-line translation in 1948. Considering Catullus' poems as at least loosely autobiographical, he reordered them in his second translation to follow Catullus' life and the 'Lesbia story'. Three selections below are attacks on Rufus. In *Carmina* 69 and 71, Catullus says Rufus' armpits smell like a goat. The goat motif is lacking in *Carmen* 77 (which Lindsay combines with *Carmen* 78b), but he suggests it in the last line of his translation.

Carmina 1, 59, 69 and 99 are from *The Complete Poetry of Gaius Catullus* (1929). *Carmina* 58, 71 and 77–8b are from *Catullus: The Complete Poems* (1948).

Carmen 1

My little book, I hold it, all my own,
bright from the binder's smoothing pumicestone –
a gift for whom? Cornelius, for you;
since from your lenient love these trifles drew
encouragement, though you'd begun to plan
the Encyclopaedic History of Man
compresst into three tomes, a task to trip
historians of lesser scholarship –
so now take this, I beg of you, and read . . .

10   Whether it's good or bad, I cannot tell –
     O Muse that stands beside me, love me well,
     and ages yet to come will surely heed.

Carmen 58

My Lesbia, Caelius, Lesbia, she –
that Lesbia once more dear to me
than self and home and family,
in lanes and crossroads milks and bilks
Remus' high-souled posterity.

Carmen 59

Rufa comes from Buonia town,
Menenius' wife, and she kneels down
mouth-high with wretched Rufus' wishes –
in the cemetery she steals
(you've seen her) offertory dishes
from the very pyre:
let a loaf roll out of the fire
down she grubs and doesn't mind
if some bristley slave of the undertaker
10   bangs her bangs her from behind.

Carmen 69

Don't wonder, Rufus, if the women all
refuse to let you make their thighs your home . . .
though with rare cloths you're hoping to forestall
their noes – with jewelry, feathers, or a comb.

They tell a dirty joke about you, sir!
that in your armpit there's a goat that stinks –
then can you wonder that a nice girl shrinks
and, when you seek to bed her, makes demur?
Chase out the goat, exterminate the stench,
10   or give up plucking at each stifled wench.

Carmen 71

If ever there was man who justly stank
and paid for lust with gout in every limb,
the man who's lying by my mistress' flank
is he; for both afflictions meet in him.
Thus I'm revenged each time they meet abed:
she's pale with nausea and with gout he's dead.

Carmina 77–78b

Rufus, I trusted you. How vain that trust.
Vain? when it cost a life of misery.
You wormed inside me, burned me with your lust,
and raped my happiness away from me.
You raped it with a cruel venom-hiss,
you snake, you wretched plague of comradeship;
and my pure girl (ah, my worst pang is this)
felt your foul spittle clammy her pure lip.
But there's a penance: I'll repay your crime:
10   embalmed in verses, you shall stink through time.

Carmen 99

I snatched a kiss, a tiny kiss today,
from you, Iuventius, tumbled in your play,
Nectarous the touch... but ah, for one whole hour,
at your shrill cruelty you forced me cower –
yes, on your anger I was crucified.
How I remember every plea I sighed;
all that long hour I made excuses while
no tear could conjure a forgiving smile:
before the kiss had brought its rush of red,
for cleansing water angrily you fled,
scopped it in palmfuls, rubbed your mouth again
that no one tincture of my heat remain...
as though my lips with brothelspit were vile.

You sold me slave to Love, you bade him beat
my body from the face down to the feet
until I oozed with torment from each pore.
The kiss's nectar wried to hellebore –
Then since there's so much pain to blot the sweet,
I swear I'll not steal kisses anymore.

STEVIE SMITH (1902–71)

Stevie Smith (Florence Margaret Smith) was a poet and novelist. She lived in a London suburb with her aunt and worked as a secretary for over thirty years during which she produced a steady stream of novels and books of poems, many accompanied by her Thurberesque line drawings. The apparent naïvety and genuine irony characteristic of her verse are evident in her version of *Carmen* 31, which achieves its effect by omitting the salutation to Sirmio at the end of Catullus' poem to end on a note of middle-class worry: who is going to pay the bills?

From *Not Waving but Drowning* (1957).

Carmen 31

Dear Little Sirmio
Catullus Recollected

Dear little Sirmio
Of all capes and islands
Wherever Neptune rides the coastal waters and the open sea
You really are the nicest.

How glad I am to see you again, how fondly I look at you.

No sooner had I left Bithynia – and what was the name of the
    other place?
And was safely at sea
I thought only of seeing you.

Really is anything nicer
10 After working hard and being thoroughly worried
Than to leave it all behind and set out for home
Dear old home and one's own comfortable bed?

Even if one wears oneself out paying for them.

LOUIS ZUKOFSKY (1904–78)

Zukofsky was born of Russian immigrant parents on New York's Lower East Side. He studied at Columbia University and supported himself for twenty years by teaching at Brooklyn Polytechnic Institute. He was a lifelong friend of Pound and Bunting, and stayed with Pound at Rapallo for a time in the 1920s, but in sensibility and poetic accent he remained an American and above all a New Yorker. His principal works include *A*, a long poem in twenty-four movements, and the translation of Catullus he wrote between 1958 and 1969 in collaboration with his wife, Celia.

The Zukofskys' preface sets out their intentions: 'This translation of Catullus follows the sound, rhythm, and syntax of his Latin – tries, as is said, to breathe the "literal" meaning with him.' Celia Zukofsky translated, parsed and scanned the Latin; Louis Zukofsky used her literal version to create a homophonic translation matching the English to the Latin sounds as closely as possible. The work was immediately controversial – detractors justly noting that Zukofsky's method often created nonsense, and admirers pointing with equal justice to his successes. The selections below include two translations of *Carmen* 8, one written in 1939, and the other from the complete translation published thirty years later. The Latin for *Carmen* 8.1–3 and *Carmen* 11 is printed before Zukofsky's homophonic translations.

From *Complete Short Poetry* (1991). The first translation of *Carmen* 8 was published in *Anew* (1946), the other selections in *Catullus (Gai Valeri Catulli Veronensis Liber)* (1969). Celia Zukofsky dates the poems as follows: *Carmina* 2 and 2a (1958), *Carmen* 8 (1939 and 1960), *Carmina* 11 and 14 (1961).

Carmen 2

Sparrow, my girl's pleasure, delight of my girl,
a thing to delude her, her secret darling
whom she offers her fingernail to peck at,
teasing unremittingly your sharp bite,
when desire overcomes her, shining with love
my dear, I do not know what longing takes her,
I think, it is the crest of passion quieted
gives way to this small solace against sorrow,
could I but lose myself with you as she does,
10   breathe with a light heart, be rid of these cares!

Carmen 2a

And for this I am grateful, as rumor had
it the quick girl was to the golden apple
that swiftly lowered her girdle long tied.

Carmen 8

Catullus viii

Miserable Catullus, stop being foolish
And admit it's over.
The sun shone on you those days
When your girl had you
When you gave it to her
   like nobody else ever will.
Everywhere together then, always at it
And you liked it and she can't say
     she didn't.
10 Yes, those days glowed.
Now she doesn't want it: why
     should you, washed out,
Want to. Don't trail her,
Don't eat yourself up alive,
Show some spunk, stand up
     and take it.
So long, girl. Catullus
     can take it.
He won't bother you, he won't
20   be bothered;
But you'll be, nights.
What do you want to live for?
Whom will you see?
Who'll say you're pretty?

> Who'll give it to you now?
> Whose name will you have?
> Kiss what guy? bite whose
>   lips?
> Come on Catullus, you can
30   take it.

Carmen 8.1–3

Miser Catulle, desinas ineptire,
et quod vides perisse perditum ducas.
fulsere quodam candidi tibi soles,

Carmen 8

Miss her, Catullus? don't be so inept to rail
at what you see perish when perished is the case.
Full, sure once, candid the sunny days glowed, solace,
when you went about it as your girl would have it,
you loved her as no one else shall ever be loved.
Billowed in tumultuous joys and affianced,
why you would but will it and your girl would have it.
Full, sure, very candid the sun's rays glowed solace.
Now she won't love you; you, too, don't be weak, tense, null,
10   squirming after she runs off to miss her for life.
Said as if you meant it: *obstinate, obdurate.*
Vale! puling girl. I'm Catullus, *obdurate*,
I don't require it and don't beg uninvited:
won't you be doleful when no one, no one! begs you,
scalded, every night. Why do you want to live now?
Now who will be with you? Who'll see that you're lovely?
Whom will you love now and who will say that you're his?
Whom will you kiss? Whose morsel of lips will you bite?
But you, Catullus, your destiny's *obdurate*.

Carmen 11

Furi et Aureli, comites Catulli,
siue in extremos penetrabit Indos,
litus ut longe resonante Eoa
    tunditur unda,
siue in Hyrcanos Arabasue molles,
seu Sagas sagittiferosue Parthos,
siue quae septemgeminus colorat
    aequora Nilus,
siue trans altas gradietur Alpes,
10 *Caesaris uisens monimenta magni,*
Gallicum Rhenum horribile aequor ulti-
    mosque Britannos,
omnia haec, quaecumque feret uoluntas
caelitum, temptare simul parati,
pauca nuntiate meae puellae
    non bona dicta.
cum suis uiuat ualeatque moechis,
quos simul complexa tenet trecentos,
nullum amans uere, sed identidem omnium
20 *ilia rumpens;*
nec meum respectet, ut ante, amorem,
qui illius culpa cedidit uelut prati
ultimi flos, praetereunte postquam
    tactus aratro est.

Carmen 11

Furius, Aurelius: comities – Catullus.
If he penetrate most remote India,
lit as with the long resonant coast's East's wave
    thundering under –
if in Hyrcania, mull of Arabia,

say the Sacae, arrow ferocious Parthians,
why even the seven gamming mouth, colored
   ichor of Nilus —
even that Transalpine graded tour magni-
fying visions of our Caesar's monuments,
Gallic Rhine, and the horrible ultimate
   mask of the Britons —
on hand, men, come whatever gods ferret and
want of us, you who're always prompt to feel with
me, take a little note now to my darling,
   no kind word dictates.
May she live, and avail herself, in the moist
clasp of one concourse of three hundred lechers,
loving no man's ever, and doomed to drain all
   men who must rupture;
no, let her not look back at me as she used to,
at her love whose fault was to die as at some
meadow's rim, the blossom under the passing
   cut of the share thrust.

Carmen 14

Not that I look to my eyes more than your love,
your kindness is to me, Calvus, immune to
your gift that's as odious as Vatinius:
how, why have I gone wrong, quipped what so luggish
to incur perdition from these deadly poets?
May he stall in his malice, your mule client,
who toted you to their misfit emporium.
I'm inclined to suspect this new award or
bonus is a sub rosa fee from that lit-
erator Sulla; not half bad, I'm lucky
you're paid, your labors have not been disparaged.
Gods, what a horrible unholy little volume
you, think! I must say *you* sent to Catullus —

not miscounting that the day he should perish
would be the First Saturnalia of all days!
No, no joke, titbit of wit can save you a bit;
when luxurious dawn comes to the bookstalls
I'll run, screen them off – Caesii, Aquini,
Suffenus, the whole venomous lot of them,
20   and with these subtleties remunerate you.
Void, vile, now be interred, and goodbye to you
ill look into hell where your dead feet led you,
incommodious cycle, pests of poets.

QUINTIN HOGG (LORD HAILSHAM) (1907–)

Quintin Hogg was a prominent politician who served variously as Leader of the House of Lords, First Lord of the Admiralty, Cabinet Minister and Lord Chancellor. Hogg's short lyrics, written primarily between 1940 and 1963, include poems on the desert war and religious themes, as well as several translations of Catullus. In the selection below he uses *Carmen* 101 to mourn the death of his own brother, Edward Marjoribanks, in a poem that quietly replaces Roman ritual with Christian liturgy and symbolism.

From *The Devil's Own Song* (1968), first printed in *The Spectator*, 29 March 1957.

Carmen 101

Edward

Over sea and land come I,
Brother dear, to say goodbye;
To hear the ancient words I dread
Muttered softly o'er the dead:

'Ash to ash and dust to dust'.
Though you hear not, speak I must
And tell your silent body how
In bitter grief I mourn you now.
Custom's servant, not her slave,
10   Stand I weeping at the grave.
Take this wreath, as tolls the bell;
Brother dear, a long farewell.

FRANK O. COPLEY (1907–93)

Copley was a classical scholar who taught for many years at the University of Michigan. He wrote scholarly works on Latin poetry and translated a wide range of classical authors. His Catullus is colloquial and slangy, in a style somewhere between e e cummings and tin-pan alley. This brash voice is generally most successful in the lighter poems and invectives. The selections below include attacks on the praetor Piso (*Carmina* 28 and 47) and two poems on the sexual activities of the undiscriminating Gellius (*Carmina* 80 and 88), as well as the cycle of poems attacking Caesar's henchman Mamurra under the insulting sobriquet 'Mentula' ('prick'), which Copley renders as 'Dickie-boy Trill' (*Carmina* 94, 105, 114 and 115).

From *Gaius Valerius Catullus: The Complete Poetry* (1957).

Carmen 24

O flowret of all the Juventiuses
not only those that are but those that were
or shall hereafter be in other years,
I'd rather you'd give the gold of Midas
to that man who has no slave nor bank-account
than let yourself be loved by him like that.
'why? isn't he nice enough' you say? he is,

he's nice, but has no slave nor bank-account.
make light of it, excuse it as you please,
fact is, he has no slave nor bank-account.

Carmen 28

Piso's pals, not a penny in your pockets,
bags all packed up and ready for departure,
good old Veranius dear old Fabullus
how're things? had enough? did that dirty devil
fill up your books with shivering and starving?
you have to write your profits in red ink, too?
just like me: I went out there with my praetor,
got one lone entry written down for profit:
> 'Memmius, you stretched me out
> And fixed me up all nice and neat
> and then backed up and took your time
> and really let me have it.'

from where I sit looks like you fared no better
you two got just as big a dose as I did.
that's what we get for suckin' round the blue-bloods.
Piso, Memmius, God and Goddess damn you,
you two blots on our country's fair escutcheon.

Carmen 40

Say
what in the world's got into you
you poor damn fool, Ravidus
what's the big idea
    running yourself head on into my verses?
are you sure you been saying your prayers right?
because I mean it's plain crazy stirring up a hassle
    with ME.

you looking for headlines?
10   are you sure you want . . . . kinda expensive this way,
        aren't they?
     well o.k. you asked for it:
        you swiped my boy
        all right my friend
           I've only this to say
        go on have fun
        because my friend
           you'll pay
              and Pay
20   and
        PAY

Carmen 47

Porcius and Socration
Piso's got two left hands
   (which what the right is doing never know)
and you're them
dandruff on the world's collar
hunger ache in its gut
are you the two
he put ahead of my good friends
Veranius and Fabullus?
10 must have been his old trouble
       (antsinthepants)
    are you the ones who get the fancy dinners
       (what a wad he blew on those)
    far far into the night?
    and my friends V and F
    are panhandling an invite
       to Greasy Joe's.

Carmen 75

look down down
if you want to find my heart, Lesbia.
you brought it down
it killed itself trying to do
what hearts are supposed to do
now it couldn't love you
if you were virtue in person
nor cease to want you
if you did everything.

Carmen 80

Gelly-gilly
Daffy-dilly,
prithee, why so pale?
in the morning
in the evening
it's the same old tale.

something's doing
something's brewing:
what is this I hear?
10   weren't our kisses
meant for misses?
yours are not, I fear.

how'd I know it?
do you show it?
here's the pitch, my friend:
Victor's dying
Victor's crying,
'What a painful end!'

Carmen 88

Gellius, dear Gellius
pray tell me what you'd call
a man who for his mother
and his sister Gave his All,
who wouldn't let his uncle
be a husband to his aunt —
can you such antics comprehend
or name — I'll bet you can't.

I'll tell you: all of Ocean's streams
from here to far Cathay
could never make him clean again
or wash his sins away
there is no greater depth of sin
to which a man could fall
not if he'd kiss his own sweet self
and Give himself his All.

Carmen 94

Dickie-boy Trill loves somebody's wife
o somebody's wife loves Dick
   which is just so
    (as who doesn't know)
as to say that a sticker will prick

Carmen 105

Dickie-boy Trill
climbed helicon hill
to fetch a pail a poesy

the muses saw
and (being quick on the draw)
they knocked him arsover noesy.

Carmen 114

Dickie-boy Trill has got a farm
at Fermo and rich is he
for on that farm he has got
   birds
Dickie-boy Trill has got
   fishes
a farm at Fermo
   cows
and rich is he
   oxen
Dickie-boy Trill
   boars
has got a
   (with a moo-moo here and a tweet-tweet there)
but I regret to state
he's no richer than before
the costs (which he forgot to remember)
are always somehow more
   (with an oink-oink here)
than what comes in
   (here a moo there a tweet)
so it's all right with me
for him to be so rich
so long as he hasn't a nickel
   (with an oink-moo here)
to rub against a dime
   (and a tweet-oink there)
and of his farm I'll sing
   I hope it brex
   his silly nex

Carmen 115

Dickie-boy Trill's got thirty acres of grass
and forty of grain, the rest is watery deep
why shouldn't he boast that he's richer than Croesus? he could:
in one fine lot he's got such a pile of wealth
pastures and grain-fields, forests and meadows and swamps
from here to the North and from there to Ocean's streams
it's all pretty big, but he beyond all is the biggest –
man? who said 'man'? just great big old dangerous Dick.

JAMES LAUGHLIN (1914–97)

Laughlin was a prolific poet, writer, and lecturer, as well as the founder of New Directions Publishing Corporation. He received numerous awards for his contributions to letters, including several honorary degrees and a Distinguished Service award from the American Academy of Arts and Letters. He published over a dozen books of poems.

His translation of *Carmen* 32 is followed by this note: 'If the elegant Latin euphemisms are converted to US colloquial, this is what the poem says.'

From *The Country Road: Poems* (1995).

Carmen 32

CATULLUS XXXII

Ipsitilla, my sweet, dear girl,
Little furnace, send word at once,
Please, that I may spend the
Afternoon with you. And if I may,
Be sure no other cocks are let

Into your henhouse. And don't
You go walking the streets;
Stay home and have ready for me
Nine of your nicest continuous
Fucks. (And don't forget the
Wine.) May I come as soon as
Possible? I've had my lunch
But I'm hot for it and my
Prick is trying to poke holes
In my shirt and the blanket.

GUY LEE (1918–)

Lee is a classical scholar and translator and a Fellow of St John's College, Cambridge. He has translated many Latin poets, including Horace, Propertius and Tibullus, as well as Virgil's *Eclogues* and the *Amores* of Ovid.

From *The Poems of Catullus* (1990).

Carmen 35

I'd like you, papyrus, to tell my comrade
Caecilius, the tender poet,
To come to Verona, leaving Novum
Comum's walls and the Larian shore.
I want him to consider certain
Thoughts of a friend of his and mine.
So if he's wise he'll eat up the road,
Though a pretty girl should call him back
A thousand times and laying both
Hands on his neck should beg him stay.
There's one now, if I'm rightly informed,
Dying of desperate love for him.

For ever since the day she read
His unfinished *Lady of Dindymus*
Fires have been eating the poor thing's marrow.
And I don't blame you, girl more learned
Than Sappho's Muse. Caecilius' *Great
Mother* is charmingly unfinished.

Carmen 57

They're a fine match, the shameless sods,
Those poofters Caesar and Mamurra.
No wonder. Equivalent black marks,
One urban, the other Formian,
Are stamped indelibly on each.
Diseased alike, both didymous,
Two sciolists on one wee couch,
Peers in adultery and greed,
Rival mates among the nymphets,
10 They're a fine match, the shameless sods.

DAVID FERRY (1924–)

Ferry is an emeritus professor of English at Wellesley College. He has published three books of verse (*On the Way to the Island*, 1960; *Strangers: A Book of Poems*, 1983; and *Dwelling Places*, 1993) as well as translations of *Gilgamesh* (1992) and Horace's *Odes* (1997).

From *Of No Country I Know: New and Selected Poems and Translations* (1999).

Carmen 101

Multas per gentes

O my poor brother, I have journeyed here,
    Through many foreign lands and foreign seas,
To come to this unhappy ceremony,
    Seeking to speak to ashes that cannot speak.
Fortune has taken you yourself away –
    Alas, my brother, cruelly taken you.

According to the custom of our fathers
    I bring these offerings for the wretched dead.
Accept, my brother, what I have brought you, weeping.
10   *Ave*, forever, *vale*, my poor brother.

PETER WHIGHAM (1925–87)

Whigham, a peripatetic poet and translator, was brought up in England, lived for a time in Italy and finally took up residence in Southern California. He translated Dante and the Dalai Lama as well as Meleager, Martial and Catullus.

Whigham was a great admirer of Pound, but also of earlier translators, particularly Landor, Symons and Burton. He states in his preface: 'As a poem is more than the sum of its constituent parts, a certain ruthlessness over details is often necessary. It is the whole poem which has to be captured and rewritten . . . the details of a poem are to be digested so that they become a part of the living grain of the new poem, not embalmed like flies in ointment.'

Whigham was more sympathetic to the long poems than most translators. The selections below include *Carmina* 65 and 66 and excerpts from *Carmen* 64. *Carmen* 65 introduces *Carmen* 66, a translation of Callimachus' poem on the lock of Queen Berenice's hair, vowed to the gods for her husband's safe return from war (it disappeared from the temple and was subsequently recognized as a constellation by the court astronomer). Whigham treats *Carmen* 64 as a Poundian Canto, using different styles and verse forms for its several sections. The selection below includes only the wedding of Peleus and Thetis (for Theseus and Ariadne, see Elton above).

From *The Poems of Catullus* (1966).

'Carmen 18'

I dedicate, I consecrate this grove to thee,
Priapus, whose home & woodlands are at Lampsacus;
there, among the coastal cities of the Hellespont,
they chiefly worship thee:
                              their shores are rich in oysters!

Carmen 32

Call me to you
at siesta
we'll make love
my gold & jewels
my treasure trove
my sweet Ipsíthilla,
when you invite
me lock no doors
nor change your mind
10 & step outside
but stay at home
& in your room
prepare yourself

'Carmen 18' printed in most modern editions as *Fragment* 1

to come nine times
straight off together,
in fact if you
should want it now
I'll come at once
for lolling on
20   the sofa here
with jutting cock
and stuffed with food
I'm ripe for stuffing
                    you,
my sweet Ipsíthilla.

Carmen 36

Volusian sheets
shit-shotten Annals
discharge the pledge
that Lesbia makes
to Holy Venus
Holier cupid:
– if I give
myself to her
alone, again,
10   discontinue
launching these
trucacious squibs,
on a pyre of
coffin chips she'll
burn the verses
of the meanest
Latin poet
read in Rome, a
votive blaze to

20   limping cuckolds . . .
Thus with her
cerulean smile
has Lesbia pledged
a heavenly troth
in *trivia*. Hear,
Maid of sea-foam
Queen of Ancon
leafed Idalia
Cyprian Golgos
30   Amathusia
reed-bound Cnidos
Epidamnus
cross-roads of the
Adriatic,
take that vow as
here fulfilled and
neither lacking
wit nor point
in the performance:
40   *burn script, blaze paper*
into the fire you
rigmarole verse,
uncouth, banal
Volusian sheets,
shit-shotten Chronicle.

36.20 *limping cuckolds* The most famous 'limping cuckold' was Vulcan, god of fire and husband of the promiscuous Venus.
36.26–7 *Maid of sea-foam/Queen of Ancon etc.* epithets of Venus

Carmen 49

Silver-tongued among the sons of Rome
the dead, the living & the yet unborn,
Catullus, least of poets, sends
Marcus Tullius his warmest thanks:

– as much the least of poets
as he a prince of lawyers.

Carmen 53

I laughed. Calvus. I laughed today
when someone in the courtroom crowd, hearing
your quite brilliant *exposé* of
the Vatinian affair, lifted his hands up
in proper amazement, and cried suddenly:
'A cock that size . . . *and it spouts!*'
I laughed. Calvus. I laughed.

Carmen 64.1–49 and 265–408

In old days
        driving through soft waters
to the River of Pheasants
to the end of the Euxine Lake
pines spring from Pelion
        carrying picked men
Argives each like a tree
        hearts set on the Colchian pelt

---

64. 8 *Colchian pelt* the golden fleece

                of gold, daring to track
10   salt deserts in a fast ship
            cutting blue waves with firwood blades
            for whom the indweller of the arx
                        the queen of hill-castles
            had made hull poop & sail
                        – volatile under light winds –
            binding firmly the pine plaits to the curved underprow
            the first boat to experience innocent sea –
            Amphitrite.
                        As the moving waves took the keel
20   the water, chopped with oars, grew white
            and from the runnels of foam faces peered
            of Nereids, wondering. Then
            and not since
                        men with their own eyes
            saw the bare bodies of nymphs
                        in broad daylight
            caught in the marbled runnels of foam
            as far down as the nipples . . .
            So Peleus was stirred towards Thetis
30   so Thetis came to a woman's bridal
            and Jove gave his blessing.
                        O heroes
            brides nymphs oreads
                        born in a golden time
            before the tribe of gods had gone from earth
            I call on you in my poem
                        standing with Peleus
            Pillar of Thessaly
                        blest beyond most in their bride-torches
50   whom Jove himself
                        author of gods and goddesses

64.10 *fast ship* the Argo, built by Athena ('indweller of the arx', 12) from pines on Mt Pelion   **64.12** *arx* citadel, here the Acropolis of Athens

has given one of his girls,
>and Thetis
prettiest of mermaids
>touched as her own,
whom Tethys & old Ocean
>girdling all that we stand on –
have yielded a granddaughter.
>On the day
60 the longed-for light leaps up
Thessaly gathers in concourse
>gift-bearing guests
a laughing crowd
>their hearts in their faces
converge on the Palace.
>Cieros is empty
Phthiotic Tempe deserted
>the houses in Crannon
Larissa's walls
70 >abandoned –
flocking into Pharsalia
>packed under Pharsalian roofs
the crowds gather.
>No man tills the field
the bullock's neck grows soft.
>Not for many days shall the pronged hoe
rake among the vine-roots,
>or the pruning hook lessen
the olive tree's deep shade.
80 >Oxen do not turn the lumps of loam,
>red rust flakes the neglected plough.
But in the royal halls
>wherever you look

64.67 *Phthiotic Tempe* place-names chosen for their literary associations, but geographically inaccurate. Tempe is a beautiful valley in northern Thessaly, while Phthiotis is in southern Thessaly.

as room unfolds into room
> silver & gold gleam

an effulgence of ivory,
> carved thrones,

glittering cups on the long tables
the whole building thrums with the splendour of royal goods,
and there, in the middle,
> inlaid with Indian tooth

and quilted with arras,
> > the divan of the small goddess

> the arras ochred with rock-lichen &

> tinctured with stain of rose shell-fish.

[. . .]
Such the stitches worked in the wedding quilt,
such the splendid figures embracing the divan.
The young guests from Thessaly
their eyes filled with the tapestry
gradually ebb
> from courts & corridors,

the demi-gods are due;
> it is a dawn figure,

Aurora climbs
> to the threshold of the day-sojourning sun,

Zephyr
> flicks the flat water into ridges

with a morning puff,
the sloped waves
loiter musically
> later the wind rises

& they rise,
> they multiply,

they shed the sun's sea purple as they flee.
In this way
> the crowd scatters from the royal crannies,

the mortal guests disperse to their own homes.

And now, Chiron,
    first to arrive,
carrying from Mount Pelion
    green gifts
of Thessalian buds
    from fields & alps
from river banks
    where the light west wind
has unsealed them.
    It is the centaur's *potpourri*.
They luxuriate
    through the wedding rooms
with a confused fragrance.
And behind Chiron,
Peneus
    bearded with rushes
from Tempe
    whose girdling woods
are a river roof.
    He brings
store of beech
    dripping roots,
& laurel
    like a girl's flanks,
he brings the plane tree
    that is restless,
the piercing cypress
    & the poplar
supple in the wind,
its tears of amber
for flame-shrouded Phaeton.
    The river god

64.145 *the poplar* After Phaeton's fiery death, his weeping sisters were transformed into poplar trees and their tears hardened into amber.

150   heaps the foliage
              outside & in
          until the house
              is dressed
          for a bride's bower-bed.
              Next, Prometheus
          patron of crafts
              & seer
          still showing
              the faint cicatrices
160   Jove's penance
              paid on the cliff-face
          in Caucasus,
              rock-chained
          arms & legs
              thirty years . . .
          And then follows Jove,
              Juno,
          their issue –
              only Apollo
170   the archer
              & his twin sister, Artemis,
          have spurned
          the bride-ale & wedding torches
          and are left to haunt Heaven.

          The gods have disposed
              their white forms
          at the wedding tables.
              It is bride-hymn time.

---

64. 155 *Prometheus* Bound by Jupiter to a cliff in the Caucasus for giving the gift of fire to mankind, he was reconciled with Jupiter for warning him against marriage with Thetis, who was destined to bear a son mightier than his father.

The Parcae prepare
180   to intone
the prophetic song.
   The white shift
wrapping their palsy
   is alive,
it is red-hemmed
   at the ankles,
and their white hair
   is bound
with a red cloth.
190   Their deft fingers
manipulate
   the eternal thread,
one hand on the distaff
the other carding
   with upturned fingers
the spindle wool,
drawing the thread
   downwards,
twirling the whorl
200   as the thread lengthens.
and stooping
   with mauve lips
to bite the rough ends off
   so that the bits hang
from the withered skin.
   An osier basket bulges
with new-shorn fleece . . .
   the wool whirrs
and the clear voices ring
210   in Epithalamion

64.179 *The Parcae* the Fates

for Thetis,
   her bride-doom
time-sealed.

'Emathian bulwark, son of Jove,
whose acts augment his born worth,
accept the sisters' wedding truth.

Inexorably, fate follows thread,
from spindle to the shuttle running.

Fair-fortuned star that draws the bride
220 to groom, that yields the longed-for wife
whose mastery of love will drown
his heart, who settling to the drawn-
out marriage sleep will make her arms
light cushions for his heavy neck.

Inexorably, fate follows thread,
from spindle to the shuttle running.

Not yet such love as Peleus
For Thetis holds (& she for him)
Has been – or such a grove of love.

230 *Inexorably, fate follows thread,*
from spindle to the shuttle running.

A child, Achilles, void of fear:
foe known face-on not fleeing, first
in racing, in hunt fleeter than
the fleet-foot stag, whose hooves strike flame.

64.214 *Emathian bulwark* Peleus, not a 'son of Jove', as Whigham translates, but rather 'dear to Jupiter'

Inexorably, fate follows thread,
from spindle to the shuttle running.

No warrior dare confront Achilles
where the Trojan rivers stream with
240   Trojan blood, and the Greeks raze stone
from stone of Troy, ten years consumed.

Inexorably, fate follows thread,
from spindle to the shuttle running.

The women at the gravesides weep
his deeds, their hair is loose, coated
with ash-dust, their ageing bosoms
showing fist marks of their sorrow.

Inexorably, fate follows thread,
from spindle to the shuttle running.

250   As the farmer's scythe in close-packed
cornstalks, stripping the yellow field,
his fierce blade crops Troy's men-at-arms.

Inexorably, fate follows thread,
from spindle to the shuttle running.

Scamander by quick Hellespont
will watch his valour swell, its width
shrink with slaughter-stooks, while its deep
course warms with the issuing blood.

---

64. 255 *Scamander* a river of Troy choked with the corpses of Trojans slain by Achilles
64.257 *stooks* bundles or shocks, as of corn or grain

Inexorably, fate follows thread,
260 *from spindle to the shuttle running.*

And Polyxena, death-given,
too shall watch . . . and watch the earth-tomb
rise, where her maiden limbs will fall.

Inexorably, fate follows thread,
from spindle to the shuttle running.

Once Chance lets slip the Greeks inside
the sea-born belt of stone, the young
girl's blood will soak the barrow mound,
who crouches to the two-edged sword
270 & pitches, a headless trunk, forward.

Inexorably, fate follows thread,
from spindle to the shuttle running.

But now the joining of their loves,
as Peleus accepts his nymph, &
Thetis lightly yields to wedlock

Inexorably, fate follows thread,
from spindle to the shuttle running.

And dawn light finds the nurse who tries
today's neck fillet, her mother reads
280 the sign & smiles: the goddess was
not coy in love – young fruit will follow.

Inexorably, fate follows thread,
from spindle to the shuttle running.'

64.261 *Polyxena* a princess of Troy sacrificed on Achilles' tomb

This song
   of happy wedding-fates
the Parcae sang
   to Peleus
in old days.
   For once
when piety had place on earth
   the gods themselves
stood at our chaste doors
   or drank at the bride-ales
of mortal heroes.
   On Holy Feasts
Jove from his bright throne
saw the earth littered with a hundred bulls.
The wine-god on Parnassus
   goading his dishevelled troop
was hailed
   with altar smoke
from happy Delphos
   where the rasping Thyiades
had emptied street & square.
   Athene, Mars or Artemis
appeared
   in the death-tussle
and lit men's hearts.
   To-day ill wreaking rules.
Man's piety is fled.
   The loveless child neglects its parent's death
   a brother's blood trickles from brothers' hands
   the first son's girl attracts the father's lust
   who seeks a step-dame & a son's demise
   unwittingly the youngster mounts his mother
   her vicious incest spurning the house-kin
   spirits: laws bouleversé, and the welter
   such, those of Hill-Heaven have withdrawn their care.

No longer do they deign
to keep our bride-ales, or
reveal themselves to us
in the light of common day.

Carmen 65

Although entangled in prolonged grief
severed from the company of the Muses
and far from Pieria
    my brain children still-born
myself among Stygian eddies
the eddies plucking at the pallid foot
of a brother
    who lies under Dardanian soil
stretched by the coastland
    whom none may now hear
none touch
    shuttered from sight
whom I treasured more than this life
and shall –
    in elegies of loss
plaintive as Procne crying under the shadow of the cypress
for lost Itylus,
    I send, Hortalus, mixed with misery
Berenice's Lock –
    clipped from Callimachus
for you might think my promise
had slipped like vague wind through my head

65.16 *Procne* the nightingale. Procne killed her son Itylus to punish her husband for his rape of her sister, Philomela. The sisters were later transformed into birds. Catullus follows a version in which Procne was changed into a nightingale and Philomela into a swallow.

or was like the apple
    unavowed
the girl takes from her lover
    thrusts into her soft bodice
and forgets there . . .
    till her mother takes her off guard –
she is startled,
        the love-fruit trundles ponderously across the floor
and the girl, blushing, stoops gingerly
                            to pick it up.

Carmen 66

Who scans the bright machinery of the skies
& plots the hours of star-set & star-rise,
this or that planet as it earthward dips,
the coursing brightness of the sun's eclipse,
who knows the dreams that fill Endymion's head
& draw sly Cynthia to his Latmian bed –
palace astronomer, whose gaze is set
more earnestly on Heaven than on *Debrett*,
by you this soft effulgence first was seen
who knew at once the ringlets of the Queen,
those ringlets Berenice with bridal care
pledged when the King left for the Syrian war
(the suppliant Queen with tender arms outspread
the King still swollen from the marriage bed),
who carries with him marks of sweeter strife,
the night's clear traces of a virgin wife!

66.5 *Endymion* a mortal man loved by *Cynthia*, goddess of the moon
66.7 *palace astronomer* Conon, the court astronomer of Ptolemy III
66.8 *Debrett, Debrett's Peerage of England, Scotland and Ireland* (first issued 1803) lists the pedigrees of noble families.

Are brides averse to Venus (as they show)
or are their tears transparencies of woe
brilliantly shed amidst the wedding scene
effective bar to *you know what I mean*?
Their tears are false. I saw a bride's tears shed
when wartime took her husband from her bed.
Still wedded to the Queen's resplendent hair
I witnessed Berenice's crude despair.
And does she wail a so-called 'brother' gone,
or that she lies in bed at night alone,
her body wasted with intensive fire,
her soul devoid of all save one desire?
The proof is here, for virgin she displayed
a spirit commoner in man than maid.
When her betrothed preferred her mother's charms
she saw him slain, couched in Apáme's arms,
procuring by such resolute despatch
her present Kingdom (with a King to match).
Then why this gale of wife-forsaken sighs,
the trembling tears brushed from the brimming eyes?
What God is this, unless the God of Love,
who cannot brook his servants' long remove?
For Ptolemy, all Egypt's altars smoke
and hecatombs of bullocks loose their yoke,
while I, a ransom from a loving head,
secure a husband's swift return to bed,
who conquers Syria, the Euphrates crosses,
views India & returns with trifling losses.
Whisked hence by Venus, lo! these few hairs set
in starry payment of the royal debt.
  And yet with grief, O Queen, I left your hair,
a grief attested by your own coiffure,

66.25 *'brother'* Ptolemy and Berenice were cousins, but the Egyptian king and queen were conventionally described as brother and sister.
66.32 *Apáme* Berenice's mother

> by which I vow (& none vows there in vain)
> no hair exists that scissors can't obtain.
> Scissors & hair? Before the touch of steel
> the tallest mountains have been known to reel.
> Athos itself, the Guardian of the Coast,
> bent to the pickaxe of the Persian host,
> whereat the Thian forbears of your crown
> watched a fleet passing & a mountain drown.
> For women's locks what help, when such as these
> yield to the metal of the Chalybes?
> A plague on smithies, be they crude or fine,
> cursed be the smelter, cursed the teeming mine!
>
>   My loss was freshly mourned, when Venus sent
> black Memnon's brother with Divine intent.
> The winged familiar mounts; he fans the air;
> he bears me upwards through the darkening sphere
> until in Heaven he lays me safe at rest
> in the chaste dove-cote of Cytherea's breast.
> Translated thus, at Queen Arsínoe's word,
> I join (though wet with tears) the golden horde.
> No more shall Ariadne's Crown alone
> gleam from the threshold of the Heavenly Throne:
> these holy spoils (with hers) must share from now
> th' immortal honours of a mortal brow.
> The older stars make room. The Gods declare
> th' apotheosis of a lock of hair.
>
>   Shielding the Virgin from the Lion's wrath
> (below the Bear that glisters in the North)

66.54 *Persian host* the army of Xerxes, who dug a canal through the Point of Athos on his expedition against Greece in 483 BC
66.58 *Chalybes* legendary inventors of iron-working
66.62 *black Memnon's brother* the wind Zephyr, brother of the Ethiopian prince Memnon
66.66 *Cytherea* the deified Queen Arsinoe (sister and second wife of Ptolemy II), worshipped as Venus (*Cytherea*)

trampled by night upon the Milky Way
to kindly Tethys then restored by day,
westward I wheel, leading slow Boötes on
loth to sink seawards e'er the night has gone.
Unlooked-for Fate! 'Tis ill to tempt the Maid –
more abject still to leave the Truth unsaid,
or, fearful of a God's offended smart,
forbear to lend expression to the heart.
Know: less a source of gladness than of sighs
my elevation to the brilliant skies,
my heavenly lustres shine (to me) less clear
than those that hung from Berenice's ear,
who used to smooth me with sweet oils & scent
though not with myrrh, nor married ornament.

Pour then for me, upon your bridal night,
before you doff your silks & quench the light,
before your eager bosom you yield up,
the mingled fragrance of the onyx cup,
onyx, whose contents have so often led
to the chaste dalliance of the marriage bed.
Let the false tokens of unwedded lust
degraded sink into the wasteful dust.
Favoured the bride whose offerings I accept,
her husband constant, she in love adept.

When, Berenice, you come to Venus' rites
amid the cerem'ny of palace lights,
when gazing upwards (in the cause of Love),
you fix your eyes upon the stars above,
recall the 'simple' scents I knew in life
& pour the perfumes proper to a wife.

Let but Aquarius with Orion shine,
the stars fall inward and this Lock Divine
be placed once more on that fair head of thine!

66.81 *the Maid* Nemesis, who punishes presumption

JAMES K. BAXTER (1926–72)

Baxter was New Zealand's best-known modern poet. A deeply religious and troubled man, he embraced both Catholicism and Maori spiritual values and worked for social change. In the 1960s he moved to Jerusalem, a Maori village and Catholic mission on the Wanganui River, North Island, where he established a community. Baxter both imitated and responded to Catullus in a sequence of fourteen poems that he called *Words to Lay a Strong Ghost: after Catullus*. His imitation of *Carmen 3* appears below. Two others from the sequence are included in the Appendix.

From *Runes* (1973).

Carmen 3

The Budgie

Pyrrha's bright budgie who would say,
'Pretty fellow! Pretty fellow!'
For bits of cake from her hand is now
Silent in the underworld.

We buried him beside the rhubarb
Ceremoniously in a box
That once held winklepickers – Death,
You've got a hard gullet!

Pyrrha's eyes are red – partly on account of
10 The bird, and partly for herself,
Because nothing desired can last for long –
That's why she's crying.

JAMES MICHIE (1927–)

Michie studied both Classics and English at Oxford and went on to a career as a poet and editor. He has also translated Horace (1963) and Martial (1973).

From *The Poems of Catullus* (1969).

Carmen 25

> Thallus, you punk, you're soft as a wee rabbit
> Or goose-feathers or an ear-lobe, you're as slack
> As a cobweb or an old man's floppy phallus,
> And yet by moonlight you're a hard man, Thallus;
> When the attendants doze, you have the habit
> Of pouncing quicker than a hurricane. Thief,
> Give back that cloak of mine you nabbed, give back
> My Thynian tablets and my handkerchief
> From Saetabis, which in full public view
> You flaunt as your own heirlooms – fool! Unglue
> Them from your talons instantly and hand
> Them back, or else I'll use the whip to scrawl
> Shame on those namby-pamby paws and brand
> Those lambkin buttocks till you writhe and skip
> And stagger startled, like a little ship
> Caught in a big sea by an angry squall.

Carmen 33

> Of all our bath-house thieves the cleverest one
> Is you, Vibennius, with your pansy son.
> (The old man's fingers suffer from a heinous
> Itch, but the boy's as grasping with his anus.)

Why not deport yourselves, go anywhere
The weather's horrible? For all Rome's aware
Of Father's pilferings, and believe me, Sonny,
That hairy rump won't make you any money.

Carmen 37

Baboon companions of that nasty inn
Nine posts down from the temple of the twin
Brothers who wear the skull-caps, do you think
That you're the only real men? That we stink,
The rest of us, like goats? That only you
Have the prerogative and the tools to screw
The girls in Rome? Because a hundred strong,
Or two hundred, you sit there in a long
Half-witted row, do you think I wouldn't dare
10 To bugger the whole lot of you on one chair?
Think what you like; for I intend to scrawl
Obscenities all over your front wall.
For Lesbia, who has broken from my clutch
(And no girl ever will be loved as much
As I loved her), whom I fought other men
Such long, hard battles for, has made your den
Her home. Owners of wealth or a good name,
You're all her lovers now, and, double shame,
So is each half-baked lecher, every randy
20 Alley cat; at the head of them that dandy,
Egnatius, prince of the long-haired crew,
That son of rabbit-ridden Spain – yes, you
With the two points that make you so alluring:
Thick beard and teeth scrubbed white with Spanish urine.

37.2–3 *twin Brothers* Castor and Pollux

Carmen 55

Please tell me – that's if you don't mind
Me asking – how am I to find
The holes and corners where you hide?
I searched the Lesser Campus, tried
The Circus Maximus and shrine
Of Jupiter on the Capitoline,
Combed all the bookshops, then waylaid
The girls in Pompey's colonnade,
Begging for you, but met wide-eyed,
10   Innocent looks on every side.
Desperate, I asked, 'What have you done,
You bad girls, with Camerius?' One,
Teasing me, flaunted a bare breast:
'Here he is, in this rosy nest!'
You keep such a stand-offish distance
That one needs Hercules' persistence
To track you down these days, my friend.
Divulge, disclose where you intend
To be in future; come, commit
20   Yourself, be reckless, out with it!
Is it that you've spent all day sleeping
Snug in those creamy girls' safe-keeping?
If lips and tongue stay locked and chained,
You waste the whole crop love has gained:
Venus likes speech to be loose-reined.
By all means be discreet – providing
That I'm the one you confide in.

Carmen 67

CATULLUS
From a husband and his father you've earned good
Opinions, door. Greetings. God bless your wood!
When old man Balbus owned the house, it's said,
You served him well; but now he's laid out dead
And you're a married man's door, people say
You serve the son in an ill-natured way.
Tell me, then, why you've changed, why you've discarded
Your old allegiance to the place you guarded.

DOOR
So please Caecilius, who now owns my keys,
It's not my fault, let folk talk as they please.
No one can say I've failed on any score:
Blame, though, is always laid at someone's door.
When dirty work's found out, they all exclaim,
'It's your fault, Door.' Doors always get the blame.

CATULLUS
A single word won't put you in the clear:
Prove it for anyone to see and hear.

DOOR
How can I? No one cares enough to seek
The truth.

CATULLUS
I do. Don't shilly-shally. Speak!

DOOR
Well, first of all, when people said our bride
Came to us with her maidenhead, they lied.
Although her former husband, whose effete
Equipment dangled like a limp-leaved beet

And couldn't reach his tunic, never laid
A hand on her, they say his father played
A foul trick in the bride-bed and defiled
The poor old house, fired either by a wild
Incestuous lust or simply by the need
To make up for his weak boy's lack of seed,
30 Since someone with a bit of strength and juice
Had to be found to tug her girdle loose.

CATULLUS
There's fatherly love! What an amazing chap
To piss into his own son's married lap!

DOOR
But that's not all that Brescia has to tell –
Brescia beneath Cycnaea's citadel,
Past which the Mella dawdles, golden-brown,
Dear mother of Verona, my home town:
She cites Postumius and Cornelius too,
With whom the girl did what wives shouldn't do.

CATULLUS
40 'But how do you know this?' someone will object.
'You're fixed to the lintel, Door, here to protect
Your master's threshold; you can't gad about
Listening: your job's just letting in and out.'

DOOR
It's that I've often heard her with her maids
Furtively whispering of her escapades,
Naming the men I've named – as if a door
Were deaf and dumb! She mentioned, furthermore,
Somebody else, whose name I shan't divulge
For fear his angry ginger eyebrows bulge.

67.36 *the Mella* a river near Brescia

He's a tall fellow who once had to face
A grave charge of paternity — a case
Of a lying belly, for no birth took place.

Carmen 87

No woman can
Truthfully aver
That any man
Ever loved her
As I love you.

No lover bound
By pledge of heart
Was ever found
True on his part
As I was true.

Carmen 93

Caesar, I have no great desire
To stand in your good graces,
Nor can I bother to enquire
How fair or dark your face is.

Carmen 95

At last my Cinna has brought his *Smyrna* out,
Nine long years after it was first begun;
Hortensius, on the other hand, can spout
Ten thousand verses in the space of one.
Smyrna will travel far, to the wave-grooved bed
Of the river Satrachus, and still be read

Till Time itself grows grey about the head.
Volusius' *Annals*, though, will drop stone-dead
In their own native Padua and make
10   Endless supplies of paper to wrap hake.
My friend's small masterpiece speaks to my heart:
Let the crown clap Antimachus' windy art.

Carmen 98

Of you, if anyone, it can be said
'Beware the windbag and the dunderhead',
Malodorous Victius. Given a chance, you'd use
That tongue to lick a slave's arse or his shoes.
If you want to put the lot of us to death,
Open your mouth: you'll do it with one breath.

Carmen 110

Good mistresses are praised: they take their hire
And honour their side of the bargain later.
You, Aufillena, cheat me, you're a liar,
Not half so much a lover as a hater;
   You like to take and never give –
   And that's a vicious way to live.

An honest woman would by now have kept
Her promise (a nice girl would never make it);
But, Aufillena, greedily to accept
10   Presents to seal a contract and then break it
   Puts you below the grasping whore:
   She pays the flesh that's haggled for.

Carmen 111

To marry, Aufillena, and stay true
Is for a wife to be praised above all others.
Better, though, take all comers than, like you,
Sleep with your uncle and breed cousin-brothers.

RODNEY GOVE DENNIS
(1930–   )

Dennis is a poet and translator as well as emeritus curator of manuscripts at the Houghton Library of Harvard University. In addition to his many books and articles on the Houghton collections, he has published a translation of a work of the Christian Kabbalah: *The Epistle of Secrets*, and two collections of his own poetry.

Carmina 41 and 43 are from *Persephone* 4.1 (1998), *Carmen* 51 from *Persephone* 2.1 (1996) and *Carmen* 65 from *Persephone* 2.2 (1996).

Carmen 41

Ameana, fucked about,
Would squeeze ten thousand out of me,
Has a nose that sticks way out
And a boy friend credit free.

Call for the doctors and the friends,
You with responsibility.
What the reflecting bronze portends
The girl's deranged and cannot see.

Carmen 43

O your nose isn't small, not at all,
and your eyes aren't dark. Just remark
those feet and hands. Your mouth's not dry.
Why keep trying to talk refined?
Mind, your boyfriend's out of money.
Funny, the province thinks you're fair.
There they say you're like my honey.
The times are dumb. And then some.

Carmen 51

A man like that seems to me simply godlike,
more than godlike, if you don't mind my saying so,
sitting across from you, repeatedly getting to
    see you and hear you

laughing so nicely. It made foolish me
just go crazy, for when I first saw you,
Lesbia, I suddenly felt . . .

but my words got jumbled, and little flames
went through my arms and legs, my ears
began ringing, and then twin nighttimes
    clothed my eyes.

It's idleness, Catullus, that's your main problem.
You love being idle and acting badly;
and it was idleness back then that brought down the kings and
    their rich cities.

Carmen 65

To Hortalus

Consumed, Hortalus, by a mastering grief,
called from the company of the clever Muses
with a mind so buffeted by misfortune
and helpless to pursue their fair offspring –
Just now, by Lethe's water, a moistening wave
washed over my brother's dear pale foot
whom by the Rhoetean beach the Trojan soil
weighs down, so snatched from my eyes –
Shall I never see you again, brother more dear
10 than life? Certainly I'll always love you,
always sing your death in such songs
as Procne sang deep in the woods' thick shade
about Itys, about her own son's death –
But even in this sadness, Hortalus,
I send you a Callimachean poem
(lest you might think your words escape my mind,
entrusted to the undependable breeze)
which, as an apple given secretly
falls out of a girl's chaste lap,
20 hidden forgotten under her soft dress,
dislodged at mother's entrance, slips away
and rolling suddenly downward, makes, perceived,
a rosy hue rush to her sad face.

FREDERIC RAPHAEL (1931–) and KENNETH McLEISH (1940–97)

Raphael has written stories, screenplays, and biographies of Byron and Somerset Maugham. McLeish translated Euripides and Aristophanes and published books for children and on travel, reading, music and Greek and Roman culture. They collaborated on translations of Aeschylus' *Oresteia* (1979) as well as Catullus.

The selections below include not only frank and inventive renderings of some of Catullus' most scurrilous invectives, but also a sympathetic translation of *Carmen* 68, one of his most learned and Alexandrian productions. Most modern scholars would divide *Carmen* 68 into two distinct poems, a letter to Manius or Mallius and an expression of gratitude to Allius for his services to Catullus and his mistress. Raphael and McLeish treat it as a single poem addressed to Mallius, presenting the letter (lines 1–43) in a more colloquial voice. Catullus does not name his mistress; Raphael and McLeish call her Lesbia.

From *The Poems of Catullus* (1979).

Carmen 15

Myself and the one I love, Aurelius,
I put under your protection.
So grant me this modest favour:
If ever you have wanted
To keep just one thing chaste
(Or even roughly pollution-free),
Keep this young man so for me.
I don't mean just from the plebs –
They don't bother me much.
10 A virgin's safe in the rush-hour:
No room to mix business with pleasure.
Quite frankly, it's you that I fear:

You prick, you've a hard reputation –
You've got it in for all the boys.
As far as I'm concerned, keep it up,
Wherever, whoever you like,
As long as it's not around here.
Look, one simple exception:
In my view, it isn't a lot.
So: if you get any nasty ideas,
You sod, and dare to get cracking
(Tempting that soft head into your noose),
I give you a solemn warning:
You'll wish you'd had a different end.
I'll lash you up with the door open
And stuff your back passage with fish
(Mullet garnished with radishes),
Prescribed suppository.

Carmen 68

You sent me a tearful letter – I have it here:
Crushed by fortune . . . utterly distraught . . .
A shipwrecked sailor on a foam-washed beach . . .
Feet poised on the threshold of death . . .
You ask me to drag you back, to offer your heart
Some ease. *Venus torments me . . . I toss and turn . . .*
I'm alone, in a single bed . . . I try reading . . .
The old, sweet songs . . . the Muses will lull me asleep . . .
But they don't. You lay down the old songs,
And ask me for a new love-song, a friend's gift.
Dear Mallius, don't think me unsympathetic.
I understand – and I know the duty
Friend owes friend. But like you, I too
Am 'crushed by fortune'; *my* heart's 'awash with care'.
I spent the flowery spring of youth
In studying (beginning the day I came of age).

My subject: love. I learned every game
The laughing goddess plays, who mixes joy and care.
I was a good student, promised well –
20 Until he died, and stole my joy.
O dear brother, stolen away,
My life's light, I died, I went to the grave
With you; my happiness (kept alive alone
In loving you, alive) died with your death.
When you died I gave up my studies,
Withdrew from my courses, abandoned
All my researches into pleasure.

So when you write, *Things must be bad,*
Catullus, there in Verona: even here in Rome
30 *The best people warm themselves – in a widow's bed . . .*
Things aren't that bad in Verona,
Not bad like that at all.
You ask me for a friend's gift, Mallius.
Please understand, my grief gives me no gifts
To give. Here in Verona, I've no desk
Bulging with manuscripts: my desk –
My youth! – I left behind in Rome,
And here I live from a single trunk.
All this to explain why this time
40 I can't deliver the goods: no lack
Of affection, no shirking of obligations –
I simply can't supply
Goods (at the moment) not in stock.

And yet, I must speak out: I must tell
Every detail of Mallius' unstinting friendship.
Take up the story, Muses: even when
These sheets grow old, keep them alive –

68.30 *widow's bed* Clodia (Catullus' 'Lesbia') was a widow

> Don't let the immemorial flight of time
> Darken them into blind obscurity,
> Or spiders weave lofty, insubstantial webs
> Round Mallius' immortality.

50

> When two-faced Venus had my heart in thrall,
> Scorched through with passion, shaken and convulsed
> With volcanic tides of love, that kept my eyes
> Misty with weeping, my cheeks as dewed with tears
> As a rivulet on a lofty mountain-side
> That bubbles down from rock to mossy rock
> (A stream that soon, tumbling to the valley floor,
> Will make its way past stately poplar trees,
> Refresh the traveller sweating on his way
> And slake the parched fields' thirsty furrows):
> Such was my state — as sailors lost at sea
> In a crow-black storm cry out in desperate need
> To Castor and Pollux for a gentler breeze —
> Such was my state: My rescuer, Mallius.
> He found us a private place, my love and me,
> A secret house where we might safely love.
> Then in she walked, my goddess, with steps as sure
> As a virgin bride: worn doorstep, fair white feet . . .
> I remember, her sandal squeaked (an omen).

60

70

> Like Laodamia, when she first set foot
> In doomed Protesilaus' house, hot with love,
> In a union unsanctified by sacrifice
> Or the pacific ceremonial of heaven.
> (O lady Nemesis, may I never act
> In such hot haste, without my lords' approval.)
> Later (husband lost) Laodamia learned
> How the thirsty altar must drink holy blood

68.72 *Protesilaus* the first Greek killed at Troy

Before a bride submits to her lusty groom.
80 He went; she waited; winter came and went
And came again, filling her starving heart
With love unsatisfied, teaching her to live
Without her husband, snatched (as the Fates well knew)
For ever, that day he went to fight at Troy.

Troy! With Helen's rape as bait to draw
The leaders of Greece, a clarion-call to death;
Troy! Mass grave of Europe and Asia,
Bitter dust of heroes and heroic pride;
Troy! You stole my unhappy brother too,
90 Stole him away. O dear brother, stolen away,
My life's light, I died, I went to the grave
With you; my happiness (kept alive alone
In loving you, alive) died with your death.
You lie, not reverently in a familiar tomb
With those who loved you, but far away
In Troy, foul Troy, Troy at the end of the world,
That clawed you down to lie in foreign earth.
They flocked there then, the choice young men of Greece;
They left their hearths and homes, and flocked to Troy
100 To stop Paris taking his pleasure in Helen,
Unchallenged pleasure in a bed of ease.
And for this – for this! fair Laodamia,
Your husband (dearer than life, than breath itself)
Was snatched away: your love and his, climbing
To climax in melting passion, was plunged
From the high peaks to the chilly depths – a pit
As deep, as fathomless, as Hercules once dug
(Hercules, Greek-named 'son of Amphitryon')
At Pheneus, at the foot of Mount Cyllene,
110 Dug to drain the marsh, and dry the fertile soil,
Dug through the very marrow of the mountain
As soon as the Stymphalian birds were dead,

CARMEN 68 · FREDERIC RAPHAEL AND KENNETH McLEISH

    Struck with unerring arrows, as his cruel lord
    Had ordered: his obedience opened the gates
    Of Olympus to him, won him Hebe's love.
    That pit was deep; but deeper still the pit
    Engulfing your lofty love, humbling your pride.
    Your husband was dear to you, dearer far
    Than a grandson born to an only daughter,
120 Born to warm an old man's feeble heart,
    Born at last to inherit an old man's wealth,
    To enter his name on the tablets of the will
    (Stripping the joy from the circling next-of-kin
    Who hover like vultures round the old man's head).
    White doves, they say, are loyal lovers,
    Devoted lovers, snatching kisses
    With impetuous, darting beaks, their love
    A flame fiercer than in any woman's heart –
    Fiercer than any flame but yours, Laodamia,
130 As you lapped your lovely lover then.
    Like Laodamia, my Lesbia, then,
    My shining passion, ran to my arms
    While Cupid fluttered happily above,
    Her smiling page-boy, dressed for a wedding.
    And now, you say, Catullus is not enough
    For her, she warms others in her widow's bed?
    I must allow her a few indiscretions:
    I'll not play the fool, the slave of jealousy.
    Remember: Juno, queen of heaven, knew
140 Her flighty lord's multifarious affairs,
    Knew them all, and choked her anger back.
    No point in mortals outdoing the gods;

68.113 *cruel lord* Eurystheus, to whom Hercules was enslaved, commanded him to perform his famous labours

68.115 *Hebe's love* Hercules gained immortality as a reward for his labours and married Hebe ('Youth').

No point in playing the palsied cuckold –
She did not come to me on her father's arm
(To that house, smelling of Syrian musk!);
She came secretly, at night, and gave me
A priceless gift, stolen from her husband's lap.
No, I am satisfied: enough for me
If she counts *my* days red-letter days.

150 There, Mallius. A love-poem. A friend's gift,
My best return for generous help.
Your name will live for ever now, free of rust,
Today, tomorrow and tomorrow and tomorrow,
Let the gods grant as many tomorrows
As ever Justice granted the pure in heart.
God bless you, Mallius. Long life to you;
Long life to the house you lent us,
The ground and beginning of all our bliss.
Like a true friend, you gave me happiness:
160 My mistress, dearer to me than all the world,
My daylight, focus of all my life and love.

Carmen 86

QUINTIA VOTED TOPS

                    Granted, she's a star:
Tall, blonde, good figure.
I'm not saying she hasn't her points.
They don't add up to beautiful, that's all.
Big girl, big talent, she lacks the clinching spark.
Lesbia is beautiful. The beauty of beauties.
What have the others got?
                    She's got it all.

Carmen 97

No (so help me God), I never discriminated in any way
Between the smell of A's mouth and the smell of his arse.
In no respect was the former nicer than the latter, or vice versa.
I was wrong: the arse is nicer, much.
In that it comes without teeth. The mouth has teeth, eighteen
    inches long,
Like pegs stuck in a rickety cart to stop the manure falling out.
Another comparison: when he smiles, his grin spreads out
Like a cunt on a straddling mule having a steamy piss.
And this is your big man with the girls. A fucking charmer.
10 Put him on the treadmill: let him play the donkey there.
A woman who could stomach him – she's just the girl we want
To lick the arse of the public hangman when he's got the trots.

Carmen 106

PRETTY BOY SEEN WITH AUCTIONEER

Rumour says, going, going, gone.

Carmen 108

For Cominius. By popular decision

Suppose your venerable old age were to be
Terminated on grounds of moral turpitude.
I've a strong feeling that your tongue might be ripped out
(No one likes it) and given to a peckish vulture.
A black-throated crow could enjoy your dug-out eyes,
Your tripe the dogs, and wolves could lick the plates.

Carmen 113

When Pompey was first consul, Cinna, two men
Frequented the First Lady. Now he's consul again
The same two are at it again – with a thousand more
Up to the same. Fucking inflation again.

Carmen 116

In anxious, constant search I racked my brains
    For poems of Callimachus to send
You, Gellius – to please by taking pains,
    And bring your short, sharp missives to an end.
A waste of time (I see that now): my pleas
    Were useless. Fine! Sharp-shoot away: your aim
Is poor, I pirouette aside with ease.
    And *I* shoot bull's-eyes, sure to kill, or maim.

ROBERT CLAYTON CASTO
(1932–   )

Casto has translated Racine's *Britannicus* for performance and published several volumes of poetry. In his version of *Carmen* 63, Casto does not translate the last three lines, but uses them as an epigraph. (For a translation see Hunt above.)
  From *Arion* 2 (1968).

Carmen 63

Attis
after Catullus 63

Dea magna, dea Cybelle, dea domina Dindymi,
procul a me tuus sit furor omnis, hera, domo:
alios age incitatos, alios age rabidos.   – Catullus LXIII

... And cast his loins upon the Phrygian shore
and split 'em with a stone,
Attis who once was young and brown,
and at a crossroads of that land
his soft seed tickling the Asian sand
hoisted under his bloody thumb
the timbrel the light mysterious drum
which is the sign of Cybelè
and with his fingers slippery and numb
struck those vacant hollow skins
and piped with white lips mincingly
to that sensual sodality:

– Strike, brother bodies! strike and throng;
if you could see her angry eyes
in a dream as I have done,
vivid and famous, you would dance!
and her white fastidious hands
stronger than laws of Galilee or Rome,
you would not soon lament your distant home
nor (following my custom) that you took
the dissipated traffic of the seas
into the precincts of this sacred land
and here unmanned
your vicious parts in diffidence of love
and all those soft cooperative lusts

addressed by weaker men
– now let the silver cymbal and the crude
insinuating Phrygian flute
sound through these mounting shelves of spurted vine
30 the advent of the corybantic train
to the great Mother on the highland plain!

2
Up the raw hills where monster images
skim the red woodland and the speckled pine,
he raced those wild anatomies,
the moist she-misters, and they twitched
in service on the grass's lip
all rare with frenzy dancing and divine
until upon a black plateau
where casually the gristled snow
40 begins to seep
and squalid roosts of great birds crop,
they steaming drop
from hunger and from weariness.
                              They sleep
as now the silver person of the moon
moves out upon the single hemispheres
and spans the savage masses of the night.

3
But when the sun within the eastern house
pierced the ambiguous hedges and hard land,
50 Attis arose in wonder, hot and dry,
and stood before the stubble-lands of the Queen
and saw his caked and bloody thigh
and saw his loss, the fervid epicene
and with a cry
down through the mosses and the creaking vines
plunged in the morning

CARMEN 63 · ROBERT CLAYTON CASTO

    down to the sea
    and at the shore wept piteously:
    — My country far away! my fatherland!
60   And I like a poor fool on this bone of sand!
    I? I to be empty? I to be less than dross?
    I to be set apart? to be cheap? to be lost?
    where is my home? my parentage? my cause?
    what cause have I? what sorry shape have I?
    where are the thresholds warm with frequent friends?
    for mine were the kisses and the limpid vows,
    pink easy melons and the colloquial grape,
    and all the milkyoung flowers of puberty
    sang at the native chambers of my house
70   in previous dawn:
    and have I sought
    these dunes, these forests, and this twisted lawn
    and done the grisly absence at my groin
    to be her jockey-handmaid and listless concubine?
    Now to the regions and corrosive dens
    where sun or snow makes burst or blasts the flesh
    henceforth I pass:
    the forests and the grass,
    the very solid earth its equipoise,
80   the scarfed boar and night-crawlers of the brush,
    the hooded worms and weasels of this land,
    she-goats, black wings, and humid tusks,
    shall be my eager enemy!
    and I will thrust
    among these throttled bulbs and pits
    my dancing nerves:
                        you belly of Dindymus!
    what once I sought to do,
    or having been in dreams wake now to be,
90   now I am sick for; and I am sorry too.

4
The enormous she,
she heard him where she sat, regent of Force,
among the worn pavilions of her place
and in her face,
hideous and pure, a silent kind of rage
began to work and smart
and her weedy paps and corrugated heart
and her crossed wombs and unimpeded thighs,
the looped and central fleshes of her frame
that fold the generations of the moss,
and all her rooted functions heaved from shame
and wrath! and as her groans began to toss
and chiefly sound,
from rugged ditches of great sacrifice,
from ropy shacks and vacant lots,
pockets and hutches of her holy space,
raced all the stifled priestlings of her rites
with sensitive offerings in their hands
to drop before her oriental glance:
she sweeping down
her towered head, unleashed
the brazen yoke of each brown beast
that slavered at her feet and cried:

– Go chase him from the branches of the sea
for he would dance and still be free:
go drive him up: THERE IS NO REMEDY.

5
Now with their gorgeous claws they tear the brush
and streaking through the ripe personal wilderness
down through the lichens and the dented brakes,
down to the beaches and the lifted dunes,
they burst where Attis shakes

    with sorrow by the smooth spaces of the sea:
    and they lunge
    to rip the tender youngster and they roar:
    his form a dancing jelly as they come,
    he leaps along the clotted shore,
    along the rank fields up into the swamps,
    pursued to the grottoes and stiff secret nests
    up, up into the wasted hills,
130 up to the vacant reaches of the cliffs
    pursued, pursued, extravagant and sore
    pursued
            and dancing dancing evermore.

DOROTHEA WENDER (1934–)

Dorothea Wender, a classical scholar and translator, is an emeritus professor at Wheaton College in Norton, Massachusetts. She is the author of *Last Scenes of the Odyssey* (1978) and has translated Hesiod and Theognis for Penguin.

From *Roman Poetry: From the Republic to the Silver Age* (1980).

Carmen 16

I'll bugger you, Aurelius Swishy-tail,
I'll shove it down your throat, Queen Furius!
Because I've written poetry which seems
'A little soft' – you think I'm queer like you.
A poet and his verse are different things:
He should be decent, but his poetry
Need not. His verses, if they're rather 'soft'
Or shocking, and are able to excite
The readers' itchy parts, have wit and charm

10 Not for the little boys, but hairy men
    Who don't know how to swish their tails like you.
    I write of many thousand kisses – you
    Read it, and think that I'm effeminate:
    I'll bugger you; I'll shove it down your throats!

Carmen 39

Egnatius has such pearly teeth
He's smiling all the time.
He goes to court; some orator
Describes a heinous crime,
The crowd is moved to passion, but
He's smiling all the while.
There's weeping at a funeral:
What does he do but smile?
He smiles at everything. I think
10 It is a foul disease,
It isn't cosmopolitan
It really doesn't please.

Take warning, good Egnatius! If
You had been born in Rome
Or if you were a Sabine or
If Tibur was your home,
If you were a stingy Umbrian,
A fat Etruscan man,
A toothy, black Lanuvian
20 Or Transpadane (my clan)
Or any hygienic sort
Whose habits are not vile
I still don't think that I would want
To see you *always* smile.
Of all inanities there are

There's nothing more inane
Than empty smiling. And, what's worse
My friend, you come from Spain.
And Spaniards use their urine

30 As a handy dentifrice,
So when your smile is bright, we know
That you've been drinking piss!

Carmen 84

Arrius said 'hadvantage' for
'Advantage', and for 'ambush',
He thought it most grandiloquent
To shout, distinctly, '*Hambush!*'
He got the trait from Mother
And her various relations;
Her parents, her free brother,
All had great aspirations.

He went abroad, to Syria,
10 We thought that we were blessed;
Language was soft and smooth again,
Our ears had a nice long rest.
When suddenly the frightening news
Arrived that since our man
Had crossed the Ionian Sea, it was
Now called 'HIONIAN'.

ROBERT MEZEY (1935–)

Mezey is poet in residence at Pomona College. He is the author of several volumes of poetry and translations.

Earlier versions of *Carmen* 32 and *Carmen* 51 were published in *The Lovemaker* (1961). *Carmen* 89 appears here in print for the first time.

Carmen 32

Ipsithilla, my pet, my favorite dish,
Plump, wanton little coney, how I wish
You'd bid me join you for a noonday nap
And let me spend this scorcher in your lap.
How does that sound? Then see nor man nor mouse
Opens your little gate. Don't leave the house.
Just change the sheets, break out your bread and wine,
And one by one, my puss, we'll tear off nine
And melt away in joy. Want to know how?
10   Then let me come immediately, for now,
Swollen with lunch and dreams, catching your scent,
I watch my tunic hoisted like a tent.

Carmen 51

That man seems to me almost a god, or even
– Dare I say it? – surpasses the gods, he who,
Sitting turned towards you continually
    Watches and catches

Your dulcet laughter – all of which drains my senses,
For always when I turn and face you, Lesbia,
Not a breath remains in my mouth, not a sound,
    Nothing is left me,

But my tongue thickens as a thin flame travels
10   Down along nerve and vein, with a mute thunder
My ears ring, and my eyes go dark under
    Wave after wave . . .

Idleness, Catullus, idleness weakens you.
In idleness you take too drugged a pleasure –
Idleness, that has brought down powerful princes,
    Prosperous kingdoms.

Carmen 89

Jerry's lost weight – and why not? Have you seen his mother?
Such a lively performer at her age, so pretty, so giving –
And his succulent sister? and uncle, a man who, like mother,
Just can't say no? And girls, girls by the dozen,
All of them kissing cousins, – when does he eat and sleep?
Well, even if he cut back, kept it all in the family,
Touched only what mustn't be touched – he'd still be thin.

HUMPHREY CLUCAS (1941–   )

Clucas is a poet and a composer. He has published essays on A. E. Housman (1995) and several volumes of poetry.

    Carmina 33, 48, 50 and 56 are from *Agenda* 26 (Autumn–Winter 1978–9). *Carmina* 38 and 81 are from *Versions of Catullus* (1985).

Carmen 33

First of all the bath-house filchers –
Father Vibennius, and son.
One's an itchy-fingered lecher,
One's a randy-ended queer.

The devil take them: everyone's
Disgusted by those groping fingers,
No-one wants that hirsute bum.

Carmen 38

Things aren't well with me, friend –
Not well at all. They're pretty rough,
In fact, and worse daily. Hourly,
I should say. And though a morsel
Of comfort wouldn't cost much,
What have you done about it? No
Word? I'm losing patience, friend.
Console me – send me a few lines.
Fill them with crocodile tears.

Carmen 48

Three hundred thousand times, Juventius,
I'd kiss your sweet eyes; never enough
Kissing – thick as the ripe ears
Of corn in a good harvest. If you'd yield.

Carmen 50

A day that was all holiday,
Licinius; a day of games –
Sophisticated, by arrangement;
A day scribbling epigrams.
Each followed his quick fancy,
Now one metre, now another,
Taking turns, while the wine and laughter
Flowed. I came away so roused

By your sharp wit, Licinius,
That I couldn't eat, or sleep either.
Open-eyed, I spent a restless
Night tossing around my bed,
Longing for dawn – another meeting,
More talk. But when at last
I could lie still, half-alive
And quite exhausted, I wrote this,
My friend, so that you'd know my need.
Don't be proud – and don't refuse
My invitation. Nemesis
Is a strict goddess, quick to punish.
Take care not to offend her.

Carmen 56

What an absurd thing, Cato!
You'll laugh. Laugh with Catullus, then.
Cato, it's too ridiculous.
I found a boy banging his girl;
I was so stirred – forgive me, Venus –
That I drew my own rod, and served him right.

Carmen 81

Couldn't you find in all Rome, Juventius,
Someone a little smarter than your friend
From back-of-beyond – that hole Pisaurum –
To shower your favours on? He's pale yellow,
Like a gilded statue. And you'd prefer
Him, to me? with an unjaundiced eye?

BENITA KANE JARO (1941–)

Benita Kane Jaro is a novelist with a special interest in the late Roman republic. Her Roman novels include *The Door in the Wall* (1994) and *The Key* (1988), a fictional biography of Catullus built around translations of the poems.

From *The Key* (1988).

Carmen 37

Whorehouse tavern, and you band of friends
at the ninth pillar from the Brothers in the Hats
do you think you're the only ones with pricks,
the only ones allowed to do the girls?
That everyone else stinks like a goat?
Line up, then, a hundred,
two hundred, more, stupid, on your chairs –
do you think I can't screw you all myself?
where you sit? on one bench?
10 Believe it, for I'll put the names on the tavern wall:
my girl, gone from my arms,
lives there with you now,
though I loved her as no woman has been loved.
Well, you all love her too, rich men, men of rank –
Even, to her shame, you little creeping lechers
and you, long-haired son of rabbity Iberia,
with such a lovely beard
and teeth you brush with Spanish piss.

37.2 *Brothers in the Hats* the Temple of the twins Castor and Pollux, who are usually depicted wearing felt caps

Carmen 52

Why wait, Catullus? Die now.
Nonius, that tumor, sits in the magistrate's chair
Which Vatinius is perjuring himself to buy.
Why wait, Catullus? Die now.

Carmen 80

What can I say, Gellius, about why
that pink mouth is paler than snow
when you get up in the morning,
when you wake from your soft sleep
in the middle of the day?
I don't know: is the rumor true
that you dine at noon on a boy's big thing?
I do know this: poor Victor's exhausted haunches
prove your meal —
that and the snow
around your lips.

CHARLES MARTIN (1942–)

Martin is a poet and translator. He has published a study of Catullus (*Catullus*, 1992) as well as several volumes of poetry.
From *The Poems of Catullus* (1979, 1990).

Carmen 11

Aurelius & Furius, true comrades,
whether Catullus penetrates to where in
outermost India booms the eastern ocean's
    wonderful thunder;

whether he stops with Arabs or Hyrcani,
Parthian bowmen or nomadic Sagae;
or goes to Egypt, which the Nile so richly
    dyes, overflowing;

even if he should scale the lofty Alps, or
10 summon to mind the mightiness of Caesar
viewing the Gallic Rhine, the dreadful Britons
    at the world's far end –

you're both prepared to share in my adventures,
and any others which the gods may send me.
Back to my girl then, carry her this bitter
    message, these spare words:

May she have joy and profit from her cocksmen,
go down embracing hundreds all together,
never with love, but without interruption
20   wringing their balls dry;

nor look to my affection as she used to,
for she has left it broken, like a flower
at the edge of a field after the plowshare
    brushes it, passing.

Carmen 27

Waiter, Falernian! That fine old wine, boy:
pour me another bowl & make it stronger.
— Postumia, the mistress of these revels,
loaded as the vines are, she's laid the law down:
go elsewhere, water. Go to where you're wanted,
spoiler of wine, go — pass your sober days with
sober people. Up Bacchus, undiluted.

Carmen 47

Well, if it isn't Pestilence & Famine,
sinister hirelings of mobster Piso!
Has that licentious prick picked you two over
my dear Fabullus & Veraniolus?
And does he feed you lavishly at banquets
while it's still light out? While my poor companions
lurk at the crossroads, looking for some action?

Carmen 79

Lesbius is pretty: boy, is he ever! Why Lesbia'd rather
   have him than you, Catullus, and your whole family!
Let prettyboy Lesbius sell us all — if he can find even three
   men of good taste to take his vile kiss when they meet him.

JANE WILSON JOYCE (1947–)

Jane Wilson Joyce, a poet and translator, is a professor of classics at Centre College, Danville, Kentucky. She has published two volumes of poetry and a translation of Lucan and is now completing a translation of Statius' *Thebaid*.

From *Latin Lyric and Elegiac Poetry*, Diane J. Rayor and William W. Batstone, eds. (1995).

Carmen 32

Pleasepleaseplease, DEAR little lady-oh,
my fancy-tickler, my clever-puss,
ask me to take my siesta at *your* house.
And, if you *do* ask me, it'd be
Highly Desirable for you to arrange
to have the side door left unlocked
and *not to go out yourself*: no,
you stay home and get ready for our
Nine Continuous Fornifuckations.
10   But seriously – if you've got plans,
ask me *NOW*: I've had my breakfast
(protein aplenty), and I'm just lying here
on my back, making the bedclothes bulge.

Carmen 73

Don't even *want* to expect anything from anyone
   or think someone can be made conscientious.
All deeds are thankless, no kindness shown ever wins
   a medal – no, it's just *tiresome*, it's *meddling*.
So say I, speaking as one hard-hit – and by whom?
   the man who claimed I was his one and only friend.

Carmen 83

Lesbia gives me (husband right there!) a good tongue-
    lashing —
  an act which affords that fathead the rarest
felicity. Oxbrain! you don't get it. If she cold-
  shoulders us, she's cured; but, because she's
squawking a blue streak, (A) she remembers and (B) what's
    more
  to the point — she's enraged. Cold talk, hot pants.

Carmen 109

Proposal, dear heart, or proposition? that this love
  we share shall be ours, ours alone, forever.
Ye mighty Gods, enable her to make a promise
  honestly, to speak sincerely and from the heart,
that we, for all our days, may jointly constitute
  one couple, under God, indivisible . . .

MARCIA KARP (1948–)

Marcia Karp has translated Sappho and is writing about the making of volumes of poetry in English.

From *Partisan Review* (Winter 1996).

Carmen 101

Brother

Multas per gentes . . . frater
    CATULLUS

Driven through people and people and places
    I am come to this terrible service   brother
so I might give you your last gift   the death gift
    might talk to your ashes   might listen in vain for their voice
Since your life took you from me   seized you
    unjust   brother   misery   took you from me
now   as we were taught by our parents   here
    I offer my last gift   a death gift
take it   wrapped only in brotherly tears
10   and always   my brother   now I have found you   farewell

ANNE CARSON (1950–)

Anne Carson, a poet and translator, is in the classics faculty at McGill University. Her most recent work is *Autobiography Of Red: A Novel In Verse* (1998). Of her Catullus translations she says: 'the following bear about the same relation to translation as Francis Bacon's paintings do to mug shots. He says they are very close.'

From 'Catullus: Carmina', *The American Poetry Review* (Jan./Feb. 1992).

Carmen 43

Salve Nec Minimo Puella Naso:
Hello Not Very Small Nosed Girl
Here Catullus compares an unnamed girl to his own love

Your nose is wrong.
Your feet are wrong.
Your eyes are wrong your mouth is wrong.
Your pimp is wrong even his name is wrong.
Who cares what they say, you're not –
Why can't I
Live in the nineteenth century.

Carmen 46

Iam Ver Egelidos Refert Tepores: Now Spring
Here Catullus greets the spring

Now spring unlocks.
Now the equinox stops its blue rages quiet
As pages.
I tell you leave Troy leave the ground burning, they did.
Look we will change everything all the meanings
All the clear cities of Asia you and me.
Now the mind isn't she an avid previous hobo?
Now the feet grow leaves so glad to see whose green baits.
Awaits.
10   Oh sweet don't go.
Back the same way go a new way.

Carmen 50

Hesterno Licini Die Otiosi:
Yesterday Licinius At Our Ease
Here Catullus addresses Licinius with affection

I guess around sunset we started to drink.
And lay on the floor writing lines
For songs that cold
Night smell coming in
The window I left about four went
Home.
Opened the fridge.
Closed it lay down got up.
Lay down.
10   Lay.
Turned.
Not morning yet.
I just want to talk to you.
Why does love happen?
So then I grew old and died and wrote this.
Be careful it's worldsharp.

Carmen 86

Quintia Formosast Multis:
Quintia Is Beautiful To Many
Catullus compares a certain Quintia to his own love

There was a whiteness in you.
That kitten washed in another world look.
Good strong handshake for a girl but.
But.

HUGH TOLHURST (1966–)

Tolhurst is an Australian poet and translator. His free versions, which he calls 'Unfaithful Translations', bring Catullus into the world of contemporary Australia.

From *Filth and Other Poems* (1997). *Carmina* 2 and 3 first appeared in *Scriptorium* 2 (1997), *Carmen* 7 in *Antipodes* 7 (1993).

Carmen 2

Her blue tit, her lapis jewel,
you are the bird she would admit
the nest of her breast or the soft
landing of her fingertips.
You never tap at the window mistaken for rain,
You never translate at a typewriter, waiting;
she teases you to nip her more & more
& toys with you to evade an hour
    If I were you, blue tit,
       I'd sing sad as Nick Cave,
a bird in the hand is worth Sydney or the Bush.

Carmen 3

Sing, choirs of radios,
the tenderest play a dirge,
my girl's wild friend is dead;
the blue tit, the lapis jewel
she loved more than her eyes.

2.10 *Nick Cave* an Australian rock star sometimes called 'the prince of darkness' for his mordant and unhappy lyrics

That charm of a bird held her
as a child touches mother,
never sang from the tree
but flitting about her skin
picked tunes for her alone.
Now broken wings glide no beat
& a one-way ticket touches ground:
shame on the circling sparrowhawk
whose talons shred a lovely thing;
shame on you, misprized blue tit,
your crime that her cool christmas eyes
crash out rose & thorny red from crying.

Carmen 7

You ask how many of your worldly kisses
are enough for me, Lesbia, enough & more?
One kiss for every grain of sand swept
down the coast from Seven Apostles
past Apollo Bay, to Point Danger;
a number glowing like southern skies
in points to star your eyes below midnight,
the dashboard legend of illicit miles:
to find your lips as many times
might quiet Tolhurst's madness:
no barman could squeeze the measure,
no satellite eavesdrop the amount.

Carmen 51

To me he seems charmed as a god
or, if legal, charmed above gods,
seated by you repeatedly
    gazing, getting

your sweet laugh. Unhinged by love
his senses fly: on seeing you,
Lesbia, my voice loses power
> (can't think to speak)

but my tongue lies flat, subtle fires
10 break burning down my limbs, my ears
ring deaf, at once two pitch black nights
> close down my lights.

Easy, Catullus, your demise;
easy your excess, your desire.
How else do great cities, kings, fall
> but easily?

APPENDIX:
Some poems that would not have been written without Catullus

SIR WALTER RALEGH
(*c.* 1552–1618)

From *The Poems of Sir Walter Ralegh* (1951).

cf. *Carmina* 5 and 7

To his Love when hee had obtained Her

Now Serena bee not coy;
Since wee freely may enjoy
Sweete imbraces: such delights,
As will shorten tedious nightes.
Thinke that beauty will not stay
With you allwaies; but away;
And that tyrannizing face
That now holdes such perfect grace;
Will both chaing'd and ruined bee;
10   So fraile is all thinges as wee see,
So subject unto conquering Time.
Then gather Flowers in theire prime,
Let them not fall and perish so;
Nature her bountyes did bestow
On us that wee might use them: And
Tis coldnesse not to understand

What shee and Youth and Forme perswade
With Oppertunety, that's made
As we could wish itt. Lett's then meete
Often with amorous lippes, and greet
Each other till our wantonne Kisses
In number passe the dayes Ulisses
Consum'd in travaile, and the starrs
That looke upon our peacefull warrs
With envious lustere. If this store
Will not suffice, wee'le number o'er
The same againe, untill wee finde,
No number left to call to minde
   And shew our plenty. They are poore
That can count all they have and more.

ROBERT HERRICK (1591–1674)

From *The Poetical Works* (1956).

cf. *Carmen* 5

from *Corinna's going a Maying* (lines 57–70)

Come, let us goe, while we are in our prime;
And take the harmlesse follie of the time.
   We shall grow old apace, and die
   Before we know our liberty.
   Our life is short; and our dayes run
   As fast away as do's the Sunne:
And as a vapour, or a drop of raine
Once lost, can ne'r be found againe:
   So when or you or I are made
   A fable, song, or fleeting shade;

> All love, all liking, all delight
> Lies drown'd with us in endlesse night.
> Then while time serves, and we are but decaying;
> Come, my *Corinna* come, let's goe a Maying.

cf. Carmen 72

To his Booke

> While thou didst keep thy *Candor* undefil'd,
> Deerely I lov'd thee; as my first-borne child:
> But when I saw thee wantonly to roame
> From house to house, and never stay at home;
> I brake my bonds of Love, and bad thee goe,
> Regardlesse whether well thou sped'st, or no.
> On with thy fortunes then, what e're they be;
> If good I'le smile, if bad I'le sigh for thee.

THOMAS RANDOLPH (1605–34/5)

Randolph lost his finger to a sword in a tavern brawl.
From *The Poems and Amyntas* (1917).

cf. Carmen 5.4–6

On the losse of his finger

> How much more blest are trees then men,
> Their boughes lopt off will grow agen;
> But if the steel our limbs dissever,
> The joynt once lost is lost for ever.

>   But fondly I dull fool complain,
>   Our members shall revive again;
>   And thou poor finger that art dust
>   Before the other members, must
>   Return as soon at heaven's command,
> 10 And reunited be to th' hand
>   As those that are not ashes yet;
>   Why dost thou then so envious sit,
>   And malice Oaks that they to fate
>   Are tenants of a longer date?
>   Their leafes do more years include
>   But once expir'd are nere renew'd.
>   Therefore dear finger though thou be
>   Cut from those muscles govern'd thee,
>   And had thy motion at command,
> 20 Yet still as in a margent stand,
>   To point my thoughts to fix upon
>   The hope of Resurrection:
>   And since thou canst no finger be
>   Be a deaths head to humble me,
>   Till death doth threat her sting in vain,
>   And we in heaven shake hands again.

ABRAHAM COWLEY (1618–67)

'Sitting and Drinking' is from *The English Writings of Abraham Cowley: Poems* (1905). 'Love Given Over' is from *The Collected Works of Abraham Cowley*, vol. 2.1 (1989).

---

20 *margent* book margin (where readers and printers often drew a pointing finger to mark an important or memorable passage)

cf. *Carmen* 4

from *Sitting and Drinking in the Chair, made out of the Reliques of Sir Francis Drake's Ship* (lines 18–50)

2

What do I mean? What thoughts do me misguide?
As well upon a staff may Witches ride
    Their fancy'd Journies in the Ayr,
As I sail round the Ocean in this Chair:
    'Tis true; but yet this Chair which here you see,
For all its quiet now, and gravitie,
Has wandred, and has travailed more,
Than ever Beast, or Fish, or Bird, or ever Tree before.
In every Ayr, and every Sea't has been,
'T has compas'd all the Earth, and all the Heavens 't has seen.
Let not the Pope's it self with this compare,
This is the only Universal Chair.

3

The pious Wandrers Fleet, sav'd from the flame,
(Which still the Reliques did of *Troy* persue,
    And took them for its due)
A squadron of immortal Nymphs became:
Still with their Arms they row about the Seas,
And still make new and greater voyages;
Nor has the first Poetick ship of *Greece*,
(Though now a star she so Triumphant show,
And guide her sailing Successors below,

---

13 *pious Wandrers Fleet* the fleet of Aeneas, escaping captured Troy
16 *A squadron of immortal Nymphs* Aeneas' ships were transformed into sea nymphs in *Aeneid IX*
19 *the first Poetick ship of Greece* the *Argo*

Bright as her ancient freight the shining fleece;)
Yet to this day a quiet harbour found,
The tide of Heaven still carries her around.
Only *Drakes* Sacred vessel which before
    Had done, and had seen more,
    Than those have done or seen,
Ev'n since they Goddesses, and this a Star has been;
As a reward for all her labour past,
30   Is made the seat of rest at last.
    Let the case now quite alter'd be,
And as thou went'st abroad the World to see;
    Let the World now come to see thee.

cf. *Carmen* 8

Love given over

1

It is *enough*; enough of time, and pain
  Hast thou consum'd in vain;
  Leave, wretched *Cowley*, leave
  Thy self with *shadows* to deceave;
Think that *already lost* which thou must *never gain*.

2

Three of thy lustiest and thy freshest years,
  (Tost in storms of *Hopes* and *Fears*)
  Like helpless *Ships* that bee
  Set on fire i'th' midst o'the *Sea*,
10 Have all been *burnt in Love*, and all been *drown'd in Tears*.

3
Resolve then on it, and by force or art
   Free thy unlucky *Heart*;
   Since *Fate* does disapprove
   Th' ambition of thy *Love*.
And not one *Star* in heav'n offers to take thy part.

4
If e're I clear my *Heart* from this desire,
   If e're it home to 'his breast retire,
   It ne'r shall wander more about,
   Though thousand beauties call'd it out:
A *Lover Burnt* like me for ever *dreads the fire*.

5
The *Pox*, the *Plague*, and ev'ry *smal disease*,
   May come as oft as *ill Fate* please;
   But *Death* and *Love* are never found
   To give a *Second Wound*,
We're by those *Serpents bit*, but we're *devour'd by these*.

6
Alas, what comfort is't that I am grown
   Secure of be'ing *again* orethrown?
   Since such an *enemy* needs not fear
   Lest any else should quarter there,
Who has not onely *Sack't*, but quite *burnt down* the *Town*.

ANDREW MARVELL (1621–78)

From *The Poems and Letters of Andrew Marvell* (1971).

cf. *Carmen* 5

To his Coy Mistress

    Had we but World enough, and Time,
This coyness Lady were no crime.
We would sit down, and think which way
To walk, and pass our long Loves Day.
Thou by the *Indian Ganges* side
Should'st Rubies find: I by the Tide
Of *Humber* would complain. I would
Love you ten years before the Flood:
And you should if you please refuse
10 Till the Conversion of the *Jews*.
My vegetable Love should grow
Vaster than Empires, and more slow.
An hundred years should go to praise
Thine Eyes, and on thy Forehead Gaze.
Two hundred to adore each Breast:
But thirty thousand to the rest.
An Age at least to every part,
And the last Age should show your Heart.
For Lady you deserve this State;
20 Nor would I love at lower rate.
    But at my back I alwaies hear
Times winged Charriot hurrying near:
And yonder all before us lye
Desarts of vast Eternity.

Thy Beauty shall no more be found:
Nor, in thy marble Vault, shall sound
My ecchoing Song: then Worms shall try
That long preserv'd Virginity:
And your quaint Honour turn to dust;
And into ashes all my Lust.
The Grave's a fine and private place,
But none I think do there embrace.
   Now therefore, while the youthful hew
Sits on thy skin like morning dew,
And while thy willing Soul transpires
At every pore with instant Fires,
Now let us sport us while we may;
And now, like am'rous birds of prey,
Rather at once our Time devour,
Than languish in his slow-chapt pow'r.
Let us roll all our Strength, and all
Our sweetness, up into one Ball:
And tear our Pleasures with rough strife,
Thorough the Iron gates of Life.
Thus, though we cannot make our Sun
Stand still, yet we will make him run.

---

29 *quaint Honour* a pun, since both *quaint* and *honour* are also used as substantives to denote the female pudenda
44 *Thorough* through

ALEXANDER POPE (1688–1744)

From *The Rape of the Lock and Other Poems* (1940).

cf. *Carmen* 66

from *The Rape of the Lock* (canto iii.171–8)

What Time wou'd spare, from Steel receives its date,
And Monuments, like Men, submit to Fate!
Steel cou'd the Labour of the Gods destroy,
And strike to Dust th'Imperial Tow'rs of *Troy*;
Steel cou'd the Works of mortal Pride confound,
And hew Triumphal Arches to the Ground.
What Wonder then, fair Nymph! thy Hairs shou'd feel
The conqu'ring Force of unresisted Steel?

THOMAS TWINING (1735–1804)

Twining's 'parsonage at Fordham had a moat or piece of water of sufficient capacity for a small boat which was built for him at Twickenham, and became a source of much amusement'.

From *Recreations and Studies of a Country Clergyman of the Eighteenth Century* (1882).

cf. *Carmen* 4

from *The Boat* (lines 1–30, 77–9 and 95–106)
(An imitation of the 'Dedicatio Phaseli' of Catullus)

The boat which here you see, my friends,
Sharp as a needle at both ends,
A bean-shell for my wife and me,
Deep loaded when it carries three;
A mongrel thing – pray take a view –
Between a boat and a canoe:
This *boat* (for we will not defame,
Nor quarrel for an empty name)
Protests and vows, and if you'll have it,
10 Is ready to make *affidavit*,
That she's the fleetest little thing
That ever flew on wooden wing.
On Father Thames she calls to say
If any bark e'er cut its way
So swiftly through his liquid glass,
But she, with ease, would quickly pass,
And, whether urged by oar or wind,
Would scuddle by, and leave behind.
This Father Thames will say; and she
20 Full many a day has joy'd to see
How oft the god would rise and stare,
Shake from his eyes his weedy hair,
To her in pleased attention turn,
Leaning his elbow on his urn,
And smile, and look so grimly merry,
To see his fav'rite little wherry,

---

3 *bean-shell* Catullus' boat is called a *phaselus*, 'bean pod', from its characteristic shape

>   And mark how deftly over all
>   Her floating sisters great and small,
>   With all their oars, and all their sail,
> 30   The plaything boat would still prevail.
>   [. . .]
>   'But, ah!' she cries, 'how changed the scene!
>   Troy *was* – and I, alas! *have been*.
>   Nor swifter ev'n myself can glide,
>   With ev'ry aid of wind and tide,
>   Than happy days and youthful prime
>   Fly down the rapid stream of time.
>   I, who was born on *Thames's* shore,
>   In Thames's stream first dipp'd my oar,
>   Each feat forgot of youthful praise,
> 40   Doom'd, the remainder of my days,
>   Instead of *Thames's* ample flood,
>   To paddle in a pond of mud!
>   Fair Twit'nam, gay-frequented scene
>   Where ev'ry evening deck the green
>   Bag-wigs, and swords, and negligees,
>   [. . .]
>   Exchanged for Fordham's rustic nook,
>   The lonely walk, the silent book,
>   The quiet lane, so grassy green,
>   Where waddling geese alone are seen,
>   [. . .]
> 50   The antique Pars'nage, undermined
>   By rats, and shaking to the wind;
>   Ducks, chickens, goslings, pigs, and cows,
>   The Parson, and the Parson's spouse!'

---

43 *Twit'nam* Twickenham

GEORGE ELLIS (1753–1815)

Ellis parodies *Carmen* 45 in an anti-Whig satire on a political meeting at the Whig Club at the Crown and Anchor Tavern on the birthday of Charles James Fox (24 January 1798). The Duke of Norfolk presided, proposing the toast: 'Our Sovereign's Health – the Majesty of the People.' Fox, the Whig leader, was a supporter of the French Revolution. John Horne Tooke was a friend of Tom Paine, and had been imprisoned in 1778 for raising a subscription for the Americans in the Revolutionary War.

From *The Anti-Jacobin*, 5 February 1798.

cf. *Carmen* 45

Acme and Septimius; or, the Happy Union Celebrated at the Crown and Anchor Tavern

Fox, with Tooke to grace his side,
Thus address'd his blooming bride –
'Sweet! Should I' e'er, in power or place,
Another Citizen embrace;
Should e'er my eyes delight to look
On aught alive, save JOHN HORNE TOOKE,
Doom me to ridicule and ruin,
In the coarse hug of *Indian* Bruin!'
    He spoke; and to the left and right,
10   NORFOLK hiccupp'd with delight.
Tooke, his bald head gently moving,
    On the sweet patriot's drunken eyes
    His wine-empurpled lips applies,
And thus returns in accents loving:

---

8 *Indian* a reference to Fox's bill on India (1783)

'So, my dear CHARLEY, may success
At length my ardent wishes bless,
And lead, through discord's low'ring storm,
To one grand RADICAL REFORM!
As, from this hour I love thee more
Than e'er I hated thee before!'
    He spoke, and to the left and right,
    NORFOLK hiccupp'd with delight.
With this good omen they proceed;
Fond toasts their mutual passion feed;
In Fox's breast HORNE TOOKE prevails
Before rich IRELAND and SOUTH WALES;
And Fox (unread each other book),
Is Law and Gospel to HORNE TOOKE.
    When were such kindred souls united!
    Or wedded pair so much delighted?

SAMUEL TAYLOR COLERIDGE (1772–1834)

From *The Complete Poetical Works* (1912).

cf. *Carmen* 3

The Death of the Starling
Lugete, O Veneres, Cupidinesque – Catullus

Pity! mourn in plaintive tone
The lovely starling dead and gone!
    Pity mourns in plaintive tone
The lovely starling dead and gone,

---

26 *rich IRELAND and SOUTH WALES* the Clerkship of the Pells in Ireland and auditorship of South Wales

Weep, ye Loves! and Venus! weep
The lovely starling fall'n asleep!
Venus sees with tearful eyes –
In her lap the starling lies!
While the Loves all in a ring
Softly stroke the stiffen'd wing.

WALTER SAVAGE LANDOR
(1775–1864)

From *The Poetical Works of Walter Savage Landor* (1937).

cf. *Carmen* 4

The vessel which lies here at last
Had once stout ribs and topping mast,
And, whate'er wind there might prevail,
Was ready for a row or sail.
It now lies idle on its side,
Forgetful o'er the waves to glide.
And yet there have been days of yore
When pretty maids their posies bore
To crown its prow, its deck to trim,
And freight it with a world of whim.
A thousand stories it could tell,
But it loves secrecy too well.
Come closer, my sweet girl! pray do!
There may be still one left for you.

cf. *Carmen* 21

Imitation of the Manner of Catullus

Aurelius, Sire of Hungrinesses!
Thee thy old friend Catullus blesses,
and sends thee three fine watercresses.

There are who would not think me quite
(Unless we were old friends) polite
To mention whom you should invite.

Look at them well; and turn it o'er
In your own mind . . . I'd have but four . . .
Lucullus, Cesar, and two more.

Written in a Catullus

Among these treasures there are some
That floated past the wreck of Rome;
   But others, for their place unfit,
     Are sullied by uncleanly wit.
   So in its shell the pearl is found
     With rank putridity around.

On Catullus

Tell me not what too well I know
About the bard of Sirmio . . .
    Yes, in Thalia's son
Such stains there are . . . as when a Grace
Sprinkles another's laughing face
    With nectar, and runs on.

LEIGH HUNT (1784–1859)

Hunt recalls Catullus' Attis to protest against the treatment of the *castrato* singer Velluti on his appearance in London.

From *The Examiner*, 7 August 1825.

cf. *Carmen* 63

From Velluti to his Revilers (lines 1–15, 143–63, 260–70 and 371–80)

Velluti, the lorn heart, the sexless voice,
To those who can insult a fate without a choice.

    You wrong your manhood, critics, and degrade
Your just disdain of an inhuman trade,
When, in your zeal for what a man should be,
You wreak your shuddering epithets on me.
Scorn, as you will, the trade; you cannot err;
But why with curses load the sufferer?
Was I the cause of what I mourn? Did I
10 Unmake myself, and hug deformity?
Did I, a smiling and a trusting child,
See the curst blow, to which I was beguil'd?
Call for the knife? and not resist in vain,
With shrieks convulsive and a fiery pain,
That second baptism? bloody and profane?
[. . .]
How often have I wept the dreadful wrong,
Told by the poet in as pale a song,
Which the poor bigot did himself, who spoke
Such piteous passion when his reason woke! –
20 To the sea-shore he came, and look'd across,
Mourning his native land and miserable loss. –

Oh worse than wits that never must return,
To act with madness, and with reason mourn!
I see him, hear him, I myself am he,
Cut off from thy sweet shores, Humanity!
A great gulf rolls between. Winds, with a start,
Rise like my rage, and fall like my poor heart:
Despair is in the pause, and says 'We never part.'
'Twas ask'd me once (that day was a black day)
30 To take this scene, and sing it in a play!
Great God! I think I hear the music swell,
The moaning bass, the treble's gibbering yell;
Cymbals and drums a shatter'd roar prolong,
Like drunken woe defying its own song:
I join my woman's cry; it turns my brain;
The wilder'd people rise, and chase me with disdain!
[. . .]
Alone! alone! no cheek of love for me,
No wish to be wherever I may be
(For that is love): – no helpmate – no defence
40 From this one, mortal, undivided sense
Of my own self, wand'ring in aching space;
No youth, no manhood, no reviving race;
No little braving playmate, who belies
The ruffling gibe in his proud father's eyes;
No gentler voice – a smaller one – her own –
No – nothing. 'Tis a dream that I have known
Come often at mid-day. – I waked, and was alone.
[. . .]
Yet as the bird who, in his prison born,
Never knew tree, or drank the dewy morn,
50 Still feels a native sweetness at his tongue,
And tow'rds his woodland shakes a glittering song;
So the sweet share of nature left in me
Yearns for the rest, but yearns with harmony;

And through the bars and sorrows of his fate
Hails his free nest, and his intended mate.
Love's poorest voice shall loving still be found,
Though far it strays and weeps, – a solitary sound.

PERCY BYSSHE SHELLEY
(1792–1822)

From *The Complete Poetical Works* (1927).

cf. *Carmen* 51

from *To Constantia, Singing* (stanza III)

Her voice is hovering o'er my soul – it lingers
    O'ershadowing it with soft and lulling wings;
The blood and life within those snowy fingers
    Teach witchcraft to the instrumental strings.
My brain is wild, my breath comes quick –
    The blood is listening in my frame,
And thronging shadows, fast and thick,
    Fall on my overflowing eyes;
My heart is quivering like a flame;
    As morning dew, that in the sunbeam dies,
    I am dissolved in these consuming ecstasies.

ALFRED, LORD TENNYSON
(1809–92)

From *The Poems of Tennyson* (1987).

Hendecasyllabics

O you chorus of indolent reviewers,
Irresponsible, indolent reviewers,
Look, I come to the test, a tiny poem
All composed in a metre of Catullus,
All in quantity, careful of my motion,
Like the skater on ice that hardly bears him,
Lest I fall unawares before the people,
Waking laughter in indolent reviewers.
Should I flounder awhile without a tumble
Through this metrification of Catullus,
They should speak to me not without a welcome,
All that chorus of indolent reviewers.
Hard, hard, hard is it, only not to tumble,
So fantastical is the dainty metre.
Wherefore slight me not wholly, nor believe me
Too presumptuous, indolent reviewers.
O blatant Magazines, regard me rather –
Since I blush to belaud myself a moment –
As some rare little rose, a piece of inmost
Horticultural art, or half coquette-like
Maiden, not to be greeted unbenignly.

cf. *Carmen* 51

from *Eleänore* (stanza viii)

But when I see thee roam, with tresses unconfined,
While the amorous, odorous wind
   Breathes low between the sunset and the moon;
     Or, in a shadowy saloon,
On silken cushions half reclined;
       I watch thy grace; and in its place
     My heart a charmèd slumber keeps,
       While I muse upon thy face;
     And a languid fire creeps
       Through my veins to all my frame,
   Dissolvingly and slowly: soon
        From thy rose-red lips MY name
Floweth; and then, as in a swoon,
   With dinning sound my ears are rife,
     My tremulous tongue faltereth,
   I lose my colour, I lose my breath,
   I drink the cup of a costly death,
Brimmed with delirious draughts of warmest life.
   I die with my delight, before
       I hear what I would hear from thee;
     Yet tell my name again to me,
I *would* be dying evermore,
So dying ever, Eleänore.

cf. *Carmina* 31 and 101

Tennyson wrote this poem on a visit to Sirmio in 1880, only a few months after the death of his brother Charles.

'Frater Ave atque Vale'

Row us out from Desenzano, to your Sirmione row!
So they row'd, and there we landed – 'O venusta Sirmio!'
There to me through all the groves of olive in the summer
   glow,
There beneath the Roman ruin where the purple flowers grow,
Came that 'Ave atque Vale' of the Poet's hopeless woe,
Tenderest of Roman poets nineteen-hundred years ago,
'Frater Ave atque Vale' – as we wandered to and fro
Gazing at the Lydian laughter of the Garda Lake below
Sweet Catullus's all-but-island, olive-silvery Sirmio!

cf. *Carmen* 63

Tennyson described these rhythms as 'a far-off echo of the *Attis* of Catullus'.

from *Boädicéa* (lines 1–16)

While about the shore of Mona those Neronian legionaries
Burnt and broke the grove and altar of the Druid and Druidess,
Far in the East Boädicéa, standing loftily charioted,
Mad and maddening all that heard her in her fierce volubility,
Girt by half the tribes of Britain, near the colony Cámulodûne,
Yelled and shrieked between her daughters o'er a wild
   confederacy.

---

1 *Desenzano* a town on Lake Garda
2 '*O venusta Sirmio!*' 'O delightful Sirmio!', a quotation from *Carmen* 31

'They that scorn the tribes and call us Britain's barbarous
   populaces,
Did they hear me, would they listen, did they pity me
   supplicating?
Shall I heed them in their anguish? shall I brook to be
   supplicated?
10 Hear Icenian, Catieuchlanian, hear Coritanian, Trinobant!
Must their ever-ravening eagle's beak and talon annihilate us?
Tear the noble heart of Britain, leave it gorily quivering?
Bark an answer, Britain's raven! bark and blacken innumerable,
Blacken round the Roman carrion, make the carcase a skeleton,
Kite and kestrel, wolf and wolfkin, from the wilderness, wallow
   in it,
Till the face of Bel be brightened, Taranis be propitiated.'

ALGERNON CHARLES SWINBURNE (1837–1909)

Swinburne uses themes from *Carmen* 63 to contrast present-day weakness and the full-blooded passions of antiquity. The selection begins with an apostrophe to Priapus, now broken and ignored.

From *The Complete Works* (1925).

from *Dolores* (stanzas 41–4)
Notre-Dame Des Sept Douleurs

What broke off the garlands that girt you?
   What sundered you spirit and clay?
Weak sins yet alive are as virtue
   To the strength of the sins of that day.

For dried is the blood of thy lover,
    Ipsithilla, contracted the vein;
Cry aloud, 'Will he rise and recover,
    Our Lady of Pain?'

Cry aloud; for the old world is broken:
    Cry out; for the Phrygian is priest,
And rears not the bountiful token
    And spreads not the fatherly feast.
From the midmost of Ida, from shady
    Recesses that murmur at morn,
They have brought and baptized her, Our Lady,
    A goddess new-born.

And the chaplets of old are above us,
    And the oyster-bed teems out of reach;
Old poets outsing and outlove us,
    And Catullus makes mouths at our speech.
Who shall kiss, in thy father's own city,
    With such lips as he sang with, again?
Intercede for us all of thy pity,
    Our Lady of Pain.

Out of Dindymus heavily laden
    Her lions draw bound and unfed
A mother, a mortal, a maiden,
    A queen over death and the dead.
She is cold, and her habit is lowly,
    Her temple of branches and sods;
Most fruitful and virginal, holy,
    A mother of gods.

---

6 *Ipsithilla* the woman invited to a sexual rendezvous in *Carmen* 32
18 *oyster bed* at Lampsacus, the home of Priapus (see '*Carmen* 18')

Evocations of *Carmen* 101

from *Ave atque Vale* (stanza 18)
In memory of Charles Baudelaire

For thee, O now a silent soul, my brother,
    Take at my hands this garland, and farewell.
    Thin is the leaf, and chill the wintry smell,
And chill the solemn earth, a fatal mother,
    With sadder than the Niobean womb,
    And in the hollow of her breasts a tomb.
Content thee, howsoe'er, whose days are done;
    There lies not any troublous thing before,
    Nor sight nor sound to war against thee more,
For whom all winds are quiet as the sun,
    All waters as the shore.

To Catullus

My brother, my Valerius, dearest head
Of all whose crowning bay-leaves crown their mother
Rome, in the notes first heard of thine I read
    My brother.

No dust that death or time can strew may smother
Love and the sense of kinship inly bred
From loves and hates at one with one another.

---

5 *Niobean womb* Niobe's twelve children were killed by Apollo and Artemis and she wept until she turned to stone.

To thee was Caesar's self nor dear nor dread,
Song and the sea were sweeter each than other:
How should I living fear to call thee dead,
    My brother?

ARTHUR SYMONS (1865–1945)

From *Knave of Hearts. 1894–1908* (1913).

cf. *Carmen* 86 (and Symons' translation of it)

Lesbia in Old Age

You see these shrunken arms, this chin,
A sharp bone wrapped about with rags
Of scrawled and wrinkled parchment skin;
This neck now puckered into bags
Was seamless satin at the first;
And this dry broken mouth a cup
Filled up with wine for all men's thirst;
This sodden hair was lifted up
In coils that as a crown were curled
About a brow that once was low,
As any woman's in the world;
And these two eyes of smouldering tow
That scarcely light me to this hearth
Were as two torches shaken out
To be a flame upon the earth.
What is it that he said about
Beauty I stole, to be my own,
All beauty's beauty? Look at this:
Finger by finger, to the bone,
His lips and teeth would bite and kiss

These joints of these abhorred hands,
These cheeks that were not always thus;
What was it that he said of sands
And stars that could not count for us
Our kisses? Let us love and love,
My Lesbia: yes, and I shall live,
A hungering, thirsting shadow of
That love I gave and could not give.
I gave him pleasure, and I sold
30   To him and all men; he is dead,
And I am infamous and old,
And yet I am not quieted.
Take off your curses from my soul:
Can not Catullus pity me
Although my name upon his scroll
Has brought him immortality?

W. B. YEATS (1865–1939)

From *The Collected Poems of W. B. Yeats* (1951).

The Scholars

Bald heads forgetful of their sins,
Old, learned, respectable bald heads
Edit and annotate the lines
That young men, tossing on their beds,
Rhymed out in love's despair
To flatter beauty's ignorant ear.
All shuffle there; all cough in ink;
All wear the carpet with their shoes;

All think what other people think;
All know the man their neighbour knows.
Lord, what would they say
Did their Catullus walk that way?

EDNA ST VINCENT MILLAY
(1892–1950)

From *Second April* (1921).

cf. *Carmen* 3

Passer Mortuus Est

Death devours all lovely things;
    Lesbia with her sparrow
Shares the darkness, – presently
    Every bed is narrow

Unremembered as old rain
    Dries the sheer libation,
And the little petulant hand
    Is an annotation.

After all, my erstwhile dear,
    My no longer cherished,
Need we say it was not love,
Now that love is perished?

DOROTHY PARKER (1893–1967)

From *Death and Taxes* (1931).

cf. *Carmen* 3

From a Letter from Lesbia

> . . . So, praise the gods, at last he's away!
>   And let me tend you this advice, my dear:
> Take any lover that you will, or may,
>   Except a poet. All of them are queer.
>
> It's just the same – a quarrel or a kiss
>   Is but a tune to play upon his pipe.
> He's always hymning that or wailing this:
>   Myself, I much prefer the business type.
>
> That thing he wrote, the time the sparrow died –
> 10   (Oh, most unpleasant – gloomy, tedious words!)
> I called it sweet, and made believe I cried;
>   The stupid fool! I've always hated birds . . .

WILLIAM D. HULL, II (*fl.* 1940)

The poem below is the first of six sections of Hull's 'In Memoriam'. The other sections are entitled 'Victoria', 'Mae West', 'Mrs F.D.R.', 'Boswell' and 'Griffes'.
 From *Sewanee Review* 48 (1940).

Griffes Charles Tomlinson Griffes (d. 1920), an American impressionist composer

In Memoriam I
Catullus

flower of evil
rooted in a rotting rome

pure lyricist
vituperative ranter

possessor of something fine
haunter of the gutters

impetuous swallow
with wings
clipped

10 you wrote
odi et amo
to lesbia
and lesbia got more
elsewhere

ALLEN TATE (1899–1979)

From *Collected Poems, 1919–1976* (1977).

Adaptation of a Theme by Catullus
From the translation by Aubrey Beardsley
Carmen CI

Past towns, states, deserts, hills and rivers borne
By the first plane, brother, I've come today,
A spirit, to linger at your spiritless clay
That sleeps well-dressed beyond the reach of scorn:

> Not glad, lifeless tycoon, nor sorry feel
> For neither Bull nor Bear attends your way –
> Ah vanity of speech, what should I say?
> The grave encloses you with technical zeal
> For Chance, swift giver, may just as swiftly take.
> 10 Accept these costly wreaths for my own sake
> (Death asks no entrance fee to let you in)
> And for the decent sense of heaven and hell:
> Take them, and think not much on mortal sin.
> Now brother, time being money, I say farewell.

R. P. BLACKMUR (1904–65)

From *From Jordan's Delight* (1937).

cf. *Carmen* 4

Phasellus Ille

> This little boat you see, my friends, has not,
> as once Catullus' pinnace could repeat,
> a history of deep-sea peril sought;
> for her no honoured peace, no earned retreat.
> Too narrow for her length in beam, unstable
> and unseaworthy, her strakes and transom leak;
> although no landsman, even, would call her able,
> I float her daily in our tidal creek.
>
> I do not need the bluster and the wail
> 10 in this small boat, of perilous high seas
> nor the blown salt smarting in my teeth;
> if the tide lift and weigh me in his scale
> I know, and feel in me the knowledge freeze,
> how smooth the utter sea is, underneath.

REX WARNER (1905–86)

From *Poems and Contradictions* (1945).

cf. Carmina 76 and 8

Difficult suddenly to lay down love
of long standing. Difficult, but must be done
and no more remembered the time when love was begun
in the spring daffodils and the cherry blossom above,
and above the blossom the windwashed and fleeting sky,
and the clasped hands, and words panted out through
gates of the soul and body both. Then you
loved, I am sure, you loved and so did I.
Then the sun shone and the heart and the lip trembled,
the voice and the eyes and limbs threw spark to spark.
Then we went together: then truly the sun shone,
and the face was true that had not yet dissembled.
O now let the mind's face too rest in the dark.
Let memory be dark. Lay down what is done.

JOHN COTTON (1925–)

From *Ambit* 89 (1982).

cf. Carmen 31

from *Catullus at Sirmio* (lines 1–31)

I suppose I am obliged
To haunt this place,
Sharing the silence

And companionship of lizards
Whose stillness absorbs the light.
You have to be sharp to catch us.
Though I drift, while they flick,
Whipping out of sight
Between ancient crevices.
Then, you have to bring me with you,
Although you pay to come here.

The heat mounts.
The protection of walls
Lost in the absence of roofs,
We retreat to the shade
Of the olive's two-toned uniform.
The sawing of crickets falters,
The dusty scent of rosemary fades,
While below, the lake flashes
The merest movement of air
At this prick of land
Pushing up

Into Garda's somnolence.
This was the peace it brought
After Asia and the trauma
Of that everlasting farewell
To a brother's young ashes.
And we set it down: apple of islands,
The leave taking that still echoes,
The words are there.
Is that immortality enough?

JAMES K. BAXTER (1926–72)

From *Words to Lay a Strong Ghost: after Catullus*, in *Runes* (1973).

cf. *Carmen* 63

The Wound

It is not women only
Who lose themselves in the wound of love –
When Attis ruled by Cybele
Tore out his sex with a flint knife,

He became a girl. Blood fell
In flecks on the black forest soil –
So it was for me, Pyrrha,
And the wound will ache, aches now,

Though I hear the flute-players
And the rattling drum. To live in
Exile from the earth I came from,
Pub, bed, table, a fire of hot bluegum,

The boys in the bathing sheds playing cards –
It's hard to live on Mount Ida
Where frost bites the flesh
And the sun stabs at the roots of trees,

No longer a man – Ah! don't let
Your lion growl and run against me,
Cybele's daughter – I accept
Hard bondage, harder song!

cf. *Carmen* 68

The Friend

As those cold waters rise at Rainbow Springs
Endlessly from the underworld
(So deep a fountain that the divers cannot
Find its beginning in the groins of earth;

So strong a current that the coins they drop
Spin sideways onto ledges) –
As those fish-breeding waters flow
Under tidy bridges

Bringing some peace to the time-sick traveller –
10   Your friendship, Allius,
Has lifted for a half day from me
The manacles of Cybele.

THOMAS McAFEE (1928–)

From *My Confidant, Catullus* (1983).

Alas, but not too literally

Catullus,
I have no Caesar
To declaim. Look at us:
Never at war
Yet fighting
War after war.
Nothing, not a thing

       I write will be read
       By any Head
10   Of State.
       I might say, 'I berate
       You heartily, Senator
       And President.'
       But I wouldn't be sent
          For, reprimanded, or
       Cajoled, or commanded
       To ease up. Instead,
       As I told you, I wouldn't be read.
       I'm deader than Clodia's sparrow, Catullus.

cf. *Carmina* 2 and 3

To Lesbia's Sparrow

Fly, sparrow, back to the breast
Of Lesbia. You have worried me
Long enough at my window. She
Has grieved, she says. Better, go
To Catullus: he has made such a
Fool of himself, wanting to touch
The bird that touched Lesbia's breast.
Go anywhere. I'm sick of you.
You've made a fool of everybody.

JULIA BUDENZ (1934–)

From 'Roman Sonnets', from *The Gardens of Flora Baum*, a poem in five books. Sonnet 1 appears here for the first time in print. Sonnet 2 is from *Rhino: The Poetry Forum*, 1998. Sonnet 3 is from *The American Voice* 45 (1998).

cf. *Carmen* 5

Roman Sonnet 1

A sonnet is a little conversation
With all the sonnets that have gone before.
Will rhyme reply to rhyme forevermore
In a perpetual continuation,

Or might this evening see, seal, the cessation
Of twinklings that a new dawn must abhor
And tinklings that, delight to noons of yore,
Fade to dim irritants of iteration?

The loved and lovely ladies lived and died.
10   Autumns glowed gold, burned bronze, and iced to iron.
Those roses were the roses of their time,

Those snows the tears of yesteryears that cried
Down all the Alps and into their – no, my – urn.
Catullus kissed and kissed without a rhyme.

Roman Sonnet 2

We give a million kisses and then give
A thousand and then give a million more
And mix the millions with the thousands, for
Our kisses let us love and let us live

Our little life, Catullus wrote. The priv-
Ilege of art is alteration, or
I have betrayed my trust as a translator.
My mood has been a mere indicative.

Give, he commanded. Let us, he exhorted.
I do not push my will or waste my wishes.
Each sun rolls like the penny of brief luck.

Before the Ultimate must come unstuck,
Before Dawn's lucent blossom be aborted,
O Fortune, Fortune, give me many kisses.

Roman Sonnet 3

Millions of kisses, swift and lyrical,
Measured in Latin meters though no rhyme
Numbered the pulse of their lovely chime
Numbered upon another principle

That rendered them no less invincible
Despite all loss of count, all loss of prime,
All loss of gloss in blossoms out of clime,
Still hold the potence of their miracle.

Pull down the book, pull out the dictionary,
Dust off the grammar, move a finger slowly
Along the letters. Must there be a rift

In twenty centuries? The missionary
Crossing the seas of ages glimpses, holy,
Millions of kisses, lyrical and swift.

DAVID VESSEY (1944–)

From *the Ice Age and Other Poems* (London, 1973).

Lesbia in Orco

Reading Catullus on the Northern Line
in Fordyce's edition (which omits the obscene),
I wondered if Lesbia would have got out at Hampstead
or come on with me to Golders Green.

Somehow I don't picture her
on the platform at Bank,
jostled in a smoking carriage
by that man who stank

of '*The Daily Telegraph*' and Players plain.
Perhaps I am wrong
there may be somewhere a Lesbia
worthy of song

from Gaius Valerius Catullus, who
counts her kisses like stars in the sky:
but for some reason
she escapes my eye

as I read his *carmina* on the Underground.
She must be as rare
as the nymph who picked up Peleus
near Weston-super-Mare

as he sailed in the Argo on a virgin sea.
(But isn't that Attis in a shiny suit
asking a dame to dance with him
to the sound of dinning cymbal and of shrilling flute?)

Who? Lesbia? I know her: she went to Leicester Square
and hurried through to Soho in the evening rain,
where she helps the sons of Romulus
drink Japanese champagne.

ENGLISH EDITIONS

Anthologies and Collections

The Adventures of Catullus and History of his Amours with Lesbia Intermixt with translations of his Choicest Poems by Several Hands. London, 1707.

A. H. Bullen. *Poems, Chiefly Lyrical, from Romances and Prose-tracts of the Elizabethan Age*. London, 1890.

Robert H. Case, ed. *English Epithalamies*. London and Chicago, 1896.

A Collection of Poems: viz. The Temple of Death by the Marquis of Normanby. An Epistle to the Earl of Dorset, etc. Second edn, London, 1702.

Edward Doughtie, ed. *Lyrics from English Airs*. Cambridge, Mass., 1970.

John Dryden. *Examen Poeticum: Being the Third Part of Miscellany Poems, Containing a Variety of New Translations of the Ancient Poets Together with Many Original Copies by the Most Eminent Hands*. London, 1693.

The Gentleman's Journal: or the Monthly Miscellany 1–3 (1692–94).

The Oxford Book of Latin Verse, ed. H. W. Garrod. Oxford, 1912.

Alexander Pope. *Pope's Own Miscellany, Being a reprint of Poems on Several Occasions 1717 containing new poems by Alexander Pope and others*, ed. Norman Ault. London, 1935.

Diane J. Rayor and William W. Batstone, eds. *Latin Lyric and Elegiac Poetry: An Anthology of Translations*. New York and London, 1995.

F. Kinchin Smith and T. W. Melluish, eds. *Catullus: Selections from the Poems*. London, 1942.

Nahum Tate. *Poems by Several Hands, and on Several Occasions collected by Mr. Tate*. London 1685.

Individual Poets and Translators

Franklin Pierce Adams. *Weights and Measures*. New York, 1917.
Nicholas Amhurst. *Poems on Several Occasions*. London, 1720.
Maurice Baring. *Have You Anything to Declare? A Notebook with Commentaries*. New York, 1937.
James K. Baxter. *Runes*. Oxford, 1973.
Aubrey Beardsley. 'Carmen CI'. *The Savoy*. 1896.
R. P. Blackmur. *Poems of R. P. Blackmur*, ed. Denis Donoghue. Princeton, 1977.
Alexander Brome. *Poems*, ed. Roman R. Dubinsky. 2 vols. Toronto, 1982.
Tom Brown et al. *A Collection of Miscellany Poems, Letters, etc.* London, 1699.
Julia Budenz. 'Sonnet 2 from "Vision"'. *Rhino: The Poetry Forum*. 1998.
—. 'Sonnet 3 from "Vision"'. *The American Voice* 45 (1998).
Basil Bunting. *The Complete Poems*, ed. Richard Caddel. Oxford, 1994.
Richard Francis Burton and Leonard C. Smithers. *The Carmina of Caius Valerius Catullus Now first completely Englished into Verse and Prose, the Metrical Part by Capt. Sir Richard F. Burton, K.C.M.G., F.R.G.S., etc., etc., etc., and the Prose Portion, Introduction, and Notes Explanatory and Illustrative by Leonard C. Smithers*. London 1894.
John Cotton. 'Catullus at Sirmio'. *Ambit* 89 (1982).
George Gordon, Lord Byron,. *Fugitive Pieces*. [Newark], 1806.
—. *Complete Poetical Works*, ed. Jerome J. McGann. 7 vols. Oxford, 1980–93.
Thomas Campion. *The Works of Thomas Campion*, ed. Walter R. Davis. London, 1969.
Anne Carson. 'Catullus: Carmina'. *The American Poetry Review* 21.1 (Jan./Feb. 1992) 15–16.
Robert Clayton Casto. 'Attis: after Catullus 63'. *Arion* 2 (1968) 603–7.
George Chapman. *The Poems of George Chapman*, ed. Phyllis Brooks Bartlett. New York, 1941.

Humphrey Clucas. 'Versions of Catullus'. *Agenda* 16, nos. 3 and 4 (1978–9) 22–38.

—. *Versions of Catullus*. London, 1985.

Samuel Taylor Coleridge. *The Complete Poetical Works of Samuel Taylor Coleridge*, ed. Ernest Hartley Coleridge. Oxford, 1912.

Thomas Cooke. *Mr. Cooke's Original Poems, with Imitations and Translations*. London, 1742.

Frank O. Copley. *Gaius Valerius Catullus: The Complete Poetry*. Ann Arbor, 1957.

Abraham Cowley. *The Complete Works in Verse and Prose*, ed. Alexander B. Grosart. 2 vols. Edinburgh, 1881.

—. *The English Writings of Abraham Cowley: Poems*, ed. A. R. Waller. Cambridge, 1905.

—. *Essays, Plays, and Sundry Verses*, ed. A. R. Waller. Cambridge, 1906.

—. *The Essays and Other Prose Writings*, ed. Alfred B. Gough. Oxford, 1915.

—. *The Collected Works of Abraham Cowley*, eds. Thomas O. Calhoun, Laurence Heyworth and J. Robert King. Newark, Delaware, 1989– .

James Cranstoun. *The Poems of Valerius Catullus translated into English Verse*. Edinburgh, 1867.

Richard Crashaw. *The Complete Poetry of Richard Crashaw*, ed. George Walton Williams. New York, 1972.

—. *The Poems English, Latin, and Greek of Richard Crashaw*, ed. L. C. Martin. Oxford, 1927.

Rodney Gove Dennis. ['Translations of Catullus'.] *Persephone* 2.1–2 (1996) and 4.1 (1998).

[George Ellis.] 'Acme and Septimius; or, the Happy Union'. *Poetry of the Anti-Jacobin*, ed. Charles Edmonds. Third edn, New York and London, 1890.

Charles Abraham Elton. *Specimens of the Classic Poets in a Chronological Series from Homer to Tryphiodorus*. 3 vols. London, 1814.

David Ferry. *Of No Country I Know: New and Selected Poems and Translations*. Chicago, 1999.

Eugene Field. *Second Book of Verse*. Chicago, 1892.

James Elroy Flecker. *The Collected Poems of James Elroy Flecker*, ed. J. C. Squire. New York, 1916.

John Hookham Frere. *The Works of the Right Honourable John Hookham Frere in Verse and Prose*, ed. W. E. Frere. 3 vols. Second edn, London, 1874.

John Gay. *The Beggar's Opera*, in *Dramatic Works*, ed. John Fuller. Vol. 2. Oxford, 1983.

W. E. Gladstone and Lord Lyttelton. *Translations*. Second edn, 1863.

John Glanvill. *Poems: Consisting of Originals and Translations*. London, 1725.

Horace Gregory. *The Poems of Catullus*. New York, 1931.

Thomas Hardy. *Poems of the Past and the Present*. London and New York, 1902.

—. *The Complete Poetical Works of Thomas Hardy*, ed. Samuel Hynes. 5 vols. Oxford, 1982–95.

Robert Herrick. *The Poetical Works of Robert Herrick*, ed. L. C. Martin. Oxford, 1956.

Quintin Hogg (Viscount Hailsham). *The Devil's Own Song and Other Verses*. London, 1968.

—. 'Edward'. *The Spectator*, 29 March 1957.

William D. Hull. 'In Memoriam'. *Sewanee Review* 48 (1940).

Leigh Hunt. 'Atys the Enthusiast; A Dithyrambic Poem translated from Catullus, with Prefatory Remarks'. *The Reflector* 1 (1810).

—. *The Feast of the Poets*. London, 1814.

—. *Foliage, or Poems Original and Translated*. Philadelphia, 1818.

—. 'Velluti to his Revilers'. *The Examiner*, 7 August 1825.

—. *The Poetical Works of Leigh Hunt*, ed. H. S. Milford. London, 1923.

Benita Kane Jaro. *The Key*. New York, 1988.

Ben Jonson. eds. C. H. Herford and Percy and Evelyn Simpson. 11 vols. Oxford, 1925–52.

—. *Ben Jonson: The Complete Masques*, ed. Stephen Orgel. New Haven and London, 1969.

—. *Ben Jonson*, ed. Ian Donaldson. Oxford, 1985.

Marcia Karp. 'Brother'. *Partisan Review*, Winter 1996.

George Lamb. *The Poems of Caius Valerius Catullus Translated, with a Preface and Notes.* 2 vols. London, 1821.
Walter Savage Landor. 'The Poems of Catullus'. *Foreign Quarterly Review,* July, 1842.
—. *The Complete Works of Walter Savage Landor,* eds. T. Earle Welby and Stephen Wheeler. 16 vols. London, 1927–36.
—. *The Poetical Works of Walter Savage Landor,* ed. Stephen Wheeler. 3 vols. London, 1937.
James Laughlin. *The Country Road: Poems.* Cambridge, Mass., 1995.
Guy Lee. *The Poems of Catullus.* Oxford, 1990.
Jack Lindsay. *The Complete Poetry of Gaius Catullus.* London, 1929.
—. *Catullus: The Complete Poems.* London, 1948.
[William James Linton.] *In Dispraise of Woman – Catullus with Variations.* Appledore Private Press, Hamden, Conn., 1886.
Robert Lloyd. *Poems by Robert Lloyd.* London, 1762.
Richard Lovelace. *The Poems of Richard Lovelace,* ed. C. H. Wilkinson. Oxford, 1930.
F. L Lucas. *Poems, 1935.* Cambridge and New York, 1935.
Thomas McAfee. *My Confidant Catullus.* Mt Carmel, Conn., 1983.
Hugh Macnaghten. *The Story of Catullus.* London, 1899.
—. *Verse Ancient and Modern.* London, 1911.
—. *The Poems of Catullus Done into English Verse.* Cambridge, 1925.
Charles Martin. *The Poems of Catullus.* Baltimore and London, 1990.
Sir Theodore Martin. *The Poems of Catullus Translated into English Verse.* London, 1861.
Andrew Marvell. *The Poems and Letters of Andrew Marvell,* third edn, ed. H. M. Margoliouth, rev. Pierre Legouis with E. E. Duncan-Jones. Oxford, 1971.
George Meredith. *The Poems of George Meredith,* ed. Phyllis B. Bartlett. 2 vols. New Haven and London, 1978.
Robert Mezey. *The Lovemaker.* Iowa City, Iowa, 1961.
James Michie. *The Poems of Catullus.* London, 1969.
Edna St Vincent Millay. *Second April.* New York and London, 1921.
Michel de Montaigne. *The Essays: or Morall, Politike and Millitarie Discourses,* trans. John Florio. London, 1603.

ENGLISH EDITIONS

Thomas Moore. *Odes of Anacreon Translated into English Verse.* Philadelphia, 1804.

—. *The Poetical Works of Thomas Moore.* London, 1841.

[John Nott.] *The Poems of Caius Valerius Catullus in English Verse.* 2 vols. London, 1795.

John Oldham. *The Poems of John Oldham*, ed. Harold F. Brooks. Oxford, 1987.

Dorothy Parker. *Death and Taxes.* New York, 1931.

Henry Peacham. *Period of Mourning Disposed into sixe Visions in Memorie of the late Prince, Together with Nuptiall Hymnes in Honour of this Happy Marriage betweene the Great Princes Frederick, Count Palatine . . . and Elizabeth onely Daughter to our Soveraigne His Majestie.* London, 1613.

Alexander Pope. *The Rape of the Lock and Other Poems*, ed. Geoffrey Tillotson. London, 1940.

Ezra Pound. *Lustra of Ezra Pound.* London, 1916.

—. *The Translations of Ezra Pound.* London, 1970.

—. *Collected Early Poems of Ezra Pound*, ed. Michael John King. New York, 1982.

Ezra Pound and Marcella Spann, eds. *Confucius to Cummings: An Anthology of Poetry.* New York, 1964.

Sir Walter Ralegh. *The Poems of Sir Walter Ralegh*, ed. Agnes M. C. Latham. Cambridge, Mass, 1951.

—. *The History of the World*, ed. C. A. Patrides. Philadelphia, 1971.

Thomas Randolph. *The Poems and Amyntas*, ed. John Jay Perry. New Haven and London, 1917.

Frederic Raphael and Kenneth McLeish. *The Poems of Catullus.* Boston, 1979.

Samuel Say. *Poems on Several Occasions.* London, 1745.

Percy Bysshe Shelley. *The Complete Poetical Works*, ed. Thomas Hutchinson. London, 1927.

Samuel Sheppard. *The Loves of Amandus and Sophronia, Historically Narrated.* London, 1650.

Sir Philip Sidney. *The Complete Works of Sir Philip Sidney*, ed. A. Feuillerat. Cambridge, 1922.

—. *The Poems of Sir Philip Sidney*, ed. William A. Ringler, jun. Oxford, 1962.

John Skelton. *John Skelton: The Complete English Poems*, ed. John Scattergood. Harmondsworth, 1983.

Christopher Smart. *The Poetical Works of Christopher Smart*, eds. Karina Williamson and Marcus Walsh. Oxford, 1980– .

Stevie Smith. *Not Waving but Drowning*. London, 1957.

Mary Stewart. *Selections from Catullus*. Boston and Toronto, 1915.

Jonathan Swift, *The Works of Jonathan Swift D. D.*, ed. George Faulkner. Dublin, 1746.

—. *The Poems of Jonathan Swift*, ed. Harold Williams. 3 volumes. Oxford, 1958.

—. *The Complete Poems*, ed. Pat Rogers. Harmondsworth, 1983.

Algernon Charles Swinburne. *The Complete Works of Algernon Charles Swinburne*, eds. Edmund Gosse and Thomas James Wise. 20 vols. New York and London, 1925.

Arthur Symons. *Knave of Hearts. 1894–1908*. London, 1913.

—. *From Catullus, Chiefly Concerning Lesbia*. London, 1924.

—. *Poems: Volume Three*. London, 1924.

Allen Tate. *Collected Poems, 1919–1976*. New York, 1977.

Nahum Tate. *Poems Written on Several Occasions. The Second edition Enlarged*. London, 1684.

Alfred, Lord Tennyson. *The Poems of Tennyson*, ed. Christopher Ricks. 3 vols. Berkeley and Los Angeles, 1987.

Hugh Tolhurst. *Filth and Other Poems*. North Fitzroy, Victoria, 1997.

Thomas Twining. *Recreations and Studies of a Country Clergyman of the Eighteenth Century*. London, 1882.

David Vessey. *The Ice Age and Other Poems*. London, 1973.

[William Walsh.] *Letters and Poems, Amorous and Gallant*. London, 1692.

Rex Warner. 'Contradictions, 1937–40', in *Poems and Contradictions*. London, 1945.

Dorothea Wender. *Roman Poetry: From the Republic to the Silver Age*. Carbondale, Ill., 1980.

Peter Whigham. *The Poems of Catullus*. Harmondsworth, 1966.

W. B. Yeats. *The Collected Poems of W. B. Yeats*. New York, 1951.
Louis Zukofsky. *Anew*. Prairie City, Ill., 1946.
—. *Catullus (Gai Valeri Catulli Carmina)*. London, 1969.
—. *Complete Short Poetry*. Baltimore and London, 1991.

INDEX OF POEMS TRANSLATED

The translators are listed chronologically by date of birth.

Carmen 1
John Nott 75
Mary Stewart 158
James Elroy Flecker 164
Jack Lindsay 175

Carmen 2
Walter Savage Landor 88
Charles Abraham Elton 93
Louis Zukofsky 180
Hugh Tolhurst 255

Carmen 2a
Louis Zukofsky 181

Carmen 3
Nahum Tate 36
Anonymous in *The Gentleman's Journal* 49
Walter Savage Landor 88
Charles Abraham Elton 94
George Gordon, Lord Byron 124
G. S. Davies 146
James K. Baxter 215
Hugh Tolhurst 255

Carmen 4
Anonymous (1717) 69
James Elroy Flecker 164

Carmen 5.4–6
Sir Walter Ralegh 3

Carmen 5
Thomas Campion 11
Ben Jonson 14
Anonymous (1612) 24
Richard Crashaw 25
Anonymous in *The Gentleman's Journal* 50
Samuel Taylor Coleridge 86
Eugene Field 148

Carmina 5 and 7
Ben Jonson 15

Carmen 6
James Cranstoun 140

Carmen 7.7–12
Thomas Moore 107

Carmen 7
Thomas Campion 11
John Oldham 39
Hugh Tolhurst 256

Carmen 8
Thomas Campion 13

INDEX OF POEMS TRANSLATED

Thomas Cooke 59
Arthur Symons 152
Louis Zukofsky (2 translations) 181, 182

Carmen 9
Hugh Macnaghten 149

Carmen 10
John Hookham Frere 82
Walter Savage Landor 89

Carmen 11
Thomas Moore 107
Louis Zukofsky 183
Charles Martin 248

Carmen 12
John Nott 75–6

Carmen 13.1–8
Walter Savage Landor 90

Carmen 13
Richard Lovelace 27
James Cranstoun 140

Carmen 14
Sir Theodore Martin 131
Louis Zukofsky 184

Carmen 14a
Hugh Macnaghten 150

Carmen 15
Frederic Raphael and Kenneth McLeish 226

Carmen 16
Sir Richard Burton 137
Dorothea Wender 239

Carmen 17
Charles Badham 129

'*Carmen* 18'
Peter Whigham 196

'*Carmen* 20'.5–14
Walter Savage Landor 92

'*Carmen* 20'
George Lamb 122

Carmen 21
Adventures of Catullus 63

Carmen 22.20–21
Robert Herrick 24

Carmen 22
Anonymous (1693) 52
Walter Savage Landor 91

Carmen 23
Adventures of Catullus 64
John Nott 76
Franklin P. Adams 162

Carmen 24
Frank O. Copley 186

Carmen 25
John Nott 77
James Michie 216

Carmen 26
Adventures of Catullus 65
Sir Theodore Martin 133
Ezra Pound 166

Carmen 27
James Cranstoun 141

INDEX OF POEMS TRANSLATED

Hugh Macnaghten 150
Charles Martin 249

Carmen 28
Sir Theodore Martin 133
Frank O. Copley 187

Carmen 29
Adventures of Catullus 66
John Nott 78

Carmen 30
Thomas Cooke 60

Carmen 31
Anonymous (1717) 71
Leigh Hunt 109
Thomas Hardy 145
Stevie Smith 179

Carmen 32
George Lamb 117
James Laughlin 192
Peter Whigham 196
Robert Mezey 242
Jane Wilson Joyce 250

Carmen 33
James Michie 216
Humphrey Clucas 243

Carmen 34
Mary Stewart 159

Carmen 35
Anonymous (1693) 53
Guy Lee 193

Carmen 36
George Lamb 117

Peter Whigham 197

Carmen 37
James Michie 217
Benita Kane Jaro 246

Carmen 38
Leigh Hunt 110
Humphrey Clucas 244

Carmen 39
John Hookham Frere 84
Dorothea Wender 240

Carmen 40
Frank O. Copley 187

Carmen 41
George Lamb 119
Rodney Gove Dennis 223

Carmen 42
George Lamb 119

Carmen 43
Sir Richard Burton 138
Arthur Symons 153
Mary Stewart 160
Ezra Pound 166
Rodney Gove Dennis 224
Anne Carson 253

Carmen 44
Sir Theodore Martin 134

Carmen 45
Abraham Cowley 33
Charles Abraham Elton 95
Leigh Hunt 110

Carmen 46
George Lamb 120
Sir Richard Burton 136
Hugh Macnaghten 150
Horace Gregory 169
Anne Carson 253

Carmen 47
Horace Gregory 170
Frank O. Copley 188
Charles Martin 249

Carmen 48
Richard Lovelace 27
Adventures of Catullus 67
George Gordon, Lord Byron 125
Humphrey Clucas 244

Carmen 49
Richard Lovelace 28
Christopher Smart 72
Peter Whigham 199

Carmen 50
Mary Stewart 160
Humphrey Clucas 244
Anne Carson 254

Carmen 51.5–12
Sir Philip Sidney 4
Matthew Gwinne 6

Carmen 51
George Gordon, Lord Byron 125
The Right Hon. W. E. Gladstone 126
Arthur Symons 153
Basil Bunting 173
Rodney Gove Dennis 224
Robert Mezey 242

Hugh Tolhurst 256

Carmen 52
Benita Kane Jaro 247

Carmen 53
Peter Whigham 199

Carmen 54.1–5
Sir Richard Burton 139

Carmen 54
George Lamb 121

Carmen 55
James Michie 218

Carmina 55 and 58b
Nahum Tate 37

Carmen 56
Humphrey Clucas 245

Carmen 57
Adventures of Catullus 67
Guy Lee 194

Carmen 58
Adventures of Catullus 68
Nicholas Amhurst 54
Jack Lindsay 176

Carmen 59
Jack Lindsay 176

Carmen 60
Arthur Symons 154

Carmen 61.1–40
Samuel Sheppard 22

INDEX OF POEMS TRANSLATED

Carmen 61.209–13
Hugh Macnaghten 151

Carmen 61
Henry Peacham 18

Carmen 62.1–3 and 62–65
George Chapman 9–10

Carmen 62.39–48
John Gay 48

Carmen 62.39–58
Ben Jonson 16

Carmen 62
Anonymous (1702) 55

Carmen 63
Leigh Hunt 112
Robert Clayton Casto 235

Carmen 64.1–28
Basil Bunting 173

Carmen 64.1–49 and 265–408
Peter Whigham 199

Carmen 64.38–277
Charles Abraham Elton 96

Carmen 64.143–8
Thomas Cooke 61

Carmen 64.269–75
Walter Savage Landor 92

Carmen 64.405–6
Matthew Gwinne 6

Carmen 65.19–24
Matthew Gwinne 7

Carmen 65
Peter Whigham 210
Rodney Gove Dennis 225

Carmen 66.15–18
Matthew Gwinne 7

Carmen 66
Peter Whigham 211

Carmen 67
James Michie 219

Carmen 68
Frederic Raphael and Kenneth
   McLeish 227

Carmina 68.20, 23–4, 21–2, 25–6
   and 65.[9]–11
Matthew Gwinne 8

Carmen 68.125–8
Matthew Gwinne 8

Carmen 69
Richard Lovelace 28
Jack Lindsay 176

Carmen 70
Sir Philip Sidney 5
Richard Lovelace 29
George Lamb 122
William James Linton 128

Carmen 71
Jack Lindsay 177

INDEX OF POEMS TRANSLATED

Carmen 72
William Walsh 40
Thomas Moore 108

Carmina 72 and 85
Richard Lovelace 29

Carmen 73
Mary Stewart 161
Jane Wilson Joyce 250

Carmen 74
Horace Gregory 170

Carmen 75
Richard Lovelace 30
Frank O. Copley 189

Carmen 76.17–26
F. L. Lucas 168

Carmen 76
Samuel Say 45
William Walsh 40
Maurice Baring 157

Carmina 77–78b
Jack Lindsay 177

Carmen 79
James Cranstoun 142
Charles Martin 249

Carmen 80
Frank O. Copley 189
Benita Kane Jaro 247

Carmen 81
Humphrey Clucas 245

Carmen 82
Richard Lovelace 30

Carmen 83
John Glanvill 43
Nicholas Amhurst 55
Jane Wilson Joyce 251

Carmen 84
Dorothea Wender 241

Carmen 85
Abraham Cowley 35
Ezra Pound 167

Carmen 86
Richard Lovelace 30
Arthur Symons 154
Frederic Raphael and Kenneth
    McLeish 232
Anne Carson 254

Carmen 87
Richard Lovelace 31
James Michie 221

Carmina 87 and 75
Walter Savage Landor 92

Carmen 88
Frank O. Copley 190

Carmen 89
James Cranstoun 142
Robert Mezey 243

Carmen 90
Horace Gregory 171

INDEX OF POEMS TRANSLATED

Carmen 91
John Hookham Frere 85

Carmen 92
Tom Brown 42
Jonathan Swift 44
Robert Lloyd 73

Carmen 93
Adventures of Catullus 93
Hugh Macnaghten 151
James Michie 221

Carmina 93–94
John Nott 79

Carmen 94
James Cranstoun 143
Frank O. Copley 190

Carmen 95
James Michie 221

Carmen 96
Charles Abraham Elton 106
Arthur Symons 154
Horace Gregory 171

Carmen 97
Frederic Raphael and Kenneth McLeish 233

Carmen 98
James Michie 222

Carmen 99
John Nott 80
James Cranstoun 143
Jack Lindsay 178

Carmen 101
Arthur Symons 155
Aubrey Beardsley 156
F. L. Lucas 168
Quintin Hogg (Lord Hailsham) 185
David Ferry 195
Marcia Karp 252

Carmen 102
Mary Stewart 162

Carmen 103
Richard Lovelace 31
Sir Theodore Martin 135

Carmen 104
James Cranstoun 144

Carmen 105
Frank O. Copley 190

Carmen 106
Richard Lovelace 31
John Nott 81
Frederic Raphael and Kenneth McLeish 233

Carmen 107
Arthur Symons 155

Carmen 108
Frederic Raphael and Kenneth McLeish 233

Carmen 109
Thomas Cooke 61
Jane Wilson Joyce 251

Carmen 110
James Michie 222

Carmen 111
James Michie 223

Carmen 112
John Nott 81
James Cranstoun 144

Carmen 113
Sir Theodore Martin 136

Frederic Raphael and Kenneth
    McLeish 234

Carmen 114
Frank O. Copley 191

Carmen 115
Frank O. Copley 192

Carmen 116
Frederic Raphael and Kenneth
    McLeish 234

INDEX OF TRANSLATORS AND IMITATORS

Names marked with an asterisk also appear in the Index of Poets in the Appendix.

Adams, Franklin P. (1881–1960), 162–3: *Carmen* 23
The Adventures of Catullus (1707), 62–8: *Carmina* 21, 23, 26, 29, 48, 57, 58, 93
Amhurst, Nicholas (1697–1742), 54–5: *Carmina* 58, 83
Anonymous (1612), 24–5: *Carmen* 5
Anonymous in *The Gentleman's Journal* (1692), 50–51: *Carmen* 5
Anonymous in *The Gentleman's Journal* (1693), 49–50: *Carmen* 3
Anonymous (1693), 51–3: *Carmina* 22, 35
Anonymous (1702), 55–8: *Carmen* 62
Anonymous (1717), 68–71: *Carmina* 4, 31

Badham, Charles (1813–84), 129–31: *Carmen* 17
Baring, Maurice (1874–1945), 156–8: *Carmen* 76
*Baxter, James K. (1926–72), 215: *Carmen* 3

Beardsley, Aubrey (1872–98), 155–6: *Carmen* 101
Brown, Tom (1663–1704), 41–2: *Carmen* 92
Bunting, Basil (1900–1985), 172–4: *Carmina* 51, 64.1–28
Burton, Sir Richard (1821–90), 136–9: *Carmina* 16, 43, 46, 54.1–5
Byron, George Gordon, Lord (1788–1824), 123–6: *Carmina* 3, 48, 51

Campion, Thomas (1567–1620), 10–13: *Carmina* 5, 7, 8
Carson, Anne (1950–), 252–4: *Carmina* 43, 46, 50, 86
Casto, Robert Clayton (1932–), 234–9: *Carmen* 63
Chapman, George (*c*. 1560–1634), 9–10: *Carmen* 62.1–3 and 62–5
Clucas, Humphrey (1941–), 243–5: *Carmina* 33, 38, 48, 50, 56, 81
*Coleridge, Samuel Taylor (1772–1834), 86: *Carmen* 5
Cooke, Thomas (1703–56), 59–61: *Carmina* 8, 30, 64.143–8, 109

Copley, Frank O. (1907–93), 186–92: *Carmina* 24, 28, 40, 47, 75, 80, 88, 94, 105, 114, 115
*Cowley, Abraham (1618–67), 32–5: *Carmina* 45, 85
Cranstoun, James (1837–1901), 139–44: *Carmina* 6, 13, 27, 79, 89, 94, 99, 104, 112
Crashaw, Richard 1613?–49), 25–6: *Carmen* 5

Davies, G. S. (1845–1927), 146–7: *Carmen* 3
Dennis, Rodney Gove (1930–), 223–5: *Carmina* 41, 43, 51, 65

Elton, Charles Abraham (1778–1853), 93–106: *Carmina* 2, 3, 45, 64.38–277, 96

Ferry, David (1924–), 194–5: *Carmen* 101
Field, Eugene (1850–95), 147–8: *Carmen* 5
Flecker, James Elroy (1884–1915), 163–5: *Carmina* 1, 4
Frere, John Hookham (1769–1846), 81–5: *Carmina* 10, 39, 91

Gay, John (1685?–1732), 47–8: *Carmen* 62.39–48
Gladstone, the Right Hon. W. E. (1809–98), 126–7: *Carmen* 51
Glanvill, John (1664?–1735), 43–4: *Carmen* 83
Gregory, Horace (1898–1982), 169–71: *Carmina* 46, 47, 74, 90, 96
Gwinne, Matthew (1558?–1627), 5–8: *Carmina* 51.5–12, 64.405–6, 65.19–24, 66.15–18; mosaic of verses from 68 and 65, 68.125–8

Hardy, Thomas (1840–1928), 145–6: *Carmen* 31
*Herrick, Robert (1591–1674), 23–4: *Carmen* 22.20–21
Hogg, Quintin (Lord Hailsham) (1907–), 185–6: *Carmen* 101
*Hunt, Leigh (1784–1859), 109–16: *Carmina* 31, 38, 45, 63

Jaro, Benita Kane (1941–), 246–7: *Carmina* 37, 52, 80
Jonson, Ben (1572?–1637), 13–17: *Carmina* 5, 5 and 7, 62.38–58
Joyce, Jane Wilson (1947–), 250–51: *Carmina* 32, 73, 83, 109

Karp, Marcia (1948–), 251–2: *Carmen* 101

Lamb, George (1784–1834), 116–23: *Carmina* '20', 32, 36, 41, 42, 46, 54, 70
*Landor, Walter Savage (1775–1864), 87–93: *Carmina* 2, 3, 10, 13, '20'.5–14, 22, 64.269–75, 87 and 75
Laughlin, James (1914–97), 192–3: *Carmen* 32
Lee, Guy (1918–), 193–4: *Carmina* 35, 57
Lindsay, Jack (1900–1990), 175–8: *Carmina* 1, 58, 59, 69, 71, 77–78b, 99
Linton, William James (1812–97), 127–8: *Carmen* 70
Lloyd, Robert (1733–64), 73: *Carmen* 92

INDEX OF TRANSLATORS AND IMITATORS

Lovelace, Richard (1618–57), 26–31: *Carmina* 13, 48, 49, 69, 70, 72 and 85, 75, 82, 86, 87, 103, 106

Lucas, F. L. (1894–1967), 167–8: *Carmina* 76.17–26, 101

McLeish, Kenneth (1940–97), *see* Raphael, Frederic

Macnaghten, Hugh (1862–1929), 148–51: *Carmina* 9, 14a, 27, 46, 61.209–13, 93

Martin, Charles (1942–), 247–9: *Carmina* 11, 27, 47, 79

Martin, Sir Theodore (1816–1909), 131–6: *Carmina* 14, 26, 28, 44, 103, 113

Mezey, Robert (1935–), 242–3: *Carmina* 32, 51, 89

Michie, James (1927–), 216–23: *Carmina* 25, 33, 37, 55, 67, 87, 93, 95, 98, 110, 111

Moore, Thomas (1779–1852), 106–8: *Carmina* 7.7–12, 11, 72

Nott, John (1751–1825), 74–81: *Carmina* 1, 12, 23, 25, 29, 93 and 94, 99, 106, 112

Oldham, John (1653–83), 38–9: *Carmen* 7

Peacham, Henry (1576?–1643?), 17–21: *Carmen* 61

Pound, Ezra (1885–1972), 165–7: *Carmina* 26, 43, 85

*Ralegh, Sir Walter (c. 1552–1618), 3: *Carmen* 5.4–6

Raphael, Frederic (1931–) and McLeish, Kenneth (1940–97), 226–34: *Carmina* 15, 68, 86, 97, 106, 108, 113, 116

Say, Samuel (1676–1743), 45–7: *Carmen* 76 and *Retractatio*

Sheppard, Samuel (c. 1586?–after 1653), 21–3: *Carmen* 61.1–40

Sidney, Sir Philip (1554–86), 4–5: *Carmina* 51.5–12, 70

Smart, Christopher (1722–71), 72: *Carmen* 49

Smith, Stevie (1902–71), 178–9: *Carmen* 31

Stewart, Mary (c. 1877–1943), 158–62: *Carmina* 1, 34, 43, 50, 73, 102

Swift, Jonathan (1667–1745), 44: *Carmen* 92

*Symons, Arthur (1865–1945), 151–5: *Carmina* 8, 43, 51, 60, 86, 96, 101, 107

Tate, Nahum (1652–1715), 35–8: *Carmina* 3, 55 and 58b

Tolhurst, Hugh (1966–), 255–7: *Carmina* 2, 3, 7, 51

Walsh, William (1663–1708), 40–41: *Carmina* 72, 76

Wender, Dorothea (1934–) 239–41: *Carmina* 16, 39, 84

Whigham, Peter (1925–87), 195–214: *Carmina* '18', 32, 36, 49, 53, 64.1–49 and 265–408, 65, 66

Zukofsky, Louis (1904–78), 179–85: *Carmen* 2, 2a, 8 (1939), 8 (1960), 11, 14

INDEX OF POETS IN THE APPENDIX

Names marked with an asterisk also appear in the Index of Poets and Translators.

*Baxter, James K. 294–5
Blackmur, R. P. 291
Budenz, Julia 296–8

*Coleridge, Samuel Taylor 274–5
Cotton, John 292–3
*Cowley, Abraham 264–7

Ellis, George 273–4

*Herrick, Robert 262–3
Hull, William D., II 289–90
*Hunt, Leigh 277–9

*Landor, Walter Savage 275–6

McAfee, Thomas 295–6
Marvell, Andrew 268–9
Millay, Edna St Vincent 288

Parker, Dorothy 289
Pope, Alexander 270

*Ralegh, Sir Walter 261–2
Randolph, Thomas 263–4

Shelley, Percy Bysshe 279
Swinburne, Algernon Charles 283–6
*Symons, Arthur 286–7

Tate, Allen 290–91
Tennyson, Alfred, Lord 280–83
Twining, Thomas 270–72

Vessey, David 299–300

Warner, Rex 292

Yeats, W. B. 287–8

PENGUIN CLASSICS

www.penguinclassics.com

- Details about every Penguin Classic
- Advanced information about forthcoming titles
- Hundreds of author biographies
- FREE resources including critical essays on the books and their historical background, reader's and teacher's guides.
- Links to other web resources for the Classics
- Discussion area
- Online review copy ordering for academics
- Competitions with prizes, and challenging Classics trivia quizzes

PENGUIN CLASSICS ONLINE

READ MORE IN PENGUIN

In every corner of the world, on every subject under the sun, Penguin represents quality and variety – the very best in publishing today.

For complete information about books available from Penguin – including Puffins, Penguin Classics and Arkana – and how to order them, write to us at the appropriate address below. Please note that for copyright reasons the selection of books varies from country to country.

In the United Kingdom: Please write to *Dept. EP, Penguin Books Ltd, Bath Road, Harmondsworth, West Drayton, Middlesex UB7 0DA*

In the United States: Please write to *Consumer Sales, Penguin Putnam Inc., P.O. Box 12289 Dept. B, Newark, New Jersey 07101-5289.* VISA and MasterCard holders call 1-800-788-6262 to order Penguin titles

In Canada: Please write to *Penguin Books Canada Ltd, 10 Alcorn Avenue, Suite 300, Toronto, Ontario M4V 3B2*

In Australia: Please write to *Penguin Books Australia Ltd, P.O. Box 257, Ringwood, Victoria 3134*

In New Zealand: Please write to *Penguin Books (NZ) Ltd, Private Bag 102902, North Shore Mail Centre, Auckland 10*

In India: Please write to *Penguin Books India Pvt Ltd, 11 Community Centre, Panchsheel Park, New Delhi 110017*

In the Netherlands: Please write to *Penguin Books Netherlands bv, Postbus 3507, NL-1001 AH Amsterdam*

In Germany: Please write to *Penguin Books Deutschland GmbH, Metzlerstrasse 26, 60594 Frankfurt am Main*

In Spain: Please write to *Penguin Books S. A., Bravo Murillo 19, 1° B, 28015 Madrid*

In Italy: Please write to *Penguin Italia s.r.l., Via Benedetto Croce 2, 20094 Corsico, Milano*

In France: Please write to *Penguin France, Le Carré Wilson, 62 rue Benjamin Baillaud, 31500 Toulouse*

In Japan: Please write to *Penguin Books Japan Ltd, Kaneko Building, 2-3-25 Koraku, Bunkyo-Ku, Tokyo 112*

In South Africa: Please write to *Penguin Books South Africa (Pty) Ltd, Private Bag X14, Parkview, 2122 Johannesburg*

READ MORE IN PENGUIN

A CHOICE OF CLASSICS

Adomnan of Iona	**Life of St Columba**
St Anselm	**The Prayers and Meditations**
Thomas Aquinas	**Selected Writings**
St Augustine	**Confessions**
	The City of God
Bede	**Ecclesiastical History of the English People**
Geoffrey Chaucer	**The Canterbury Tales**
	Love Visions
	Troilus and Criseyde
Marie de France	**The Lais of Marie de France**
Jean Froissart	**The Chronicles**
Geoffrey of Monmouth	**The History of the Kings of Britain**
Gerald of Wales	**History and Topography of Ireland**
	The Journey through Wales and The Description of Wales
Gregory of Tours	**The History of the Franks**
Robert Henryson	**The Testament of Cresseid and Other Poems**
Robert Henryson/ William Dunbar	**Selected Poems**
Walter Hilton	**The Ladder of Perfection**
St Ignatius	**Personal Writings**
Julian of Norwich	**Revelations of Divine Love**
Thomas à Kempis	**The Imitation of Christ**
William Langland	**Piers the Ploughman**
Sir Thomas Malory	**Le Morte d'Arthur** (in two volumes)
Sir John Mandeville	**The Travels of Sir John Mandeville**
Marguerite de Navarre	**The Heptameron**
Christine de Pisan	**The Treasure of the City of Ladies**
Chrétien de Troyes	**Arthurian Romances**
Marco Polo	**The Travels**
Richard Rolle	**The Fire of Love**
François Villon	**Selected Poems**
Jacobus de Voragine	**The Golden Legend**

READ MORE IN PENGUIN

A CHOICE OF CLASSICS

ANTHOLOGIES AND ANONYMOUS WORKS

The Age of Bede
Alfred the Great
Beowulf
A Celtic Miscellany
The Cloud of Unknowing and Other Works
The Death of King Arthur
The Earliest English Poems
Early Christian Lives
Early Irish Myths and Sagas
Egil's Saga
English Mystery Plays
The Exeter Book of Riddles
Eyrbyggja Saga
Hrafnkel's Saga and Other Stories
The Letters of Abelard and Heloise
Medieval English Lyrics
Medieval English Verse
Njal's Saga
The Orkneyinga Saga
Roman Poets of the Early Empire
The Saga of King Hrolf Kraki
Seven Viking Romances
Sir Gawain and the Green Knight

READ MORE IN PENGUIN

A CHOICE OF CLASSICS

Honoré de Balzac	**The Black Sheep**
	César Birotteau
	The Chouans
	Cousin Bette
	Cousin Pons
	Eugénie Grandet
	A Harlot High and Low
	History of the Thirteen
	Lost Illusions
	A Murky Business
	Old Goriot
	Selected Short Stories
	Ursule Mirouët
	The Wild Ass's Skin
J. A. Brillat-Savarin	**The Physiology of Taste**
Charles Baudelaire	**Baudelaire in English**
	Selected Poems
	Selected Writings on Art and Literature
Pierre Corneille	**The Cid/Cinna/The Theatrical Illusion**
Alphonse Daudet	**Letters from My Windmill**
Denis Diderot	**Jacques the Fatalist**
	The Nun
	Rameau's Nephew/D'Alembert's Dream
	Selected Writings on Art and Literature
Alexandre Dumas	**The Count of Monte Cristo**
	The Three Musketeers
Gustave Flaubert	**Bouvard and Pécuchet**
	Flaubert in Egypt
	Madame Bovary
	Salammbo
	Selected Letters
	Sentimental Education
	The Temptation of St Antony
	Three Tales
Victor Hugo	**Les Misérables**
	Notre-Dame of Paris
Laclos	**Les Liaisons Dangereuses**

READ MORE IN PENGUIN

A CHOICE OF CLASSICS

La Fontaine	**Selected Fables**
Madame de Lafayette	**The Princesse de Clèves**
Lautréamont	**Maldoror and Poems**
Molière	**The Misanthrope/The Sicilian/Tartuffe/A Doctor in Spite of Himself/The Imaginary Invalid**
	The Miser/The Would-be Gentleman/That Scoundrel Scapin/Love's the Best Doctor/Don Juan
Michel de Montaigne	**An Apology for Raymond Sebond**
	Complete Essays
Blaise Pascal	**Pensées**
Abbé Prevost	**Manon Lescaut**
Rabelais	**The Histories of Gargantua and Pantagruel**
Racine	**Andromache/Britannicus/Berenice**
	Iphigenia/Phaedra/Athaliah
Arthur Rimbaud	**Collected Poems**
Jean-Jacques Rousseau	**The Confessions**
	A Discourse on Inequality
	Emile
	The Social Contract
Madame de Sevigné	**Selected Letters**
Stendhal	**The Life of Henry Brulard**
	Love
	Scarlet and Black
	The Charterhouse of Parma
Voltaire	**Candide**
	Letters on England
	Philosophical Dictionary
Emile Zola	**Zadig/L'Ingénu**
	L'Assomoir
	La Bête humaine
	The Debacle
	The Earth
	Germinal
	Nana
	Thérèse Raquin

READ MORE IN PENGUIN

A CHOICE OF CLASSICS

Leopoldo Alas	**La Regenta**
Leon B. Alberti	**On Painting**
Ludovico Ariosto	**Orlando Furioso** (in two volumes)
Giovanni Boccaccio	**The Decameron**
Baldassar Castiglione	**The Book of the Courtier**
Benvenuto Cellini	**Autobiography**
Miguel de Cervantes	**Don Quixote**
	Exemplary Stories
Dante	**The Divine Comedy** (in three volumes)
	La Vita Nuova
Machado de Assis	**Dom Casmurro**
Bernal Díaz	**The Conquest of New Spain**
Niccolò Machiavelli	**The Discourses**
	The Prince
Alessandro Manzoni	**The Betrothed**
Emilia Pardo Bazán	**The House of Ulloa**
Benito Pérez Galdós	**Fortunata and Jacinta**
Eça de Quierós	**The Maias**
Sor Juana Inés de la Cruz	**Poems, Protest and a Dream**
Giorgio Vasari	**Lives of the Artists** (in two volumes)

and

Five Italian Renaissance Comedies
  (Machiavelli/The Mandragola; Ariosto/Lena; Aretino/The Stablemaster; Gl'Intronati/The Deceived; Guarini/The Faithful Shepherd)
The Poem of the Cid
Two Spanish Picaresque Novels
  (Anon/Lazarillo de Tormes; de Quevedo/The Swindler)

READ MORE IN PENGUIN

A CHOICE OF CLASSICS

Jacob Burckhardt	**The Civilization of the Renaissance in Italy**
Carl von Clausewitz	**On War**
Meister Eckhart	**Selected Writings**
Friedrich Engels	**The Origin of the Family**
	The Condition of the Working Class in England
Goethe	**Elective Affinities**
	Faust Parts One and Two (in two volumes)
	Italian Journey
	Maxims and Reflections
	Selected Verse
	The Sorrows of Young Werther
Jacob and Wilhelm Grimm	**Selected Tales**
E. T. A. Hoffmann	**Tales of Hoffmann**
Friedrich Hölderlin	**Selected Poems and Fragments**
Henrik Ibsen	**Brand**
	A Doll's House and Other Plays
	Ghosts and Other Plays
	Hedda Gabler and Other Plays
	The Master Builder and Other Plays
	Peer Gynt
Søren Kierkegaard	**Fear and Trembling**
	Papers and Journals
	The Sickness Unto Death
Georg Christoph Lichtenberg	**Aphorisms**
Karl Marx	**Capital** (in three volumes)
Karl Marx/Friedrich Engels	**The Communist Manifesto**
Friedrich Nietzsche	**The Birth of Tragedy**
	Beyond Good and Evil
	Ecce Homo
	Human, All Too Human
	Thus Spoke Zarathustra
Friedrich Schiller	**Mary Stuart**
	The Robbers/Wallenstein

READ MORE IN PENGUIN

A CHOICE OF CLASSICS

Aeschylus	**The Oresteian Trilogy**
	Prometheus Bound/The Suppliants/Seven against Thebes/The Persians
Aesop	**The Complete Fables**
Ammianus Marcellinus	**The Later Roman Empire (AD 354–378)**
Apollonius of Rhodes	**The Voyage of Argo**
Apuleius	**The Golden Ass**
Aristophanes	**The Knights/Peace/The Birds/The Assemblywomen/Wealth**
	Lysistrata/The Acharnians/The Clouds
	The Wasps/The Poet and the Women/The Frogs
Aristotle	**The Art of Rhetoric**
	The Athenian Constitution
	Classic Literary Criticism
	De Anima
	The Metaphysics
	Ethics
	Poetics
	The Politics
Arrian	**The Campaigns of Alexander**
Marcus Aurelius	**Meditations**
Boethius	**The Consolation of Philosophy**
Caesar	**The Civil War**
	The Conquest of Gaul
Cicero	**Murder Trials**
	The Nature of the Gods
	On the Good Life
	On Government
	Selected Letters
	Selected Political Speeches
	Selected Works
Euripides	**Alcestis/Iphigenia in Tauris/Hippolytus**
	The Bacchae/Ion/The Women of Troy/Helen
	Medea/Hecabe/Electra/Heracles
	Orestes and Other Plays

READ MORE IN PENGUIN

A CHOICE OF CLASSICS

Hesiod/Theognis	**Theogony/Works and Days/Elegies**
Hippocrates	**Hippocratic Writings**
Homer	**The Iliad**
	The Odyssey
Horace	**Complete Odes and Epodes**
Horace/Persius	**Satires and Epistles**
Juvenal	**The Sixteen Satires**
Livy	**The Early History of Rome**
	Rome and Italy
	Rome and the Mediterranean
	The War with Hannibal
Lucretius	**On the Nature of the Universe**
Martial	**Epigrams**
	Martial in English
Ovid	**The Erotic Poems**
	Heroides
	Metamorphoses
	The Poems of Exile
Pausanias	**Guide to Greece (in two volumes)**
Petronius/Seneca	**The Satyricon/The Apocolocyntosis**
Pindar	**The Odes**
Plato	**Early Socratic Dialogues**
	Gorgias
	The Last Days of Socrates (Euthyphro/ The Apology/Crito/Phaedo)
	The Laws
	Phaedrus and Letters VII and VIII
	Philebus
	Protagoras/Meno
	The Republic
	The Symposium
	Theaetetus
	Timaeus/Critias
Plautus	**The Pot of Gold and Other Plays**
	The Rope and Other Plays

READ MORE IN PENGUIN

A CHOICE OF CLASSICS

Pliny	**The Letters of the Younger Pliny**
Pliny the Elder	**Natural History**
Plotinus	**The Enneads**
Plutarch	**The Age of Alexander (Nine Greek Lives)**
	Essays
	The Fall of the Roman Republic (Six Lives)
	The Makers of Rome (Nine Lives)
	Plutarch on Sparta
	The Rise and Fall of Athens (Nine Greek Lives)
Polybius	**The Rise of the Roman Empire**
Procopius	**The Secret History**
Propertius	**The Poems**
Quintus Curtius Rufus	**The History of Alexander**
Sallust	**The Jugurthine War/The Conspiracy of Cataline**
Seneca	**Dialogues and Letters**
	Four Tragedies/Octavia
	Letters from a Stoic
	Seneca in English
Sophocles	**Electra/Women of Trachis/Philoctetes/Ajax**
	The Theban Plays
Suetonius	**The Twelve Caesars**
Tacitus	**The Agricola/The Germania**
	The Annals of Imperial Rome
	The Histories
Terence	**The Comedies (The Girl from Andros/The Self-Tormentor/The Eunuch/Phormio/The Mother-in-Law/The Brothers)**
Thucydides	**History of the Peloponnesian War**
Virgil	**The Aeneid**
	The Eclogues
	The Georgics
Xenophon	**Conversations of Socrates**
	Hiero the Tyrant
	A History of My Times
	The Persian Expedition